THE BIOGRAPHY OF
TOTTENHAM
HOTSPUR

THE BIOGRAPHY OF
TOTTENHAM HOTSPUR

JULIE WELCH

VSP

First published by Vision Sports Publishing in 2012
This revised and updated edition published in 2015

Vision Sports Publishing
19–23 High Street
Kingston upon Thames
Surrey
KT1 1LL

www.visionsp.co.uk

ISBN: 978 1909 5345 0 6

Edited by: Justyn Barnes and Jim Drewett
Copy editing: John Murray and Paul Baillie-Lane
Design: Doug Cheeseman

A CIP Catalogue record for this book is available from the British Library

Printed and bound in the UK by TJ International, Padstow, Cornwall

CONTENTS

ACKNOWLEDGEMENTS

So many people were willing to share their thoughts on Spurs with me when I was writing this that their names would fill a whole chapter in itself; in any case, most of them appear in the following pages. That said, I'd like to credit Tottenham Hotspur FC for the help I was given along the way, with special thanks going to John Fennelly. I'm also particularly grateful to Steffen Freund, Gareth Bale, Michael Dawson, Steve Perryman, Terry Dyson, Cliff Jones, Gary Mabbutt, Micky Hazard, Andy Porter, Alex Fynn, Jim Duggan and Brian Scovell. Rob White was as generous as ever with thoughts about his dad, Martin Cloake's immense knowledge of Spurs saved me from several crucial omissions and Justyn Barnes was a superb editor as well as being a joy to work with. Thanks also to Mike Kahn for his feedback.

I read a lot of books about Spurs while I was writing this, and am indebted to Bob Goodwin's *Tottenham Hotspur: The Complete Record* and Norman Giller's amusing and informative *The Managing Game*. If you haven't yet done so, I recommend you read James's Morgan's *In Search of Alan Gilzean*; Jimmy Greaves's *This One's On Me* and Chris Horrie's *Sick As A Parrot*. *Bill Nicholson: Football's Perfectionist* is Brian Scovell's absorbing and moving account of the life of 'Sir Bill' and *The Boys From White Hart Lane*, by Martin Cloake and Adam Powley, is the best book yet about the wonderful Spurs side of the late 1970s and early 1980s.

Writing the story of the club I have loved and supported since the age of 12 has felt like a great responsibility and I hope I've done it justice. And finally, wherever she is, I'd like to wave across the decades to Toni Szamek of Form 4A, The City of London School for Girls, who was the first person ever to speak the name 'Danny Blanchflower' to me. She doesn't know what she started.

Julie Welch,
October 2012

FOREWORD

by GARY MABBUTT

It's 10 May 1998, the final day of the season and we're at home to Southampton. It's not the kind of game that's going to go down in history of one of Spurs' greatest games, just a 1-1 draw with nothing much at stake. Even so, when the final whistle blows, I am choked and overcome. It's my last ever game. I'm saying goodbye. After 16 years and 619 appearances, I'll never be on this White Hart Lane pitch again.

I spent almost all of my playing career at Tottenham Hotspur. Although some tempting offers came my way, I never took them up. I loved my football here.

If the last day of my Spurs career was the saddest moment, the best was the night in May 1984, when we beat Anderlecht to win the UEFA Cup through that excellent penalty save by Tony Parks. Just as good was the moment that as Spurs captain I held aloft the FA Cup after we beat Nottingham Forest at Wembley in 1991.

I've been part of some of the best Spurs sides ever assembled, contributing to some of its greatest moments, as well as witnessing some of its most dramatic off-field dramas.

I am very proud to have played a part in Tottenham Hotspur's story for so many years. I'm proud, too, to remain still connected with the club as a Club Ambassador. I feel I belonged, and still belong, to a unique club that occupies a special place in the history of English football. From its earliest years, back in the reign of Queen Victoria, Spurs has led the way with innovation and trail blazing achievements. Its name is synonymous with style, flair, vision and entertainment. If you are interested in the history and spirit of a special club, where the game will always be about glory, you will, like me, enjoy reading this fascinating book.

Gary Mabbutt,
October 2012

CHAPTER ONE

THE WONDER
OF YOU

I t's New Year's Day 2015 and no one expected this. Not the fans, not Jose Mourinho, and definitely not Gary Cahill, who's clearly not enjoying being given the runaround by Harry Kane.

We're tearing Chelsea apart.

If you'd have said before kick-off that Spurs would be 3-1 up by half time, most people would have thought you were deranged. Paul Merson on *Sky Sports* predicted we'd be thrashed. You'd have agreed with him 18 minutes in, when Diego Costa put Chelsea one up. A goal down to the league leaders already. You could almost feel the collective slump of shoulders around the ground.

Then, on the half-hour mark, Harry Kane conjures an equaliser out of nothing, a low shot that speeds past Oscar, past Courtois. It's a classic bit of deadly flair; it's what Teddy used to do, and Big Chiv before him. Harry Kane, he's a proper Spurs striker.

Then it's mayhem, insane, delirious mayhem. On 44 minutes, Nacer Chadli's shot hits the far post and bounces out. Danny Rose comes belting up on the right and knocks us into the lead. Chelsea don't have time to regroup. A minute later, Cahill mistimes a lunge on Kane in the goal area. Andros Townsend grabs the ball and marches to the spot. He drives a wonderfully composed and deadly smash past Courtois.

The Chelsea backlash has got to come after the break, surely. But Kane strikes again. 4–1 up after 52 minutes. The mood is now a mixture of disbelief and glee and – because this is Spurs – a slight nagging fear that midnight's going to strike and the coach is going to turn back into a pumpkin. Sure enough, 10 minutes later, Chelsea make it 4–2. If it goes to 4–3 that'll be it, we'll fall apart.

Instead, Chadli seals matters on 78 minutes, his shot deflecting off John Terry to make it 5–2. Almost there. But a tap-in at the far post by Terry makes it 5–3 with three minutes to go, and as ever the final moments are the longest of your life. Your eyeballs hurt from staring at the clock. Then, at last, comes the miracle that is the bedrock of every Spurs supporter's faith. It's over. We've won.

It's been a chilly day and the wintry sun is long gone as we trek to the station and join the long queue for the train. The fans are just a crowd of shadows stretching ahead along the street. Most of us are happily anticipating *Match of the Day*, knowing it's going to be a joy to watch because Spurs have not just got three points but got them the Spurs way with swashbuckling, attacking play. But the growing dark plays tricks with your sense of time and in the twilight White Hart Lane can look much as it must have done in the 1920s when people came here to watch the FA Cup-winning side of Dimmock and Seed and Grimsdell.

Five-three. No one expected that. When was the last time anyone except Barcelona put five past Chelsea? Jose Mourinho, your boys have taken a terrible beating! Nyah-nyah-nyah Paul Merson! Flamboyant, erratic, heart-stopping, sometimes alternating between the exasperating and the sublime at breakneck speed, that was a true Spurs performance we've just witnessed. That said, a couple of new words have been creeping into the Spurs lexicon in recent seasons: resilience and backbone. The wilderness years of the 1990s have receded into memory like video recorders and mobile phones the size of bricks. Now we've got a tomorrow of glorious headlines to look forward to: 'Kane leads rout of shell-shocked Chelsea'; 'Jose takes a KANEing'; 'KANED: Harry stars as Spurs batter Jose's Blues.' This is meant to be a transitional season and, if so, we're transforming into something fabulous. The delirium of unmanageable expectations is setting in. In my mind's eye, Harry Kane accepts the Ballon d'Or, Eric Dier has become the new Bobby Moore and Arsenal have become a mid-table side.

Psychologists maintain that what happens in the brain when we are in love has similarities with mental illness, and that being in love is a form of temporary insanity characterised by intense emotions, anxiety and affection. When these intense emotions are reciprocated, people feel elated and fulfilled. Unreciprocated love leads to feelings of despondency and despair. Any Spurs fan who saw them beat Everton 2-1 at White Hart Lane in November 2014, when Roberto Soldado scored his first Premier League goal since March and was applauded off the pitch, may suddenly have found they'd got something in their eye. But two weeks later, any fan who turned up expecting them to crush drop zone candidates Crystal Palace and sat instead through a soul-numbing 0-0 found themselves crashing right back down to earth. Except that, whereas the psychologists tell us that passionate love is transitory, usually lasting between six and 30 months, being a Spurs fan is a lifelong form of helpless enslavement.

This, for instance, is how Ivan Cohen, 'Dr Hotspur' of the Spurs List newsgroup – founded by fan Bruce Lewis in the early days of email – recalls a childhood memory of his first Spurs match: 'It was in the late 1950s and my dad took me. The away team wore claret and blue, so it would have been against Aston Villa, Burnley or West Ham. You've only seen football on TV, on a little black and white screen. Then you come up the steps from outside and you see this *lush green*. I saw Dave Mackay come to take a throw-in. He had giant leg muscles and smelt of liniment. That was it. I was hooked.'

Carol Davis – if you look at the photos of the Spurs of 1962/63 bringing back the European Cup Winners' Cup from Rotterdam you can spot her as a teenager at the club gates, glorying – can take it back even further than that: 'I was born on a freezing Saturday morning in Argyle Road, Tottenham. That was on 13th December, 1947, and Spurs were playing at home to Birmingham that day. Some of the very first sounds I would have heard as a newborn baby that afternoon were the noise of the crowd at White Hart Lane, just around the corner, especially when we scored. How could I not have bonded with Tottenham Hotspur?'

It's a sentiment echoed by Alan Fisher, who writes the blog Tottenham On My Mind. 'The first time you're there, you realise it's special. I was a schoolboy and it was Jimmy Greaves. You watched him and you were spoiled. All great players have a trademark and his was that effortless glide, the ball always a yard in front of him – it was so smooth. I remember him running the length of the pitch against Newcastle – he picked up the ball and wove through as if no one was there and knocked it in. He scored twice that day. I still feel privileged to be able to sit a few yards from where I stood in the East Stand, right near the corner, everything spread out in front of you. It's boy and man in the same place.'

And this is Daniel Wynne, matchday commentator for Spurs: 'I started going as a five-year-old with my dad in 1975 and I've had a season ticket ever since, and from the day I started going it was an affliction, it was a love. All the little landmarks in my life have coincided with Spurs landmarks. The first televised league game – Spurs v Nottingham Forest on 2nd October, 1983 – was my barmitzvah weekend. On the day of my engagement party in 1991, we beat Notts County in the cup – we won 2-1, but I had to leave 15 minutes early so I missed the goals. Your parents grow old and pass on, you can change your partner, your children grow up and move out but the one constant in your life is your club.'

Spurs love is of the kind that drives you to lengths which those not intoxicated by a similar passion regard as completely bonkers. In 1967, after Spurs won the FA Cup, the comedian Peter Cook hired a Rolls-Royce to drive round the West End hooting a car horn and once, while working in the US, he flew from New York to watch them play Arsenal. Spurs lost. In the days before Irving Scholar achieved every besotted Spurs fan's dream of owning the place, he would attend every game, home and away. Then there's Morris Keston, a nonpareil among fans who has lavished time and money not simply on watching Spurs (by 2010 he had missed only two home games since 1951) but on fundraising testimonials for players and unfeasibly generous hospitality as well as, in the days before agents, providing his services, free, as their unofficial advisor.

While I was writing this book I interviewed Terry Dyson, the diminutive left-winger who was one of the stalwarts of the Double side and who scored two of the goals in Tottenham's 5-1 defeat of Atletico Madrid in the final of 1963 European Cup Winners' Cup. He made a profound observation. 'We've never been fans,' he said. 'That's why we can't understand what it's like to be a fan.'

This is what it's like.

'It doesn't matter how well we're doing, there's always a shadow of a doubt,' says the author and journalist Martin Cloake. 'Like at the Chelsea game – we were 4-1 up with half an hour to go, but when they pulled one back there can't have been a Spurs fan anywhere who didn't think, even briefly, "That's it, we've lost this."'

Here's Danny Keene of the Tottenham Supporters Trust: 'It must be the only team which, when you're 3-0 at half-time, you're anxious about the second half.' Here's Mike Leigh of *The Spurs Show*, channelling Woody Allen: 'I can live with the misery of the defeats. It's the hope I can't handle.' And here's Bernie Kingsley, another stalwart of the Tottenham Supporters Trust: 'I think frustrating is a good word because you're never quite sure what they're going to do next. You want them to win the title again so you can stop going.' 'Tottenham fans are the Eeyores of football,' says the actor Neil Pearson. 'We're never happy unless we're complaining. We're always robbed. If we aren't, we're suspicious of success.'

As for Jim Duggan of Topspurs website, it's his opinion that 3-2 is *the* Spurs score. 'Winning or losing. The thing about Spurs is that it could go either way. There's always that uncertainty. In the 2002 Worthington Cup semi-final second leg against Chelsea, it was only when we were 4-0 up that I thought, "I can relax a bit."'

'For me it's not fun to watch,' concurs Spurs' matchday announcer Paul Coyte. 'You can't enjoy it. I ache afterwards. My hands are clenched. They should sell stress balls in the Spurs Shop. But Ricky Villa's goal against Manchester City in the 1981 FA Cup Final replay was the most unbridled joy I've ever felt. Everything else disappeared. It was total amazement and excitement. *He just went on and struck it.* People who don't have football, don't have teams, don't know what that joy is. And then there was 1993, when Arsenal knocked us out in the semi-final. Everything felt so horrendous. It wasn't, "Oh, it's just another game." It affected me for ages.'

But why is it that Tottenham Hotspur has that kind of hold on us? Why do Spurs, a club based in one of the most deprived parts of London, draw their support from not just all over London and England but from destinations as far apart as Australia, Hong Kong and Scandinavia? Or as Jim Duggan puts it, 'It's Lilywhites around the globe. There are Spurs fans in each time zone. California, Mexico, Singapore, Norway. The sun never sets. Every minute of the day, someone somewhere is supporting Spurs.'

In the case of the US-based Ken Saxton, who with Simon Dodsworth and Sam Zuramel produces the weekly podcast Hotspur America, it was: 'The 125+ history, the blue collar team in the white collar town that I LOVE visiting, a team that, if they win it all, it will be so far beyond earned that it isn't funny. Not the richest team in dollars or cents or pounds and pence, but a team that does its business generally wisely. I enjoy the Shakespearean tie in that the club is named after Harry Hotspur, a Henry IV character who was cavalier in nature and wore his spurs into battle. Bandwagon potential was invitingly low as they have only qualified for the Champions League once in the Premier League era, but they are also one of the six teams never to be relegated in that same timespan. Insert "slow and steady wins the race" here. This is my team. Tottenham Hotspur. I know that being ridiculed for being a Spurs fan is part of the deal and that this team will tear my heart out more times than it will make me leap for joy, but I have made my choice. I can't wait for the glory, glory nights yet to come.'

For me, it was a lucky fluke that took me in the direction of Spurs. When I turned 11, instead of going to the local state school in the football desert of the leafy suburbs, I was sent to the City of London School for Girls, which drew a lot of its pupils from north London. Among them were three incredibly cool Jewish girls who I started going round with. Their families were part of the Spurs Jewish community, they were all manic Spurs supporters and, like Ivan Cohen, I was hooked. I wasn't allowed to go to matches so every morning at Loughton station I bought the *Daily Mirror* and *Daily Sketch* (my mum wouldn't allow them in the house because we were too posh) and drank in the deeds of the mighty Spurs on the crowded tube train on the way to school. It was the Double season. It was Danny Blanchflower and Dave Mackay, it was Cliff Jones and John White. It was Bobby Smith, the best centre-forward in England (the *Guardian* journalist David Lacey once witnessed two blokes having a punch-up on the terraces at White Hart Lane over who was better, Smith or Brian Clough. Smith scored a hat-trick, which effectively closed down the argument).

Plus Spurs had glamour and sophistication and brains. In an era when footballers were dismissed as mud-encrusted thickos, that difference was personified by their captain, Danny Blanchflower. Then there was the name. Tottenham Hotspur – just the sound of it conjured up images of daring, courage and passion. Who wouldn't have chosen Spurs when the first four letters of the north London alternative spelt something altogether less appealing?

Along the way to becoming a Spurs fan I discovered a whole load of fascinating things. I discovered that for a Christmas present Blanchflower and the team gave Fred Bearman, the chairman, a copy of *Lady Chatterley's Lover*. I found out that Terry Dyson liked to crunch on a handful of Dextrosol glucose tablets before he went out onto the pitch, whereas John White swore by a whiff of ammonia. I learned that before every game Tommy Harmer got so nervous he used to shut himself in the toilet to smoke in the mistaken belief that no one would know. I found out not just that Dave Mackay drove a Jaguar but that he'd had it resprayed maroon, which was the colour of his first club, Hearts.

I learned that when Spurs lost – though in the Double season that wasn't something that happened often – I would be reduced to a state of extreme existential despair which pervaded the whole week and would only lift if they won the following Saturday (heaven knows what the bad patch the team went through around Easter 1961 inflicted on me by way of long-term psychological damage).

I also discovered that one of Tottenham's supporters was A.J. Ayer, a real Oxbridge professor of philosophy, which as I was a rather swotty type myself impressed me even more than the fact that another Spurs fan was Bernard Bresslaw, who played all those gentle giants in a succession of *Carry On* films. (As time went on I found out that Spurs were the club of choice for a spectacularly widely-varied collection of famous people, from King Harald V of Norway to the Page 3 girl Linda Lusardi and Michael Fish the weatherman.)

Over the years, other joyous nuggets of Spurs history came my way. In 1973, for his portrayal of the ruthless mobster Doyle Lonnegan in *The Sting*, the actor Robert Shaw based his voice on that of Danny Blanchflower. In the days when young players lived in club lodgings, Stephen Carr's landlady had a parrot that could only say, 'F*** off.' She tried to work out what accent it said it in so she could find out who had taught it. Then there was the era when electronic physio equipment first came in. The club's new state-of-the-art device was applied assiduously to Paul Walsh's knee for a year before they discovered the gadget didn't work.

When I first became a Spurs supporter, I didn't really make the connection between my friends, the fact that they were Jewish, and Spurs. It was only later on that I learned that Tottenham was regarded as a Jewish club, and later still that I became curious why. After all, Arsenal and even Chelsea have their Jewish supporters. At Tottenham Hotspur, though, the Spurs Jewish community is as much part of the fabric of the club as Bill Nicholson Way and the cockerel.

Some of it, of course, is simple geography. Tottenham is close to Stamford Hill, where many Jewish people fleeing the poverty of the East End settled in the first part of the last century. More escaped Nazi persecution before the Second World War. Then there's the fact that from the early part of the 20th century the club was run by consecutive dynasties of Jewish businessmen. Fred Bearman, for instance, joined the board in 1909 and his family name was above the doors of Bearman's, the department store in Leytonstone High Street. That's gone now, but his name lives on as the man who, so legend has it, was told by Danny Blanchflower in close-season training before the start of the 1960/61 season that Spurs were going to win the Double.

'Nobody really knows how Spurs became known as a Jewish club because it was not something that was that important back in the day, but the geography must play a role,' says Ivan Cohen. 'It's an opinion, but if you're a migrant, one of the ways to integrate is to go to football. My dad went, my uncle used to go. My dad's family lived in Bethnal Green and he met my mother at the Tottenham Royal at a Jewish dance. Spurs on a Saturday afternoon, my mother on a Saturday night out. My mum was born and bred in Tottenham – her garden backed onto Arthur Rowe's garden.

'I was born in Aldgate and when I was four we moved to Hackney, where the northern part was Stamford Hill. In 1965 I went to Hackney Downs School, which had a very significant Jewish minority and where you had a very small group who supported Orient but a significant number who were Spurs or Arsenal. I don't think Spurs had more Jewish fans than Arsenal, but the wealthy ones had season tickets to Arsenal, so they were less visible, and the less wealthy ones went to Spurs and stood on the terraces.'

Daniel Wynne tells a similar story. 'My dad was a refugee – he escaped from Belgium as a 12-year-old in 1940. David Miliband's father was on the same boat. There were two boats and the other one got hit. He settled in Stamford Hill and used to walk down the road to White Hart Lane.'

But really there's no mystery about why people become Spurs fans. They're drawn to the club for the same reason I was – the way Spurs play. Every one of us has found the answer to the choice facing every Tottenham fan: which do I value more, style or not losing? Ideally we'd take both, of course, but if I hadn't decided before, then, forced as a football reporter to make frequent visits to Highbury in the 1980s, I would have been persuaded then, watching Arsenal screw out yet another 0-0 draw while my eyelids drooped.

Even for the dedicated thousands who turned up at White Hart Lane to watch George Graham's Spurs (when many rival fans during that period would have considered that an act of ill-advised masochism), there was always some special buzz that you could never have got from any other side. To quote my co-author of *The Ghost of White Hart Lane*, Rob White, on the topic of Spurs in the late 1990s: 'Ginola was not in a great Spurs side, but you'd go and watch Ginola.'

To put the question another way, how important is it to win at all costs? Tottenham's answer remains to this day the one spelt out by Danny Blanchflower: 'The great fallacy is that the game is first and last about winning. The game is about glory. It is about doing things in style, with a flourish, about going out and beating the other lot, not waiting for them to die of boredom.' Or as Gerry Francis once said, looking back resignedly on his ill-fated tenure as Spurs manager: 'In most clubs winning is what it's all about, and people are happy with that, but at Tottenham you have to win with style as well.'

'Every fan thinks their club is unique but there's something about "The Spurs Way",' says Martin Cloake. 'It's proper football, the glory stuff, the romance of the name, the swashbuckling side. There's something about Spurs that other clubs haven't got, a kind of grandness when things go right and you think life is a wonderful thing to live.'

'The Spurs Way is to play in such a way that, even when we're not winning matches, neutrals will hang on in there on *Match of the Day* because there's a really good chance you're going to see some good football,' says the journalist and editor Mat Snow. 'Even if you're a fan of another club, your attitude is that if you didn't support your team then Spurs would be a really nice club to support.'

'Spurs are unique,' says Bernie Kingsley. 'They have a unique name and a unique style. The Spurs Way is one of those completely intangible things you can't define. But you know when the team *is* playing in The Spurs Way.'

That said, ask some of the players and they'll make a pretty good stab at telling you what it's about.

'The first day I was an apprentice pro, Bill Nick said, "Son, if you keep it quick, simple and accurate you'll do well at this club," says Steve Perryman. 'And that was the basis of "push and run" and I don't think that's changed from that era through my day 30 years ago to today. I've never heard a better saying. I don't think you could put it into a short sentence any better than that.'

'Lots of ups and downs' is Gary Mabbutt's definition. 'There always are at Tottenham. When you think you're going for the title and you don't quite make it. Promising times when you don't achieve what you think you're going to. You never know with Tottenham. But The Spurs Way doesn't change. Free-flowing, entertaining, good passing. I could go on for hours – the style, the flair that's always stayed with Tottenham.'

'I was at Tottenham from the age of 12,' says Micky Hazard, 'so I'd spent almost all my life knowing and playing nothing but The Spurs Way, so moving to Chelsea after 13 years was a culture shock. I'd known nothing but these wonderful footballers – Ossie, Hoddle, Villa – people who could make the ball stand up and say good morning. Chelsea were a semi long-ball team and it took six months to get them to pass to me in midfield. The Spurs Way is the beautiful, flowing, passing game and once you've been part of it you don't want to be part of any other style.'

To echo Hazard's words, once you've watched it you don't want to know about any other club. You support Spurs because you believe. Because they maintain a playing tradition of everything that is good and inspiring and innovative about the game. Because they have flair. Because, right from the start, they were first. If you want convincing, take a look at their record. The first (and only) non-League club to win the FA Cup, in 1901. The first British club to win a European trophy – 5-1 against Atletico Madrid, in the European Cup Winners Cup in 1963. The first to sign marquee names from abroad – Ardiles and Villa, the big talents that transformed the club. The first club to float shares on the Stock Exchange, in 1983. But most of all, they were the first club in the modern era to do the Double. Which is important because it remains the greatest achievement in club football. Even now I feel a glow of childish pride when I look at the photo of Danny Blanchflower lifting the FA Cup after the final against Leicester way back in 1961. The photo doesn't tell the whole story of the sheer scale of that achievement. It doesn't need to. What comes from that picture is all the moments of brilliance, commitment and belief distilled into an image of sheer joy.

It's easy, now the Double has been achieved numerous times, to forget how hard it is to do something the first time – something that has been looked on as impossible. But great clubs are about much more than the mighty achievement of one season. The romantic attraction of Tottenham comes from its heritage. In the 2010/11 season, watching Gareth Bale's hat-trick in the San Siro against Inter Milan in the Champions League, all you had to do was mentally back-flip nearly a quarter of a century and think of the Gazza years, when *The Sunday Times* called Spurs 'The Greatest Show On Earth'. Or just before that, when David Pleat's 1986/87 side, the one with Clive Allen apparently managing the miracle of turning thin air into goals, very nearly won the title and both the domestic cups. In the end, they just missed out on all three, which is another Spurs trope. But the point I'm making is that they played in a 4-5-1 formation. Everybody's playing it now. Then, it was ground-breaking. It was another Spurs first.

A few years before that it was the Burkinshaw era, the great Spurs cup-winning side who may not have been crowned champions but, because of the way they played and the pleasure they gave us, have lingered in our memories far longer than teams from clubs who actually did. In addition to which, Burkinshaw was the coach responsible for another Spurs first. When he called in the sports psychologist, John Syer, to work with the team, it was an unprecedented step, eliciting headlines in the papers such as 'Spurs Call In The Shrinks'. These days, everyone's doing it. The same goes for his ideas on nutrition.

There have been other great Spurs sides that never won a title. There's the one that was painfully rebuilt after John White's death, the side of Alan Mullery and the G-men, Jimmy Greaves and Alan Gilzean. The one that turned into the side of Mike England and Pat Jennings, captained by the bravest and most inspiring Spur of all, Dave Mackay. He came back after breaking his leg twice to lift the 1967 FA Cup. The one that became the last great side of Bill Nicholson's, when Chivers scored and Park Lane roared. Give us a couple of years to get over what happened in 2011/12 and we'll be talking in the same way about the side of Bale and Modric, Rafa and Parker. Which was, incidentally, in the opinion of Cliff Jones, 'The best Tottenham side since the Double.'

The point is that we want Spurs to win, but we want them to win in 'The Spurs Way': with style, intelligence and invention. Spurs supporters won't put up with anything else. For us, disdain for functional, methodical football is a necessary badge of honour.

As Danny Keene says: 'One thing I love and cherish about Tottenham, the one thing which can *never* be beaten, is that we were *first*. Arsenal can build as many soulless stadiums and statues as they like but they'll never be able to equal *that*.'

Because whenever you watch Spurs, you can sense the history reaching back, beyond Hoddle and Ardiles, beyond Blanchflower, Mackay and White, even beyond Eddie Baily and Ron Burgess of the push-and-run title-winning side of 1951. Watch Spurs now and you might be able to conjure up a picture of the FA Cup winners of 1921, the team of Grimsdell and Seed and Dimmock and Bliss; the cup-winning side of 1901, led by John Cameron – okay, those images are a cloudy splodge of men in giant shin-length shorts and heavy boots, but you get the idea. There's a line of inheritance there, going back to the start of the 20th century when Spurs carried all before them. As David Lacey says: 'At Spurs, players come and go like they do at every club, but if people from 1950 and 1960 and 1980 were to come to White Hart Lane this weekend they'd still recognise the way they play. Pass and move.'

Pass and move. The Spurs Way. The brilliant, intoxicating, ground-breaking triumphs, the glamour, the performance, the breaking of the mould – the more you delve into the Spurs story the more you see that the way Tottenham play now, its identity as a club, is linked with a thick unbreakable cord to its beginnings. In 1925 it was Peter McWilliam: 'Belting the ball with an anywhere-will-do mentality has no place in the Tottenham way of doing things.' Here's Ossie Ardiles, playing five men up front and four at the back in 1993. 'I go for beauty. If you left it to me, I would play with a goalkeeper and 10 front players.'

To say that such an attacking philosophy represents the best way of winning the title has always been arguable, but it's certainly the most entertaining. Perhaps that's what draws us to Tottenham Hotspur. We're willing to trade the seasons of glorious failure for that one supreme moment when it all comes together. When it was Brown; Baker, Henry: Blanchflower, Norman, Mackay; Jones, White, Smith, Allen and Dyson.

Around the time that Spurs won the Double there was an Elvis song forever on the radio called *The Wonder of You*. It was fairly rubbish (in 2009/10 Arsenal chose it as the tune their team would run out to at the Emirates!) but more than half a century on I still remember the feeling of wonder when Danny Blanchflower had proved that nothing was impossible. You just had to believe.

That's what started my allegiance to Spurs, and that's why I want to tell its story now. It's the story of a club that from its beginnings announced itself as a ground-breaking phenomenon. A club that through one brilliant, innovative manager, Arthur Rowe, brought us push and run, and 10 years on, through another one, Bill Nicholson, the Double. A club that gave us the G-men, Glenn Hoddle, Ossie and Ricky, Archibald and Crooks, Gascoigne and Lineker. A club that led the way in commercial innovation that was to revolutionise the game. A club that with its star-studded cast brought football to a far wider audience. A club that went through an era of extravagance and over-reaching that almost led to its extinction, a time marked by turbulent boardroom battles between powerful men, before it embarked on the struggle along the long road back to stability and success. A club that throughout (aside from a brief lapse called George Graham) has remained true to its history and style. Still The Spurs Way.

To me, that's what makes the Tottenham Hotspur story special and why I want to pass it on to the new generation of fans. It's why I want to tell them not just about the recent past but about John Cameron and Vivian Woodward; Jimmy Dimmock and Arthur Grimsdell and Peter McWilliam. I want to discover the influences that made Tottenham Hotspur the club it is now, to find out the truth behind the intense rivalry with Arsenal, and to define The Spurs Way and explore why it continues to mean so much. To know that you have to understand its history. Which means going back to a small, half-forgotten patch of land called the Tottenham Marshes where it all began.

CHAPTER TWO

THE BOYS FROM TOTTENHAM MARSHES

Only the sign that says 'Lea Valley Park' in peeling paint indicates that this is more than a patch of wasteland. Shoehorned between a flyover and an HGV depot, Tottenham Marshes is one of the less-visited corners of north London. To reach it from Tottenham Hale station, you must follow a chain of pavements on the one-way system and head vaguely north-east for half a mile with a flyover looming on the right. There are no shops, nothing inspiring to look at, nor much in the way of green space, except for a little park on your left where kids are playing football. Then you pass through a concrete wilderness of high black railings, scrap metal yards and lock-ups.

Back in the mists of time, the Marshes were much bigger, stretching from Tottenham Hale to Northumberland Park. All that's left now is the northern stub, bordered by what was once the Great Eastern Railway line and the River Lea. There have been a few attempts to tart the place up but they have had limited impact – a short cycle lane, a dank underpass that you wouldn't want to use at night. Lea Valley Park itself is silent and empty, its paths bordered by wind-battered reeds and brambles sprouting a crop of fluttering plastic bags. From somewhere deep in the undergrowth come the screeches of foxes mating. It would be a long time before you confused it with Hyde Park.

Even so, to a Spurs supporter, this is a slice of hallowed ground – all that remains of Tottenham Hotspur's first home. Walk around there now, and you can imagine what it was like to play football on those bone-chilling winter afternoons 130 years ago, head-butted by freezing rain, slapped by the north-east wind and ankle-deep in mud (the Marshes were originally a flood plain of the River Lea). But the Milford Tavern in Park Lane, where the players used to change before walking a mile along a rutted track to the pitch, closed a couple of decades ago. The building is still there and its former use is commemorated in a website devoted to the nation's dead pubs.

There are other landmarks, though, several of which are still in evidence if you know what to look for. Follow the pavement back up to Tottenham High Road and you might be able to identify the location of the lamppost under which the club was founded by three schoolboys in 1882. Percy House, where the club established its first headquarters in the basement, is still standing, a listed building set back from the High Road behind white stone gateposts, a fancy gate and a scruffy front garden. The Red House, where they moved later on, remains on Tottenham High Road. These days it bears a relic of Spurs' past, not quite as old – the cockerel. Then there's White Hart Lane station, once a stop on the Stoke Newington & Edmonton Railway, and closely associated with the development of the club. As such, you feel it ought to be a more splendid place than the bleak platform where you wait after a game for the train to Liverpool Street.

It was the coming of the railway that drove the expansion of Tottenham, a place which was still not much more than a rural village when the club was founded. There were fields and market gardens where Paxton Road is now. Edmonton, a couple of miles down the track, was the kind of bucolic tableau of haycarts and cottages that's very popular on the kind of birthday card you give your granny.

In those days, 20 years before the end of the 19th century, the Hotspur Cricket Club was a small local outfit formed by a group of 11- and 12-year-old schoolboys who went to St John's Middle Class

School and Tottenham Grammar (that morphed into Somerset Comprehensive around the time Bill Nicholson was seeing out his last seasons at Spurs). Their families mostly lived in the big houses around Northumberland Park.

The boys played cricket in a field owned by the uncle of two of them, John and Peter Thompson, and the story goes that a second pair of brothers, Hamilton and Lindsay Casey, who were doing late Medieval English history at school, came up with the name Hotspur. It was a good fit, because the land on which Tottenham stood had once belonged to the estate of the Percy family, and Sir Henry Percy, son of the first Earl of Northumberland, was the Harry Hotspur immortalised by Shakespeare in Henry V, a courageous but fatally mouthy warrior who met his comeuppance at the Battle of Shrewsbury in 1403.

At the end of the summer of 1882, three of the lads hit on a way to keep the club operating in winter, by forming a football team. The legend is that the big idea came to Bobby Buckle, Hamilton Casey and John Anderson as they were mooching along Tottenham High Road and stopped to discuss it under a gas lamp about 100 yards from where White Hart Lane is now. It cost sixpence to join the team and the boys collected the first subscriptions on 5th September, 1882, which is accepted as the date of the formation of Hotspur Football Club.

The set-up for this little local football team was pretty much like it would be now – lads and dads. They collected enough sixpences to buy timber for goalposts which were knocked up and painted by the Casey brothers' father – tape was used for the crossbar – and stored at Northumberland Park station. And they got going straight away. Records survive of a Spurs match on 30th September, 1882, when they were beaten by another local outfit, the Radicals, which indicate that the scoreline was two goals to nil. The other surviving match record from that first year is the 8-1 hammering inflicted on them by an Edmonton school team called Latymer. Latymer carried on being their fiercest rivals for a couple of years until things got so tasty that the fixture was dropped.

What they were playing was basically park football, ground-sharing on a massive basis. The Marshes were a public amenity, which meant a free for all when it came to getting hold of a pitch and hanging on to it. The way they played was the way everyone did back then – lots of elaborate stuff and individual running with the ball – while wearing knickerbockers and fancy shirts which meant that they got a hard time from the local feral youth, and the fact that they were only 14 year olds didn't help. At the end of that first season, having been roughed up once too often, they got taken under the wing of a lay preacher at the Tottenham Parish Church of All Hallows, where they went to Bible classes.

John Ripsher, who had a reputation as an organiser, was warden of the Young Men's Christian Association at Percy House. It was the same sort of youth club set-up that was going on well into the 1960s, when ping-pong, orangeade and a bit of religion was laid on to give the young people of the district a wholesome distraction from hanky-panky and getting drunk on cooking sherry. In the summer of 1883, Ripsher called a club meeting in Percy House's basement kitchen. Twenty-one boys crammed in to elect him president of what was then known simply as Hotspur Football Club. John Randall, who had moved to Hotspur from the Radicals, was made captain and Billy Harston was vice-captain. Other decisions were that home matches were to be played at the Park Lane end of Tottenham Marshes, and that the club strip would be navy blue with a red shield emblazoned with the letter 'H' on the left-hand side.

You can tell from these early records that Hotspur FC was still very much a team of schoolboys. They quickly got kicked out of Percy House following a series of offences that included eating mulberries from the garden and mild bodily harm to a YMCA member, who had apparently gone down to the basement to complain about the noise from an indoor practice session and been struck by the ball. John Ripsher and the vicar found them a new base at Number 1 Dorset Villas in Northumberland Park, which had just opened as a branch of the Young Men's Church of England Society. But there was a price attached – the players had to attend church every Wednesday evening.

When Spurs manager Ossie Ardiles fielded those five forwards in the season of 1993/94, he was actually channelling an attacking tradition as old as the club. Hotspur Football Club's second season in existence began with six forwards in the side that played Brownlow Rovers. Back then the focus on attack worked out better than it did for Ossie; they beat Brownlow 9-0 and won 15 out of their 20 games that season. They celebrated the end of it by cancelling their final game in favour of heading to the FA Cup Final at the Kennington Oval to see Blackburn Rovers beat Queen's Park. And in honour of Blackburn they changed their strip to blue-and-white halves for the following season.

There was an innocence about those early years. In the faded photo of eager-looking boys that comprises the 'ORIGINAL TEAM OF TOTTENHAM HOTSPUR FOOTBALL CLUB, 1885', some of them are sprouting the beginnings of moustaches. John Thompson is there, to one side, unlike most of them smartly dressed in his day clothes. Billy Harston is kitted out in knickerbockers, a white shirt with a big collar, muddy-looking socks and boots. Bobby Buckle looks dapper and stylish, a businessman in the making. There's Hamilton Casey, slim and slightly gangly. There's John Jull, the blond straight-shouldered public schoolboy, now the captain. John Ripsher, already an old man, stands alongside the players, his grey hair and beard lending him a slight look of an Old Testament prophet.

But even then the club was outgrowing its roots. Too good for the other teams that filled the Marshes, it was taking on tougher, more organised opposition. With that came crowds of around 100 at home games. In April 1884, they had become not just Hotspur Football Club but *Tottenham* Hotspur FC, the addition made to avoid confusion with the older established Hotspur FC, based elsewhere in London, because they both kept getting mail meant for the other. Their fixture list appeared for the first time in the *Tottenham and Edmonton Weekly Herald* in 1885.

Older players were coming in, as well as players from other local sides that had split up. This provided them with enough bodies to field a regular second team. By the summer of 1885, Tottenham Hotspur had merged with The Stars, another club that had played on the Marshes, and decided to enter the London Football Association Cup. In their first competitive match, on Saturday 17th October, 1885, they were at home to a company's works team, St Albans. In front of a crowd of 400, Spurs won 5–2, and the *Tottenham and Edmonton Herald* opined that 'the whole of the Tottenham Hotspur played well together'. The hazards of playing on a public amenity were emphasised when while Billy Harston, man of the match, was carried shoulder-high to the changing room, someone nicked his coat. The cup run ended abruptly in their next fixture. At Wandsworth, against Casuals, a team made up of the best past and present public school and university players, they lost 9–0.

That same season, they were in trouble again, this time for playing cards in church. It wasn't exactly letting off fireworks in the bathroom with their mates or parking in a disabled bay but boys will be boys, and they had to move out of Dorset Villas. The long-suffering Ripsher moved them into the Red House on Tottenham High Road in time for the following season, which not only featured a run in the East End Association Cup – they reached the semi-final, where they were beaten by a soft goal by London Caledonians – but which also contained a historical encounter. On 19th November, 1886, Spurs played their first fixture against a newly-formed South London club called Woolwich Arsenal. It was a friendly abandoned due to poor light after 75 minutes, by which time Spurs were 2–1 up. To quote Topspurs' maybe not entirely impartial historian: 'Arsenal cried to the ref to get the game abandoned with 15 minutes to play, which it was – although Spurs were the moral winners, and have been ever since.'

For Spurs, playing in the cups raised their profile well beyond Tottenham. The club was now in demand for friendlies. But that cost money, and it was becoming a struggle to get by through subscriptions and donations from supporters, though they did raise £15 from a benefit concert. By this time, the club was attracting sizeable crowds to the Marshes; the 100 had expanded to 4,000 for some fixtures, which meant they had to rope off their pitch to keep everyone from spilling onto their playing area, but it was a free show. The time had come to move to their own ground where they could charge admission to games.

At the end of the 1887/88 season Tottenham Hotspur played their last fixture on the Marshes and for £17 per season rented a field — they had to share it with Foxes FC and a tennis club — behind a garden nursery in Northumberland Park. And that's when everything changed forever.

CHAPTER THREE

MONEYBALL

The story of how Tottenham Hotspur grew from a schoolboys' team to a world-famous football club is the story of what often happens when money gets involved. When you look at the 1894/95 team photo of Tottenham Hotspur Football Club, two things strike you. One is that it's no longer a boys' team. The other is that John Ripsher is no longer there.

It's not recorded whether Ripsher was shoved out or whether he graciously agreed to step down – the Victorians always liked to drape a veil over anything the faintest bit unseemly. But the tolerant, well-meaning Methodist preacher who had been the founding president of Tottenham Hotspur wouldn't have been suited at all to the football boom that was happening all around him.

The man who replaced Ripsher was a very different sort. John Oliver was a local businessman who was already top banana at another club, Westminster Criterion. You don't need an economics degree to see why Spurs had attracted his interest. In 1870 the railway had come to Tottenham and, by the time the century was heading to a close, the rural village had turned into an economically booming suburb. It had railway workers, it had police and firemen, it had a gasworks, a workforce that needed housing, and it was close enough to London to be part of that new phenomenon, the commuter belt. And the people who moved in wanted entertainment. They wanted football.

So for the 1892/93 season, Oliver roped in Tottenham to join a new league that he was promoting. The Southern Alliance was a league for leading amateur teams in the Home Counties. For competition, Tottenham had matches against Erith, Old St Stephen's, Polytechnic, Slough Town, Upton Park and Windsor & Eton. They changed their strip to red shirts and blue knickers, briefly became known as the Tottenham Reds and went on to lose only three games that season, finishing third behind Old St Stephen's and Erith. But because of the rival attraction of more lucrative cup ties, some of the clubs failed to turn up for their fixtures. After that, John Oliver's Southern Alliance collapsed.

But Oliver, who owned a carpet factory in Old Street in the City, quite obviously had big ambitions. Once in control of Tottenham Hotspur, he put up the money to build a stand at Northumberland Park in place of the pair of wagons that up until then had been the best the club could do in the way of executive boxes. Oliver's new stand had seats for 100 spectators, not to mention changing rooms, meaning the lads no longer had a 200-yard walk from and back to the Northumberland Arms before and after.

Hiring a professional trainer, Arthur Norris, Oliver set players up with jobs at his carpet factory, which at the time, along with surreptitious cash handouts, was the way to get round the rules about amateur status. The arrangement allowed Spurs to attract decent talent. Bill Julian had been Woolwich Arsenal's hard-tackling wing-half and its captain until he'd lost the armband to Sandy Robertson, a new arrival from Preston. Put out at the loss of status, Julian was one of the players to jump on board John Oliver's Spurs, which made him the first footballer to play for both clubs, though he shoehorned a couple of years at Luton in between.

While all this was going on, Oliver was also having to look elsewhere for opposition following the demise of the Southern Alliance. At that stage Spurs weren't quite ready to go for broke and apply to join the Football League where well-funded professional clubs were picking up all the top players. But they needed to be playing in a quality competition where the opposition was good enough to pull in the crowds. The FA Cup wasn't yet a feasible prospect in terms of a cup run – as the biggest knockout competition in the country, it was getting to be such a walkover for the north that two early finals were staged up there.

By now the Football Association was perturbed by the gulf in class that was opening up between the largely amateur southern clubs and the northern-based professional teams of the Football League. In the hope of beefing up the game's popularity south of Watford, it launched the FA Amateur Cup. When the 1893/94 season got under way, Spurs climbed on board and after getting through their second-round match were drawn against a side called Clapham Rovers. They never got to play the match, though.

This is what happened: Fulham had a winger called Ernie Payne, who'd been left off their team sheet for the whole of the previous season, so in October when Spurs came knocking he agreed to play for them in a fixture in the London Senior Cup. But, so the story goes, on the morning of the game he couldn't find his kit. The team found him a spare one but none of the boots on offer fitted, so they gave him 10 bob to buy a pair. Fulham threw a hissy fit. Not only had Spurs poached their player but, they claimed, in giving him money to buy boots, they'd breached amateur rules. The London FA decided that this had been 'unfair inducement'. Payne got a week's suspension and Spurs were found guilty of gross misconduct, banned from playing home and away for a fortnight, leaving Clapham Rovers to progress in the cup by default.

Described in *The Star* as 'a trumpery affair', the furore over Ernie Payne's boots had an upside, though. Many people thought the FA had gone over the top and Spurs got enormous and favourable publicity out of it. Their Christmas away game at Southampton drew a crowd of 6,000. The fact that Spurs lost 1-0 was beside the point; it convinced John Oliver that there were plenty of people prepared to pay to watch football and indirectly bankroll a professional side.

The week before Christmas 1895, the directors met in a pub called The Eagle off Tottenham High Road and, despite the objections of some of the amateurs who could see that with pros on board their playing days would be numbered, managed to push through the resolution. Oliver, their main benefactor and the man who was guaranteeing all their debts, threatened to walk out if the vote went against him. Tottenham Hotspur were now a professional club, with the stated ambition to compete with the great clubs of the era.

John Oliver was as good as his word, but it took a while longer than everyone had hoped. And to understand why that was the case requires a short detour into the football politics of the last decades of the 19th century.

Football's north-south divide drew its origins from the conflict between amateurism and professionalism. As with rugby and cricket, the game had been codified in the public schools, and when the Football Association formed in 1863 the game was looked on largely as a gentlemanly sport, dominated by the professional middle classes. The ethos was that of the muscular Christianity of the public schools, whose Old Boys filled the team sheets of famous amateur clubs like Corinthians and Pegasus and inspired the schoolboys of Tottenham Hotspur.

But north of Watford things had changed. The growth of the industrial cities meant concentrated populations of males who, before the arrival of film, cars and music, looked to football for their main source of entertainment. And what really turned football into a growth industry was the introduction in the 1870s of half-day Saturdays in the working week. For businessmen, it meant an opportunity. Ring off a field, pit two teams against each other and charge admission.

The north of England, therefore, had a head start when it came to selling tickets to football matches. The less industrialised south provided a smaller pool of potential punters and by that time the power base of English football had shifted away from the southern toffs to the industrial north and the Midlands. With more and more of these clubs turning professional, the ad-hoc fixture list of FA Cup, inter-county and ordinary matches was seen by many as an unreliable money stream. Led by the north, clubs were considering how to turn over a steady profit. Three years after it became legal to pay players in England, one William McGregor, an Aston Villa director, came up with the idea of a league competition that would provide a guaranteed number of fixtures for its member clubs. He got 11 other clubs onside and in April 1888, in a get-together at the Royal Hotel, Manchester, the directors of Accrington, Aston Villa, Blackburn Rovers, Bolton Wanderers, Burnley, Derby County, Everton, Notts County, Preston North End, Stoke, West Bromwich Albion and Wolves presided over the birth of the professional game. They called their offspring the Football League.

The first season of the Football League began a few months later on 8th September with the 12 member clubs all positioned above a line drawn north of Coventry.

So, five months after going professional and eight years on from the genesis of the Football League, Spurs applied to join. Out of 10 clubs applying to join the Second Division Football League, they got the fewest votes. You only had to look at a map of England to see why. Arsenal, still based at Woolwich, and actually a younger club – it was founded in 1886 – had already joined the Second Division in 1893, and were the only London club in the league. The other Football League chairmen didn't fancy the expense of travelling down south twice in a season so they weren't about to vote in another London club any time soon.

So Oliver put Plan B into action. At the end of the 1895/96 season, Spurs applied to join the Southern League. Having sprung up in 1894 following the collapse of the Southern Alliance, this was the main competition outside the Football and Scottish Leagues and the precursor to the Football League's Third Division. Oliver made a persuasive case that having a well-supported club like Tottenham would boost the Southern League's credentials as a rival to the Football League. The Southern League bought the argument and Spurs were allowed to go straight into the First Division.

Now comes the next strand of the story. It starts in Scotland, where the game was played in a distinctive style which we'd categorise today as 'pass and move'. It depended on teamwork and was almost the opposite of the individualistic, dribbling style common in England when the Football Association was coming into being. But in the

1870s, when Scotland started playing England in amateur internationals, the Sassenachs were given a masterclass in a passing game which was not only more watchable but played with breathtaking technical superiority.

Unmoved by the fact that the folks back home were branding them 'traitorous wretches' and 'base mercenaries', the Scots started responding to the lure of wonga in brown envelopes and then legitimate payment once the FA legalised professionalism in 1885. The impact they made upon English football was immediate and wide-ranging. The first English team ever to do the Double, Preston North End, was filled mostly with men from north of the border. So was the title-winning Sunderland side of 1892-95. Liverpool went even further. When they emerged onto the pitch for the first time in 1892, their entire team was Scottish.

Once they'd turned professional, Tottenham had got in on the act too and imported half a dozen Scots of their own. Within another six years the club had nine on their books. In the 1897/98 season, they finished third in the Southern League. And the team's successes meant top clubs like Sheffield United, Sunderland and Bolton were willing to travel to Northumberland Park for friendlies. Matches such as those brought in the crowds – between 1896 and 1899 attendances increased from an average of 2,000 to 12,000 for one fixture against Reading – but they were still lower than the committee had hoped for when Spurs had turned pro. Without enough in gate receipts, not only were the directors faced with funding ground improvements and wages themselves, they were also liable for Tottenham's debts.

In 1897, urgently needing to raise some cash, the board called in local entrepreneur and moneyman Charles D. Roberts as an advisor. Roberts had a whiff of the adventurer about him – he'd been a soldier in the Hertfordshire Yeomanry and legend had it that he had been a pitcher for the Brooklyn Dodgers baseball team. Something of a blue-sky thinker, Roberts's first brainwave was to stage a military tournament at the Northumberland Park ground. As a money-spinner, it was a wet firework, raising £100, nowhere near enough to guarantee financial stability and bring in new investment. Unfazed, Roberts advised the committee to wind up the old club, form a limited liability company and issue shares. So on 2nd March, 1898, at a meeting at Tottenham's Red Lion pub, the club became Tottenham Hotspur Football and Athletic Club Limited, offering 8,000 £1 shares and with a board of directors made up of John Oliver (chairman), Charles Roberts, Ralph Bullock, one of the Thompson brothers and Bobby Buckle.

Not a man to hang around, just 12 days later Roberts brought Frank Bretell down from the north to become the first manager of Tottenham Hotspur. A Liverpudlian with Irish blood, Bretell had been a goal-scoring forward who doubled as manager at Everton while holding down a job as reporter and football columnist for the *Liverpool Mercury*. He was also almost as indestructible as Rasputin. One incident, an on-field collison, had left him with a crushed chest that entailed two months on his back in hospital. Unbowed, he had come back and carried on in defence until he broke his leg in a match at Stanley Park. Even that hadn't deterred him. When that had mended, he had reinvented himself as a goalie.

In 1896 he hung up his boots and became manager of Bolton Wanderers. When he took over, an article in *Cricket and Football Field* magazine described him as 'to say the least, thoroughly conversant with every phase of professional football, whilst on the authority of the Liverpool press I see that his ardour in connection with theatrical galas and other sports at Anfield has contributed greatly to their success'.

The article finished by expressing the optimistic sentiments that Bolton could not be in better hands. The print on it was barely dry before Bretell upped sticks and headed for north London. One of the first things he did was to get half of Bolton's squad to join him, by offering them all £3 10s (£3.50) a week, which didn't make him fantastically popular around Burnden Park.

Nor was his popularity long-lasting around Tottenham. In February 1899, Brettell did a reverse-Harry and left Spurs for Portsmouth, who apparently offered him twice the money he was getting in north London. Already under the financial cosh by now, Tottenham limped through the rest of the season to finish in seventh place. By this time, it's obvious that the dominant figure in the boardroom was Charles Roberts, not John Oliver, whose business interests appear to have suffered from the amount of cash he was throwing Tottenham Hotspur's way. Taking advantage of his fellow director's weakened financial position, Roberts seized the opportunity to take over and move the club to a larger-capacity ground. Northumberland Park was simply not big enough anymore. The signs had been there for a couple of years. In February 1897, the FA had ordered the closure of the ground for two weeks after a pitch invasion by fans during a game against Luton when, aggrieved by Luton being given a goal that looked like a handball and then the disallowing of what should have been a late winner for Spurs, fans had attacked three Luton players. Then on Good Friday, 1898, 15,000 turned up for a home game against Woolwich Arsenal, a lot of them with a restricted view and with thousands left outside. Five people needed treatment after the collapse of the refreshment hut roof which they'd climbed on to watch the game.

Spurs had outgrown their ground so Charles Roberts acted on a rumour. Behind the old White Hart pub on Tottenham High Road was a former market garden which, it seemed, the brewers, Charringtons, might be prepared to sell. Charringtons had earmarked the land for housing development, but Roberts and Bobby Buckle convinced them that, with 4,000 customers attending a football match every Saturday, in the long term the massive spike in the White Hart's trade would be far more lucrative.

They signed the deal with Charringtons early in the summer of 1899, which left them with four months to get the new ground ready. It was going to be the finest ground in the south, or so boasted the 1900 club handbook; at 25,000 capacity it was going to be able to pack in twice as many fans as Northumberland Park. The wooden stand from the old ground was dismantled, moved and reassembled with extra seating; parking provision was made for bicycles and stabling for horses; and the pitch was 10 whole yards wider and looked after by the top groundsman in London – John Over, who had marked out the pitch for the first Test Match against the Australians at The Oval in 1880.

With the club, as usual, a bit insecure on the cash front – the move to the new ground had set them back a then eye-popping £1,200 – Roberts organised the first event on the new ground. On the August Bank Holiday another military tournament took place; the attractions on offer included show-jumping, an international fencing contest, battles re-enacted using bicycles for warhorses and a mini-sports day for players. John Cameron, one of the imported Scots who on Bretell's departure had taken over as player-manager, won the half-mile handicap and the football dribbling competition.

The first football match on the new ground – a friendly against Notts County, the oldest club in the country – took place on 4th September, 1899, one day short of the club's 17th birthday. With a nod to the club's beginnings, one of the lamppost boys, Hamilton Casey, ran the line. Charles Roberts performed the ceremonial kickoff and along with 5,000 other spectators then watched Tottenham go behind to an own goal. They weren't behind for long; Tom Pratt had levelled by half-time and in the second half David Copeland completed a hat-trick, although for the last two goals County had been reduced to 10 men as their goalkeeper was injured. Spurs won 4-1.

There remained the issue of naming the ground. It would be good to be able to recite some romantic story about how the home of Tottenham Hotspur got its name. The reality was much more banal. They trialled 'Percy Park', 'Gilpin Park' and 'Champion Park', none of which caught on. In the end people just started calling it White Hart Lane because that was the name of the access road to the ground next to the White Hart pub.

CHAPTER FOUR

THE FIRST OF
THE FIRSTS

In their last year at Northumberland Park, Spurs had adopted a new strip of white shirts and navy shorts, in tribute to Preston's Double-winning 'Invincibles' of 1888/89. The following season, now in residence at White Hart Lane, Preston showed their appreciation by knocking Spurs out in the first round of the FA Cup. But for the man embarking on his first full season in charge it was only a temporary blip. With John Cameron as player-manager, Spurs were about to embark on a period of success that would shortly see them hailed as a football phenomenon.

The 26-year-old Cameron was the first player Frank Bretell had signed on taking the job of Spurs manager. Born in Ayr and a product of Scotland's meritocratic education system, he was a classic inside-forward in the old Scottish mould, first with Ayr Parkhouse and then Queen's Park Glasgow, a club that introduced the pass-and-move game to the world and dominated Scottish football between the 1880s and early 1890s. But it also remained obdurately amateur. That and the inevitable outcome that the club was no longer pre-eminent in the game gave Cameron the impetus to become one of those 'traitorous bastards', enraging his countrymen when he left to seek his fortune at Everton. There he became Bretell's team-mate, supplementing his income by working as a clerk in the offices of the Cunard shipping line and then becoming a sportswriter. (It's beside the point, but he also possessed the kind of good looks that these days would have got him his own underwear range.)

A kind of prototype Danny Blanchflower, Cameron was a leader, an articulate and independent-minded personality who objected to the way the game's administrators treated its players as serfs. In him was detectable the same kind of bolshy, bloody-minded spirit that would later have Blanchflower locking horns with chairmen and managers. In Cameron's case, it persuaded him, while at Everton, to become one of the driving forces behind the forming of the Association Footballers' Union. The AFU, the short-lived predecessor of the PFA (it was inaugurated in 1898 and dissolved in 1901), led and lost a campaign to stop the £4-a-week cap on players' wages. Cameron's union activities earned him a reputation as a troublemaker and got him more or less blacklisted by the northern clubs who had dominated the Football League. It's not an outside bet that the timing of the offer from Southern League Tottenham was convenient.

Like Blanchflower, Cameron combined technical skill with the ability to assess and make tactical changes on the pitch. As an enthusiastic venturer into a transfer market where his union connections were useful in attracting players, he also had Bill Nicholson's ability to identify the correct man for the job, and in the same way as Nicholson's Double-winning side did, John Cameron's Spurs featured a handful of top-class players and others who raised their game alongside them. From Preston North End he brought in Sandy Tait, a courageous, ferocious-looking Scot who possessed a heavy-duty moustache, a sideline as a coal merchant and a reputation for tackles so fearsome and unyielding that he was known as 'Terrible Tait'. With him controlling things from the back, Cameron knew he had the man he wanted to take Tottenham where Charles Roberts wanted it to go.

Not the most twinkle-toed of players, Tait had everything else: positional sense, intelligent distribution and a willingness to cover for team-mates, and at White Hart Lane he aroused the same kind of deep, enduring unconditional passion in the hearts of fans that Graham Roberts would do in later times. He might have been a hard bastard, but he was their hard bastard. Along the way, he also established himself as the best left-back in the English game. In front of him was the club captain and Welsh international half-back Jack Jones, a driving, enthusiastic player in the Alan Mullery mould. By the time Cameron took over, Jones was practically the only survivor of the pre-Bretell era, but he clinched his place by forming an immediate and effective connection with two more Cameron signings. David Copeland, a moody type but intelligent and hard-working, was the goal-getter at inside-left. Outside him was the speedy, clever ball-player John Kirwan, a blond Dubliner and Ireland international who had been Cameron's partner on the left wing at Everton. These three – Jones, Copeland and Kirwan – were soon being called 'the most effective attacking triangle in the land'.

Another of Cameron's signings in the summer of 1899 had been the goalkeeper George Clawley. Arriving at White Hart Lane via Southampton and Stoke, Clawley was an innovator who would sprint out to catch crosses and corners, or clear through-balls from the feet of attackers at a time when keepers usually stuck solidly to their line.

But what was most striking about this Tottenham side is that none of them were homegrowns. Clearly Cameron liked his own folk around him – a lot were Ayrshire Scots. In contrast, the left-half Ted Hughes was Welsh and Harry Erentz was half-Danish and hailed from Dundee. Being born in Lincolnshire – as defender Tom Morris was – was as far south as any of the rest got. It was a team, though. In the summer, in an early version of bonding, Cameron revived the Hotspur Cricket Club. And during the season, if they wanted to head for the bright lights, the London Football Social Club was right by White Hart Lane station. There, between training sessions, the players could while away the time playing billiards. Sometimes the directors would drop by. It wasn't quite Chinawhite but it answered a need.

For a start, there was a lot of time to be killed. Writing in CB Fry's *Magazine*, it was the boast of Sam Mountford, the trainer, that: 'Tottenham Hotspur is the lightest trained team in existence.' Cameron's philosophy emerged a few years later in the book he published in 1908, *Association Football and How to Play it*. 'During the season, walking and some practice at kicking, with an occasional sprint, are quite enough to keep the player well.' As a training routine, it would most definitely have had Gerry Francis, Christian Gross and Juande Ramos all foaming at the mouth.

The regime worked, though. By Christmas Day, 1899, the side had chalked up 11 wins in 13 games. That included a 3-0 home win against Frank Bretell's Portsmouth, one which probably decided the season. Portsmouth and Spurs were still fighting for the Southern League title on the season's closing day. On 28th April, 1900, Spurs travelled to Kent-based New Brompton, to whom Frank Bretell had offered a win bonus. Spurs saved him the money. Goals by Cameron and Copeland gave them a 2-1 victory and the title.

Newspapers reported that Tottenham's large travelling support invaded the pitch at the final whistle and carried the players shoulder-high to the dressing room. Returning home, the team found the same jubilation. The Tottenham Town Band serenaded them as they walked up the road from the station to White Hart Lane. The London papers called them 'The Flower of the South' and the *Tottenham Herald* penned what is probably the first Spurs chant, a tribute verse which ended:

> *I care not for things political,*
> *Or which party's out or in,*
> *The only thing I care about,*
> *Is will Tottenham Hotspurs* [sic] *win.*

The club had even finished in profit. The title run had turned the finances around. When the season ended, they were in the black to the handsome sum of £71.

John Cameron had barely got the mud washed off his strip before he was back in the transfer market. Sandy Brown was a 22-year-old centre-forward who had played three seasons with Preston. You wouldn't have watched him and thought, 'This bloke's got finesse,' but the previous season he'd hit the net 29 times for Portsmouth. He was also an Ayrshire man, from the same mining village as Sandy Tait, hence his nickname 'The Glenbuck Goalgetter'. But an injury-wrecked defence meant the reigning Southern League champions made a dismal start to the 1900/01 season. The FA Cup, the start of which was delayed until February after the death of Queen Victoria kicked off a period of statutory mourning, was their only hope of silverware.

Spurs' cup record hadn't suggested they were on the brink of anything ground-breaking. They had first taken part in the competition in the 1894/95 season, going out 4-0 to Luton Town in the fifth qualifying round, and their best effort in the next five years was to reach the third round proper. Having been knocked out by Preston in 1899/1900, no one was expecting glory any time soon when Spurs drew them again in the first round of the 1900/01 competition.

But it was here, in a 1-1 draw at White Hart Lane, that Sandy Brown kicked off a run of scoring in every round in the cup. In the replay at Deepdale, his old stamping ground, he hit a hat-trick in Spurs' 4-2 win. Next up were Bury, the cup-holders and then one of the giant clubs of the north west. With 10 of their cup-winning side playing that day, Bury were one up after two minutes and Spurs were being comprehensively outplayed until Tom Smith broke away on the counter-attack and centred from the right. Brown booted that one home and then, soon after the restart, the match-winner.

With two Football League Division One sides accounted for, Spurs were beginning to drive home the point – southern sides weren't a soft touch any longer. If you were looking for proof, it was another southern club, Reading, that gave them the toughest game in the whole competition. Meeting at Reading's ground, Spurs were a goal down at half-time, but their luck was in. Kirwan got the equaliser and the ref failed to notice Sandy Tait's surreptitious handball clearance from the line. Then, in the replay at the Lane, a magical bit of goal-scoring by Copeland and two more from Brown took them to their first-ever FA Cup semi-final.

At Villa Park, a 46,000 crowd saw West Bromwich Albion wiped out by four goals from Brown in a Spurs performance that had one paper calling them 'exceedingly fine, pretty and delightful on the ball'. In the other semi, Sheffield United came off best against Aston Villa and were promptly tipped as certainties to win the cup. They had beaten Sunderland, Everton and Wolves to get to the final, and they had nine internationals in the side, including Fred Priest who had scored in three previous finals.

That year, the final was on 20th April at Crystal Palace. Spurs prepared for the biggest match in their history by staying at the Royal Forest Hotel in Chingford on the Friday night. They travelled to the game by taking a train from there to Liverpool Street and then made their way by four-in-hand horse-drawn carriage to Crystal Palace where they were greeted by what was then a world record crowd of 114,815. There's a brilliant list in *The Spurs Miscellany* book of the food stockpiled by the caterers for the occasion, which included 40 whole lambs, 55,120 portions of cake, 300lbs of whitebait and 200 ducks. Say what you like about the Edwardians, they knew how to party.

Seventy-five thousand of the fans had come down from Sheffield – South Yorkshire must have looked pretty empty that day – and, spooked by the sheer scale of the event, Spurs let United take the lead through a Fred Priest goal on 20 minutes. They came back, though. Sandy Brown equalised on the counterattack 12 minutes later and then, sent through by Cameron, put Spurs into the lead with a rising shot five minutes after the restart.

The euphoria didn't last. Sheffield United equalised with a goal that wasn't. Spurs keeper George Clawley had saved a shot from Bert Lipsham; the linesman signalled for a corner and the referee, Mr Arthur Kingscott, gave it as a goal.

Cameron wrote later that he had 'never been so furious on a football pitch as when Mr Kingscott ruled that Sheffield United had scored . . . He was the only person among a world-record attendance who thought the ball had crossed the line'. This was the first-ever FA Cup Final to be filmed and the newsreel footage rushed out to local cinemas showed that the ball was a foot in front of the line when Clawley had made the save.

There was nothing that Spurs could do. The result stood at 2-2, and a week later they met Sheffield United again in the replay at Bolton's ground, Burnden Park. The station at Bolton was being rebuilt, which gave the Lancashire and Yorkshire Railway the pretext not to offer discounted fares, and for most Spurs fans it meant the six-hour journey north was a non-starter. Even travelling from Sheffield was beyond most pockets, which meant the vast majority of the 20,470 crowd were locals.

They stood through a first half dominated by Tottenham who, having caused all the upheaval, managed to go one down just before the break when United scored on the counterattack through Fred Priest. There followed a five-minute eternity of backs-to-the-wall defending by Clawley, Erentz and Sandy Tait before the half-time whistle went.

After the restart, Cameron changed the shape. In midfield, Spurs began to match the United players. Having been on the receiving end of that late first-half pressure, the half-backs Morris, Hughes and Jones were now the ones who were in control. The attack began to operate with power and energy and with 55 minutes gone Cameron latched onto an interception by Tait, played a one-two, knocked the ball wide to Tom Smith and positioned himself to get the pass back before clipping the equaliser beyond 6ft 4in 18-stone United keeper William 'Fatty' Foulke.

Brown, muted in the first half, had a shot stopped by Foulke and put another just wide before Smith pounced onto a poor United clearance and gave Spurs the lead with 75 minutes gone. Brown's 83rd-minute header made it 3-1.

Fifteen goals, at least one in every round of the competition. No one's ever beaten Brown's record. He was one of five Scots who, with two Welshmen, one Irishman and three Englishmen, had won the FA Cup for Tottenham Hotspur. There was delirium as the Spurs fans who had managed to get there ran onto the pitch, delaying the cup presentation.

The wife of Spurs director Morton Cadman tied blue-and-white ribbons to the handles of the cup, which the players held aloft once they'd escaped the mêlée. Afterwards the ribbons were stowed away safely ready for the next FA Cup Final victory – for which the club would have to wait a couple of decades – but the tradition of tying ribbons to the handles of the FA Cup in the colours of the winning team had been born.

It was one o'clock in the morning when they arrived back at South Tottenham station, and eyewitness reports have it that the crowd welcoming them home was bigger and better than the one that had cheered the Relief of Mafeking (a decisive victory for the British in the Second Boer War) the year before. Thirty thousand people gathered to welcome the FA Cup to the ground, along with fireworks and the Tottenham Town Band playing *See, The Conquering Hero Comes*.

You have to put yourself back in that era to see what a fantastic feat this was. Tottenham Hotspur, not even a Football League side, had beaten the stranglehold of the north and the Midlands. They'd beaten four First Division clubs, come from behind to win in four out of their eight matches, and in the final had beaten the league champions of two seasons back. They were the first professional southern side to win the FA Cup. They were the only non-League side since the Football League started in 1888 to win it, too. They still are.

It was a warm day in May 2011 when Spurs played Blackpool in the game chosen to celebrate what's still *the* landmark achievement in English football: the Double of 1961. A special match programme was on sale, raising funds for the Tottenham Tribute Trust. If you wonder what that's got to do with the FA Cup win of 1901, the answer's easy. It was the Tottenham Tribute Trust who at last ensured John Ripsher was properly commemorated.

What happened to Ripsher makes sad reading. He had served the club as president from its beginnings to 1894 when he stepped down. Spurs by then were on the brink of great things; in the following few years they would move to White Hart Lane, win the Southern League and the FA Cup. But life didn't treat Ripsher so well. Just after the start of the 20th century, he moved to Dover to live with his sister and her husband William, proprietor of the Diamond Hotel in Heathfield Avenue. What happened in the following years is lost in the mists of time, but John Ripsher ended his days in the Union Road Workhouse in January 1906. Blind, suffering from severe heart problems and general ill health, he died on 24th September, 1907, aged 67. His burial place was a pauper's grave at St Mary's cemetery, Dover.

There he lay forgotten until tracked down by the author Peter Lupson in the process of researching *Thank God for Football*, a book on the origins of football clubs founded by churches. Exactly a century after Ripsher's death, the Tottenham Tribute Trust raised the funds to have a headstone featuring the club crest and motto added to his grave.

The subsequent success of the club has surpassed Ripsher's wildest imaginings. By the time he left, Tottenham was still a small London club, albeit one with wildly big ambitions and owners who were prepared to take risks. Just six years later it would be a football giant and the blueprint for the club as we know it today.

The men who gave Tottenham its shove into the future were John Oliver, Charles Roberts and John Cameron. But if Ripsher hadn't taken the boys under his wing, the club would most probably have dwindled and died out like all those other now-forgotten teams that played on Tottenham Marshes. He was at the heart of the club at its beginnings and without him all the rest would never have happened.

CHAPTER FIVE

THE HUMAN CHAIN OF LIGHTNING

Never again in Spurs' history will there be anyone like Vivian Woodward. Not that the likes of Jimmy Greaves or Glenn Hoddle or Gareth Bale are anything less than unique either, but rather that a playing career like Woodward's would be impossible to replicate now. Even back at the start of the 20th century he was one of a dying breed, an old-fashioned gentleman amateur who remained such for the whole of his footballing life. Vivian John Woodward was, quite simply, a one-off.

When Tottenham recruited him as a 21-year-old in April 1901, the term 'impact signing' hadn't been coined, but VJW was just that – the first Spurs flair player, a Jürgen Klinsmann, a glamorous crowd-magnet capable of sensational goals and almost outrageous panache, a player who you'd go along to watch in the knowledge that even if what was going on around him was mediocre, he'd come up with something special. As a striker, Woodward had everything that mattered – speed of thought, balance, a talent for clever interplay, the ability to place a shot past the keeper rather than clout the ball and hope. When he made his England debut in the 1902/03 season, scoring twice against Ireland, one journalist described him as 'the human chain of lightning, the footballer with magic in his boots'. He went on to be regarded as one of the best centre-forwards ever to play for England – his 29 goals in 23 full internationals between 1903 and 1911 was a total not topped for more than 40 years.

But there are more intriguing aspects to Vivian Woodward than the cornucopia of talents he displayed on a football pitch. Sandy Tait might have had his sideline as a coal merchant but Woodward was on another social plane entirely; an architect by profession, one who lived in Essex and had his own practice in Kennington. It follows that when he accepted the invitation to join Tottenham it was very much on his own terms.

It's one thing to decline to play because you've had a dizzying expression of interest from Chelsea and the boss goes along with your claim that your head isn't quite right, as happened with Luka Modric in the summer of 2011. Woodward, on the other hand, quite frequently didn't show up at the start of a season for the simple reason that he was committed to appearing as leading batsman and wicket-keeper for the Spencer Lawn Tennis & Cricket Club in South London (he was also effortlessly good at a bunch of other sports ranging from tennis to rollerskating). At other times his absence from the Spurs forward line was due to a self-imposed obligation to turn out for his former football club, Chelmsford City.

Nor does the roll call of idiosyncracies end there. This was a man who, in that era of bribes and bungs and cash stuffed in the toes of boots, refused all offers of payment for his services and who practically needed to be staring down the barrel of a gun before he'd agree to accept reimbursement for his train fare; a player who was held in such awe that not only team-mates but opponents called him 'sir'; and who, as a throwback to the middle of the previous century when football was a sport for gentleman from public schools – he even played in old-style knickerbockers – was rigid in his adherence to the code of fair play, forbearing, even as he received some of the era's most eye-watering, bone-cracking clatterings, to moan to the ref or roll on the ground in simulated agony. Nor did he retaliate. What's more, he wouldn't let his team-mates exact revenge on his behalf either.

But for all the glamour and excitement Woodward gave Tottenham Hotspur, one thing he couldn't bring them was major silverware. His

75 goals in 171 senior matches is a tally even Jimmy Greaves would respect, but he arrived at a time when the glory of the 1901 cup win was beginning a slow fade, and the first few seasons after the triumph at Burnden Park were turning out to be the long goodbye of John Cameron's Spurs.

There's an almost inevitable stage in the life of a football club when a great side begins to age and break up, and Tottenham Hotspur weren't immune. Spurs in the first decade of the 20th century were a nearly side at best, coming close but not close enough in the Southern League championship of 1901/02 and, in 1903/04, finishing runners-up again. Similarly, the FA Cup campaigns were making a habit of being terminated in the quarter-finals, and between 1902 and 1904 all that the club won to put in the trophy cabinet were trinkets in the form of the 1902 Sheriff of London's Charity Shield (for a face-off between the best professional and best amateur side in which they beat Corinthians at White Hart Lane) and a couple of pots from minor league competitions.

The decline coincided with the end of John Cameron's days as a player. Though he stayed on as manager, the team seemed to lose its mojo once he hung up his boots and became just another boss. Most of the players he brought south with him were heading off. Sandy Brown, the goal-machine of the FA Cup win, went back to Portsmouth in the summer of 1902 and Tom Smith retired at the same time. As for 'the most effective attacking triangle in the land', Jack Jones was transferred to Watford in 1904 and, in 1905, David Copeland went to Chelsea along with John Kirwan.

At the same time, there were changes going on behind the scenes at White Hart Lane. Back in those days, a manager generally doubled as club secretary. Cameron had been no exception, and in an attempt to relieve him of the paperwork that had begun to get him down, the board took on Arthur Turner, an accountant, to do the admin and look after the paperclips. But that wasn't all. Less helpful to Cameron's cause was that Turner had also been hired to put in train the board's plans for ground development, which meant there wasn't a lot of cash to spare for rebuilding the team. And partly as a result of this lack of funds, Cameron was finding it harder and harder to attract players of the same calibre as the ones he'd lost. The inequality of status between the Football League and the Southern League had intensified rather than diminished. Like the best modern players now demanding Champions League football as a starting point for negotiation, all the top talent was heading for the Football League.

But it probably wasn't even that which was at the heart of Cameron's dissatisfaction. What would most definitely have been unacceptable to him was Vivian Woodward's closeness to the directors. By 1907 things had got so friendly that Woodward was invited onto the board and put in charge of picking the team. History doesn't record whether Woodward had already started putting his oar in before that, but in the spring of 1907, three weeks after losing 4-0 to Notts County in the FA Cup quarter-finals and four days after going down 3-1 at Portsmouth in the league, Cameron suddenly resigned, citing 'differences with the directorate'.

The directors thought it would be a good idea to replace him with Fred Kirkham, a Preston-based referee. Kirkham might have been one of the best-known match officials of his time, but blowing a whistle on Saturdays was his only involvement with football. Mondays to Fridays had been taken up with his day job as a commercial traveller, and with the fans he was about as popular a choice as 'the man in the raincoat' 90 years later.

But the appointment begins to make a bit more sense when you learn the wider context. By the 1906/07 season, when the side had dropped to a sixth-place finish in the league, the inevitable started happening. For all Woodward's crowd-pulling skills, for all Tottenham's ground-breaking reputation as the only southern side to carry off the FA Cup, gates started falling. Charles Roberts, the old Brooklyn Dodgers pitcher, tried to bring back the crowds by establishing baseball at the stadium as a summer game. That plan didn't take off. With London fans spoilt for choice and only knick-knacks to put in the trophy cabinet, Tottenham could see their client base shrinking. Kirkham, with his connections as a referee, was brought in to grease the wheels of a renewed attempt to join the Football League.

A dozen or so years back when the Southern League had formed, the geographical split between them and the overwhelmingly northern-based Football League had made sense. It would have cost everyone too much to fulfil a fixture list involving a fortnightly journey that could have been in any direction from Plymouth to Burnley. Now the position was different. Football was a booming industry, more money was arriving in the clubs' coffers, and transport had become easier and cheaper. The argument for a unified nationwide competition, it follows, was getting to be a strong one.

For the blazers who ran the Southern League, though, the idea of a merger was definitely bad news. A unified competition would mean more than two divisions which would in turn mean more relegation dogfights, and for the Southern League, the younger and financially weaker organisation, it would bring about almost certain subordination to their counterparts up north.

With hindsight, you could see which way things were going. In the battle to protect its own interests, all the Southern League did was collude in its own downfall. In 1905, Chelsea had been formed, complete with a massive new stadium that appeared so suddenly that the residents around Stamford Bridge must have half-expected aliens to walk out of it. The new London club applied to join the Southern League but were rejected at the behest of one Henry Norris, then chairman of member club Fulham, who not surprisingly wasn't about to glad-hand this brash new rival for the gate money in south-west London. Chelsea joined the Football League instead. It's logical to assume that Tottenham were similarly hostile to the prospect of having Clapton Orient competing for bums on seats in their part of London when the latter tried to join the Southern League the following year. So Clapton, which later became Leyton Orient, followed Chelsea into the Football League instead. Then, in 1907, Fulham themselves decided to join them. All at once the Southern League was looking several clubs short of a credible competition.

In the early weeks of 1908, Charles Roberts and the rest of the Tottenham board tried to galvanise the Southern League into taking action, coming up with a raft of proposals to boost its diminishing status as a leisure attraction and money-spinner. Their suggestions were turned down. Acting on the assumption that the combination of a mould-breaking reputation and a top-flight referee as manager would make admittance a rock-solid certainty, Roberts announced that Tottenham would be leaving at the end of the season to join the Football League.

It didn't pan out that way. At the relevant Football League meeting in May 1908, with three places up for grabs, Spurs went into the ballot with Chesterfield, Grimsby Town, Lincoln City, Bradford and Boston United. Spurs finished in fifth place.

The humiliation piled up when Tottenham asked the Southern League to reinstate them. The Southern League agreed, but stated they would have to go into the Second Division. They were rescued from that mortifying climbdown only at the very last moment when Stoke resigned from the Football League while in the throes of a financial crisis. Tottenham applied to fill their place almost before whoever penned the Stoke resignation letter had time to lick the stamp. Even then, it was no shoo-in. Tottenham found themselves competing for a Football League Second Division place with Lincoln, Rotherham and Southport. They got in, but only by polling one more vote than Lincoln.

The fans didn't care how Spurs got in. They didn't care that Spurs were managerless, that the derided Kirkham had packed up and gone back to Preston, and that the team was being picked by the directors and run by the club secretary. They were there in the Football League – that was the important thing. And the main draw was still Vivian Woodward.

On a rainswept Thursday afternoon at the start of September 1908, 20,000 of them turned up for Tottenham Hotspur's first-ever Football League fixture, an exhilarating 3-0 victory over Wolves, the FA Cup holders. It was a game Spurs dominated from start to finish, going one up in six minutes, when Woodward blasted home the club's first-ever league goal. His second arrived straight from the restart. Late in the game Spurs made things safe when Tom Morris, the last man left from the cup-winning side of 1901, threaded his way past three players before blasting a 30-yard effort into the top corner.

Woodward's prolific talent meant he finished the season as top scorer.

It was his goals that won Spurs promotion to the First Division at the first attempt, though not without a nerve-shredding final week when three clubs were fighting for the two promotion places up for grabs. Spurs, West Bromwich Albion and Bolton all had to play deciders against Derby. On the Monday, West Brom lost and on the Wednesday, Tottenham drew 1-1. It was, it turned out, the game that clinched their promotion. They were up, though not as Second Division champions; Bolton took both points against Derby on the Saturday.

Except for Tom Morris, the half-back, the team that took Spurs into the Football League First Division for the first time in its history was unrecognisable from the one that had won the Southern League title back in 1900. Now there was a Geordie, Bert Middlemiss, at outside-left, providing pace and goals (13 in the promotion season); alongside him at inside-left was a Scottish kid, Bobby Steel, providing assists for him and Woodward; there was Steel's older brother, Daniel, at centre-half. Bob Hewitson, the goalie, was a Morpeth man; Joe Walton, a Morecambe lad who'd begun his career at Preston, was at outside-right. At full-back they had another Geordie, Ernie Coquet, who signed for Spurs towards the end of the 1907/08 season in a £500 deal along with Billy Minter. Minter, another early Spurs legend, was a South London boy who had spent three months on the books of Woolwich Arsenal hardly getting a first-team game. (He had no trouble getting one at Spurs, clocking up 334 appearances and 101 goals; it was another 18 years before he hung up his boots.)

With Woodward in the side, there was real optimism that Spurs could announce their arrival in the big time with a title challenge to go with the new stand that was going to be open in time for the start of the 1909/10 season. The West Stand was the work of Archibald Leitch, the brains behind all the new stadiums that had been springing up in the football boom in the first years of the new century. This was the architect and engineer who, in a 40-year spell between 1899 and the start of World War One, put his stamp on the most beautiful citadels in Britain: Goodison, Highbury, Anfield, Old Trafford, Villa Park and Craven Cottage were among those featuring his famous gabled design. With seating for 5,300 and standing room for 6,000 in front, the West Stand at White Hart Lane was the finest, most state-of-the-art stand in the south.

Way back in Spurs' history, someone had made the vague association between the battling Harry Hotspur who gave the club its name and the fighting spurs-clad cockerel that had become the Tottenham Hotspur emblem. Now one specially crafted out of copper by a local craftsman, the ex-amateur footballer WJ Scott, was hoisted on top of the apex of Leitch's signature gable. (Cockerel-trackers note: legend had it that the takings of Spurs' first-ever match at the Lane had been placed inside it, but in 1958 when it was taken down to be transferred to the East Stand and opened up, all that was found inside was a mildewy club handbook.)

But by the time the 1909/10 season opened, by the time the fans crammed into the new stand to watch Tottenham's First Division debut, by the time the gilded fowl was receiving its first paintballing by the local pigeon community, one essential component was missing.

In the spring of 1995, Alan Sugar, the chairman of Tottenham Hotspur, got a shock. Jürgen Klinsmann, the German World Cup hero whom he'd brought to the club with such glee in the summer of 1994, announced his intention of leaving at the end of the season instead of giving the club two years as Sugar insisted had been agreed. Giving an interview to the BBC about the unexpected loss of his prized asset, a ballistic Sugar threw Klinsmann's shirt on the floor.

The Spurs directors of 1909 weren't so unbecomingly incandescent, of course, when Vivian Woodward announced his retirement from top-flight football on the eve of the 1909/10 season. Outwardly, they graciously accepted that he wished to concentrate on his architectural practice while playing for lower-league Chelmsford. Except that turned out not to be the case. In November that year, Woodward returned to Division One of the Football League in the blue shirt of Chelsea.

Woodward's explanation for this quixotic decision was that the Chelsea chairman had written to him, lamenting that his attack was decimated through injury. Woodward, it appeared, had promised him that were he to leave Tottenham he would answer Chelsea's call if they needed him.

Spurs were not long in getting their revenge. The player they took on in Woodward's place was Percy Humphreys, a Chelsea discard. Spurs had struggled most of the season and needed to beat fellow relegation-romancers Chelsea in the last game of the season to avoid dropping straight back down. The final score was 2-1 and Percy Humphreys was the man who scored the winning goal that sent the Blues down instead.

Woodward's story is too absorbing to leave it there. By now in his thirties, he carried on playing for Chelsea, helping them win back their First Division place in 1911/12 before the Great War provided the horror-strewn partition between life before and life after. On 8th September, 1914, Woodward joined the Territorial Army, then trans-ferred in 1915 as a second lieutenant to the Diehards, the 17th Service Battalion (1st Football) of the Duke of Cambridge's Own (Middlesex Regiment). Granted leave to play for Chelsea against Sheffield United in the 'Khaki Cup Final' of 1915, he declined selection because he didn't want to displace Bob Thomson, who had played in the earlier rounds.

In November 1915, the Football Battalion transferred to France. Two months later, in January 1916, Woodward was wounded in the leg by a grenade blast. He returned to the trenches seven months later, but ultimately became a physical training instructor, ending his war as coach of the British Army football team. Demobbed in 1919, he went on to design the main stadium stand for the 1920 Antwerp Olympics stadium.

And he carried on playing football. One of those people who loved the game so much he was unable to let it go, he simply turned out in lower and lower leagues until the decision to stop was made for him by the toll the years had taken on his body.

When he packed up playing, Jürgen Klinsmann went off to California to live the dream with his wife and kids – most recently taking charge of the US soccer team – still worshipped by the fans, his name in the frame any time Spurs needed a new manager.

Woodward's life after his playing days were over offers a bleak contrast. He gave up his architectural practice and went back to Essex to take up dairy farming, a venture that hit the skids in the Great Depression of the 1930s. His life later on was marked by financial problems and loneliness; if your team-mates call you 'sir' it's something of a giveaway – you're not going to be one of the lads. At 70, alone, hard up and in failing health, he was moved by the FA into a nursing home in Ealing, where he died in 1954.

Woodward's refusal to be tied to any club was mirrored by his avoidance of conventional ties in his personal life; he never married. What private demons did he battle with? What kind of life did he live away from football? It's impossible to know, but for a footballer these questions are as relevant today.

Above all Woodward was the supreme example of a type that no longer exists: the gifted amateur. It's pointless to begrudge today's players their country mansions, their absorption in multi-million-pound commercial deals, their places on the rich lists alongside web entre-preneurs and budding young oligarchs. The fact is, the whole energy of the global transfer market is what gives 21st century football its drive and buzz. But sometimes when you think of Vivian J. Woodward in his Edwardian knickerbockers, refusing to take the money for his train fare while scoring some of the most magical goals ever seen at White Hart Lane, you can't help feeling a bit nostalgic.

CHAPTER SIX

HEROES AND VILLAINS

On the opening day of the 2011/12 season, the home game against Everton was postponed due to the London riots laying waste to the Tottenham High Road. The following week, Spurs lost 3–0 to Manchester United at Old Trafford. The fans had barely had time to banish the traumatic, flashing mental images of grinning United strikers when a dire start to the season continued with a 5–1 thrashing at White Hart Lane by Manchester City. No points. Bottom of the table. Yet an inexplicable frivolity was detectable in the fans' mood that afternoon. Inexplicable, that is, to anyone who didn't know the background. Yes, Modric was 'unsettled' after being linked to a move to Chelsea. Yes, it was the second-worst start to the season in Spurs' history. But brightening the immediate gloom was that at the other end of the M1, the Old Trafford scoreboard read 'Manchester United 8 Arsenal 2'.

That was Arsenal's worst defeat since 1896. That was total humiliation. Just why it should have caused so much glee among the Tottenham faithful is a story almost as old as the club itself.

In the early part of the 20th century Arsenal might have been the only club south of Birmingham in the Football League, but at the time they were stuck out in Woolwich. At the time, Woolwich Docks might have been the engine room of the Empire, but it just about required an expeditionary force to reach it from the city. The club had been formed in south London in 1886, four years after the formation of Spurs, by a group of workers at the Dial Square workshop in Woolwich Arsenal. According to the Topspurs historian, they played their first match on a field with an open sewer running through it. Even though they found a more sanitary venue after that, it wasn't only Football League teams who didn't much fancy hiking out to tufty, windblown Plumstead Marshes; most of London didn't, either. Even though the competition was lower in status, it had been Southern League Tottenham Hotspur, not Football League Arsenal, who the football fans of the capital were piling in to watch.

That state of affairs worsened for Arsenal once Spurs joined them in the Football League. Even though Spurs spent most of the 1909/10 season in the drop zone, their average home attendance was nearly double that of the powerful clubs of the Midlands and the north. And then, in 1910, after the club became so rundown and unloved it went into voluntary liquidation, a majority shareholding in Woolwich Arsenal was taken by one Henry Norris.

Norris was a property developer who made his pile building large parts of SW6 and who in due course was to become Sir Henry, Mayor of Fulham, chairman of Fulham FC, a freemason and a Conservative member of parliament. He was also an enthusiastic practitioner of the dark arts of bribery, inducements and cronyism, and in the years to come, he was to earn a lifetime ban from football for financial irregularities and fiddling his expenses (his offences included pocketing the profits from the sale of the team bus). He was, in short, a bit of a bad hat, and he was about to change the landscape of football in north London forever.

In the early part of the 20th century, while Fulham's chairman, Norris was offered the chance to move the Cottagers to Stamford Bridge, which businessman Gus Mears had recently acquired. Norris baulked at the £1,500 per annum rent, so Mears subsequently created his own team, Chelsea, to occupy the ground.

At the time, Norris was also chairman of the Southern League, membership of which he denied Gus Mears's Chelsea when they subsequently applied to join. His plot to block his rival's progress went pear-shaped, however, when the new club was accepted into the more attractive Football League instead.

A bit of a Robert Maxwell, Norris then tried to create a London superclub by merging Fulham with his newly-acquired Arsenal. The Football League, though, thwarted his plans.

Cutting his ties with Fulham, struggling to keep Arsenal from going belly-up and coveting the gates that Tottenham and Chelsea were pulling in north of the river, Norris then decided to move Arsenal to a new stadium. The site he settled on was the recreation ground of St John's College of Divinity, just down the Seven Sisters Road from Tottenham and on the tube. His cosy relationship with Randall Davidson, Archbishop of Canterbury, was no hindrance, the old clerical patsy personally signing the ground's title deed. In the face of strong objections from Spurs and Clapton Orient, not to mention their own fans in South London, Arsenal moved to their new Archibald Leitch-designed home, Highbury, in 1913 following their relegation to the Second Division. But if Tottenham were upset about Arsenal moving onto their doorstep, they had even more reason to be angry six years later, for Sir Henry wasn't finished yet.

The 1914/15 season, played out in the shadow of the First World War with players and spectators alike going off to fight, ended with Spurs finishing bottom of the First Division along with Chelsea. Arsenal, meanwhile, finished fifth in Division Two and more in debt than ever. After that, the bubble in which football existed even in those early years was no longer impregnable, and competition was suspended. In the summer of 1915, White Hart Lane was requisitioned by the Ministry of Munitions and turned into a factory for making gas masks.

The Armistice was declared on 11th November, 1918, and football was scheduled to restart the following September with an expanded Football League of 44 clubs, with 22 in each of the two divisions. For Tottenham, it looked like a reprieve. The logical assumption was that the revamped First Division would include them and Chelsea as they had been in the division at the end of the 1914/15 season before war intervened. Not so. Or at least not in the case of Spurs. Chelsea were invited back, while Derby and Preston automatically went in right as the top two Second Division finishers of the last pre-war season. The other place went to Arsenal.

How? Well, for Henry Norris, who had spent heavily on the building of the new stadium in north London, the prospect of financial ruin loomed. The only answer was to establish First Division football at Highbury, and one theory is that match-fixing scandals in the final season of football before the war, in which both Liverpool and Manchester United were implicated, were used by Norris as a weapon in his battle to get Arsenal promoted. Norris, it's suggested, demanded that the two northern clubs be punished by relegation or expulsion, and threatened to organise a breakaway from the Football League by Midlands and southern clubs if nothing was done. To placate him the League offered Arsenal a place in the First Division. A more likely story is one of backroom deals or even outright bribery. It's suggested that, rather than making threats, Norris colluded with his friend John McKenna who, as chairman of Liverpool and the Football League, recommended Arsenal's promotion to the AGM as a reward for their 'long service to League football', having been the first League club in the south.

There's a coda to this story which is too good not to be true. Nine years previously, in the close season of 1909, Spurs had gone on a tour of Argentina and Uruguay. On the way back, one of the distractions provided for the passengers on the long boat journey was a fancy dress competition. Two of the Spurs players won it by dressing as Robinson Crusoe and Man Friday, adding to the verisimilitude of their outfits by borrowing the ship's parrot as one of their props. To celebrate their victory, the parrot was presented to the club by the ship's captain. It accompanied them back to White Hart Lane where it thrived for nearly 10 years. The day it died was the day in March 1919 which saw Arsenal usurp Spurs in the First Division.

And the outcome of this masterclass in dodgy dealing, back-stabbing and parrotcide was an emnity so intense that it persists to this day.

That summer 1909 tour of South America has a place in the Tottenham Hotspur story for a second, more serious reason. Travelling with them in the club uniform of dark suit, white shirt and boater was a promising 21-year-old inside-forward called Walter Tull who, after being spotted as an amateur for Clapton, had played a few games for Spurs in the 'A' team and reserves.

The full detail of Walter Tull's inspirational and remarkable life has what it deserves – a book of its own, Philip Vasili's *Walter Tull (1888-1918) Officer, Footballer: All the Guns in France Couldn't Wake Me* – but though he was only with Tottenham for a relatively short time, the impact of his arrival as the first black outfield player in the First Division in England makes a brief resumé of his story essential here.

Tull's grandparents on his father's side were slaves on a plantation in Barbados. His father, Daniel, had been educated by missionaries, after which he left to find work as a carpenter in Britain. Towards the end of the 19th century, most black immigrants headed for major cities or seaports and Daniel settled at Folkestone where he found work as a ship's joiner and married a white Englishwoman, Alice Palmer, the daughter of a farm labourer whom he had met at a Methodist chapel. Walter, their fourth child, was born in 1888. He was seven when his mother died of cancer.

Daniel quickly remarried and started a new family with Clara, his second wife. Two years later, in 1895, tragedy struck again for Walter when Daniel died of heart disease. Twenty-seven years old, left on her own to bring up six children, Clara's only option was to put Walter and his older brother into an orphanage, the London Children's Home in Bethnal Green, founded by a Methodist minister. There Walter joined the orphanage football team while his brother Edward sang in the choir. In the autumn of 1900, Edward went on a money-raising tour with the choir and such was the quality of his voice that a Glasgow family adopted him. Walter stayed on at the orphanage for seven years, starting an apprenticeship with the orphanage's printing department while continuing to show talent as a player in its football team. Advised to try his luck with a club, he wrote asking for a trial to the local amateur side Clapton FC, who played at The Old Spotted

Dog ground in Forest Gate and had been in the Southern League until they ran into financial problems (after that they became founder members of the Isthmian League along with clubs like London Caledonians and Casuals, who had provided opposition for Spurs in their Tottenham Marshes years).

Ten weeks later, Tull was in the first team and being described as the catch of the season after the club picked up three cups with him on board. Spurs moved in on him, offering four pounds a week. It was more than he could earn in the print industry and seemed to offer enthralling possibilities. He made his first appearance for Tottenham at the game which marked their First Division debut, at home to Manchester United, the FA Cup-holders, during which he was brought down for a penalty in a 2-2 draw. Though referred to as a 'darkie', he impressed the reporters, who referred to his 'perfect coolness' and 'accuracy of strength in passing' and averred that 'Tull is very good indeed'. A week later he scored his first goal for Spurs against Bradford City.

After that, though, Tull made only eight more appearances in the first team that season. You begin to get an idea of how tough it was when you read reports of the racial abuse he endured from opposing fans. One notorious game at Bristol City featured 'language lower than Billingsgate', though he was supported by the press who called him 'a model' and 'the best forward on the field'. It wasn't enough to keep him from being put back in the reserves when the proven goal-scorer, Percy Humphreys, arrived at White Hart Lane from Chelsea that December. Neither that season nor the one following saw Tull make anything more than slow progress in winning back a regular first-team place, and his prospects of fulfilling his potential at Tottenham seemed slim. Meanwhile Spurs, looking to strengthen their defence, had been eyeing up Northampton Town's Charlie Brittan, rated as the best right-back in the Southern League, and in October 1911 Tull plus a hefty transfer fee went Northampton's way while Brittan came to Spurs.

When war broke out in August 1914, Tull was still only 25, approaching his peak, and Glasgow Rangers had started to open negotiations for him. But Tull was destined for another kind of glory. Near the end of that December he became the first Northampton player to enlist in the 17th (1st Football) Battalion of the Middlesex Regiment. Known as The Diehards, the infantry battalion was led by a former footballer, Major Frank Buckley, who survived the war to manage Wolves. One of those who served alongside Tull was Vivian Woodward.

During his military training Tull was promoted three times. In November 1914, as Lance Sergeant, he was sent to Les Ciseaux in France, close to the front lines, only to be sent home in the May of the following year with post-traumatic stress disorder. In September 1916, he went back to fight in the Battle of the Somme, in which some 420,000 British troops were killed in just four months. Here, Tull's courage and soldiering ability really stood out. In May 1917, he was commissioned as a 2nd Lieutenant, in spite of military regulations – which didn't change until the Second World War – forbidding those who were of 'non-European descent' from becoming officers.

So, 2nd Lieutenant Walter Tull became the first black officer in the British Army. Fighting on the Italian front, he was mentioned in despatches for his 'gallantry and coolness under fire'. Late, very late on in the war, he was posted to the Somme Valley and on 25th March, 1918, met his death by machine-gun fire while trying to help his men retreat. Several of his men – they included Leicester goalkeeper, Private Tom Billingham – admired him so much they attempted to retrieve his body, but under heavy fire they had to give up. Tull's body was never found and so, like thousands of others fallen in the First World War, he has no known grave. He does, though, have a memorial. It stands outside Northampton Town's Sixfields Stadium, where it does its job of reminding us that a world that can contain a Henry Norris can also contain a Walter Tull.

CHAPTER SEVEN

SUCCESS IS THE BEST REVENGE

There was a deep sense of injustice gnawing at Spurs as they prepared to face a season in the Second Division while Arsenal enjoyed the status that should have been theirs. As far as they were concerned, there was only one option open to them. Success would have to be the best revenge.

By the time the Football League programme resumed after the war, they knew they had a side good enough for the top level. More than good enough, as it turned out. This was a team that would go on to occupy a special place in the Spurs pantheon. Arthur Rowe rated it above his own 1951 side – and Bill Nicholson's Double side, even. That 1919/20 season, they bolted away with the Second Division championship with performance after performance that created a record unbeaten for 27 years: 70 points from a possible 84 (these were, of course, the days of two points for a win), 102 goals, six points clear of runners-up Huddersfield. If the Football League ever thought they could justify their decision to give their rightful place to Arsenal, Peter McWilliam's Spurs proved them wrong with knobs on.

McWilliam had been at White Hart Lane for seven-and-a-half years when Spurs were promoted. He'd been an ambitious 33-year-old in his first job when, in December 1912, he took control at a club that was financially stretched by the continuing programme of improvements to the ground and that had been managerless for four years after the departure of Fred Kirkham, a club where the directors had been picking the team and the shareholders were in open revolt. Things had not just flatlined; they had deteriorated to the extent that when McWilliam arrived the side had chalked up three draws and 10 defeats in their first 13 games. The squad he inherited featured a combination of players past their best and others technically incapable of adapting to the style of play he wanted to impose. Though he staved off relegation in his first season and started the rebuilding work, he had been unable to keep them from dropping into the Second Division at the end of the 1914/15 season. Winning promotion in the first competitive season since the war was, it followed, a welcome vindication of his methods.

And his methods were simple but non-negotiable. Key to McWilliam's success was his belief in skilled, intelligent, creative ball-players and the trust he placed in them to get it right for themselves. An Inverness-born Scotland international, his own playing experience as an attacking left-half had been at the very top level. With 'Peter The Great' in the side, Newcastle United had won three League Championship titles between 1904 and 1909 and an FA Cup in 1910. A year later, calamity struck for him during a Wales-Scotland international in the form of a leg injury so serious it finished him as a player.

Newcastle's loss was Tottenham Hotspur's gain. Arthur Rowe, who was to take the ethos forward with his own push-and-run team, said that it was McWilliam who pioneered The Spurs Way. This was a tough-minded football purist, one who disdained cheats and cloggers and whose core belief was summed up in the statement: 'The movement of men without the ball is as vital as that of the man in possession.' Thirty years on, Bill Nicholson would be reframing that as: 'When not in possession, get into position.' Pass and move.

Plus McWilliam was a smart operator in the transfer market. He was lucky in one way, mind you. Six months before he took the Spurs job, the player was already in place who was going to be *the* one to build the side around. The left-half Arthur Grimsdell had arrived in April 1912 from Watford as an 18-year-old schoolboy star. McWilliam could see straight away that here was a future captain of Spurs and England, a warrior (at the outbreak of war he was one of the first professional footballers to volunteer), a Duncan Edwards or a Bobby Moore, worth his place for his youthful leadership alone. Simultaneously confident and saturnine, Grimsdell was a presence even in his teens, a big man, one with a powerful long-range shot, a dominant force who could attack as well as he could defend. In the 1919/20 season he scored 14 goals, not to mention providing countless assists to the durable and subtly talented Jimmy Cantrell at centre-forward and Bert Bliss, the inside-left who cost Spurs a tenner from Willenhall Swifts in the Easter of 1912.

In April 1913, McWilliam made the first of his own significant signings, paying Northampton Town a record fee of £1,700 to secure the services of the 25-year-old right-winger Frederick 'Fanny' Walden. A 1937 biography by Eric Partridge asserts that Fanny was the nickname given at the time 'to those of dainty physique'. Which Walden had. His armoury of dribbling skills and tricks, though, was magical. 'His feet are quicker than his brain,' was McWilliam's verdict. It wasn't that Walden was thick, but his feet moved so fast. According to Bob Goodwin in *Tottenham Hotspur: The Complete Record*: 'It was not unknown for Walden to play the ball one side of a man and run off the pitch, onto the cinder track, and back to avoid a clumsy challenge.' It must have been like trying to pin down a gnat.

On the other wing, McWilliam deployed the winsomely good-looking Cockney boy Jimmy Dimmock, whom he'd had watched as a schoolboy and signed as a 19-year-old in May 1919. An instinctive player like Cliff Jones, Dimmock was rated by McWilliam and Arthur Rowe as one of the best outside-lefts who ever played; in one game against Newcastle he gave the celebrated defender Bill McCracken such a torrid time that in the end McCracken just shrugged and left the pitch. There was a great line written about him by a *Tottenham Herald* reporter: 'Dimmock scores goals with the casual air of someone pouring out a cup of tea at a family gathering.' Another commented: 'He always looked so handsome on the team photographs with a splendid white parting.' It's true; Dimmock's fair, wavy hair was neatly bisected on the left by a tramline that must have taken the nation's males (Dimmock was something of a hearthrob) hours of primping and glueing to emulate, but in Dimmock's case appeared to be an entirely natural phenomenon, like the Milky Way.

In the centre of defence there was Charlie Walters, who liked going forward when he got the opportunity. At right-back there was Tommy Clay, no greyhound but impeccably controlled and rarely caught out of position; McWilliam was so impressed by his performance when he saw him playing for Leicester against Spurs in a 1914 cup tie that he signed him practically while the man was taking off his boots after the final whistle. There was Scot Bob McDonald at left-back and Bill Jaques in goal. The cornerstone of it all was Bert Smith, right-half and hard man who got through mountainous amounts of no-frills work, perhaps the most significant of which was to cover for Jimmy Seed, inside-right, director of operations and genius.

Along with Grimsdell and Dimmock, Seed was one of the three world-class players of McWilliam's side of the early 1920s. A dark-haired Mackem with bright glowering eyes and a bit of the Gary Neville about him, Seed signed for Spurs midway through the 1919/20 season after McWilliam spotted him playing for the non-League Mid-Rhondda against Ton Pentre at an FA Cup preliminary round game. McWilliam had actually travelled to the Valleys to scout a Ton Pentre midfielder called Darky Lowdell. Blown away by Seed's performance, he took him on instead.

You get a strong impression of what kind of man Seed was because his life is recorded in a fantastic little book, *Jimmy Seed: My Story* (if you like odd connections, Seed's brother Angus went on to become manager of Barnsley, where he brought a young wing-half called Danny Blanchflower over to England from Belfast). At the time Seed joined Spurs he was 24 years old and for the last five of those years he'd been riding an emotional and physical rollercoaster. His parents had wanted him to become a teacher. That wasn't so easy for a working-class Northern lad back then, and he ended up in the pit like most of his mates, playing for his local side, Whitburn, until he got his big break. Just after Sunderland sprung him from the pit by signing him, the First World War broke out. He joined up and was drafted to France. The Armistice was just months away when he was gassed and sent back to England to recover. Sunderland decided the war had finished him off as a footballer and chucked him out.

Which was how Seed ended up in Tonypandy with Mid-Rhondda, assisting them to the Southern League Division Two and Welsh League titles. He cost McWilliam £250 and eternal damnation from the Mid-Rhondda fans, who couldn't believe Seed was going of his own free will and suspected a dark plot hatched between McWilliam and the club to sell Seed because they wanted the money.

McWilliam told Seed that he'd never been forgiven in Mid-Rhondda and when he went back there to take another look at Darky Lowdell he wore glasses and a false moustache. He missed out on Lowdell, who went to Sheffield Wednesday. In fact, Spurs, Jimmy Seed and Darky Lowdell weren't finished with each other yet, but that's another story.

In the 1919/20 promotion season, Spurs had gone very close to making it a promotion and cup double. Instead, in the quarter-finals, at home to Aston Villa, Tommy Clay miskicked into his own net. That was the only goal of the match. Spurs had been the better side that day, but it was Villa who went on to win the cup. Now, as the 1920/21 competition got under way, you would only have to look at the drive and determination on Grimsdell's face to realise that just getting back into the First Division wasn't enough.

Carrying off the League Championship was always going to be beyond them. They lost to Blackburn in their first game and it took them until Christmas to adjust to life in the top division. The FA Cup, though, was something else entirely. They had an easy passage through the first round against Bristol Rovers, winning 6-2. Between that and the second-round tie, Walden picked up a cartilage injury and missed most of the rest of the season. The guy who replaced him for the second-round home game was Jimmy Banks, who scored one of Spurs' four goals against Bradford City, then actually a First Division side. The other three were down to Seed, who dominated the tie and chalked up two of them within two minutes of the restart. In his autobiography, Seed recalled a post-match bollocking from McWilliam that was classic Bill Nicholson: 'That third goal of yours was a terrible shot. Why shoot from 25 yards out? You had time to walk up to the goalkeeper and push it past him like you did with the first goal.'

In the third round, away to Southend, who'd just become part of the newly-formed Third Division (what would now be League One) Spurs turned in one of those typical performances against poor opposition, struggling for an hour to hit anything like their usual form, and rescued from ignominy when Southend missed a penalty. In the end Spurs' winning score of 4-1 – the goals came from Cantrell, Bliss, Banks, and Seed – flattered them to say the least.

So Spurs were through to the quarter-finals again, and for the second year running they were drawn against Aston Villa, the glamour club of the era, the club with some of the giants of the age in the shape of Frank Barson, Sam Hardy and Billy Walker. A year back, they had been sunk by Clay's own goal. This time they got lucky. Twenty-three minutes into the game, a Dimmock centre from the right bounced awkwardly in front of Seed, who choked. 'Then suddenly I felt a terrific crash in my back,' he recalled. 'For a moment I did not know what had happened, but when a deafening roar came from the crowd I looked up to see the ball in the back of the net and a disappointed expression on Sam Hardy's face . . . Jimmy Banks had sized up the situation and spotted something was wrong with me. So he hit me and the ball at great speed as best he could. That winning goal was actually scored off Jimmy's knee!'

The two semi-finals panned out like this: Spurs had to meet Preston at Hillsborough and Cardiff drew Wolves at Anfield. Wolves needed a replay at Old Trafford to beat Cardiff. Spurs got to the final with half the effort; Grimsdell and Dimmock were unstoppable that day, overcoming two disallowed goals and the turning-down of two cast-iron penalties with a marvellous display of trademark interpassing and two goals by Bert Bliss.

The weather on the day of the Stamford Bridge final was on the apocalyptic end of the spectrum. There was a 72,805 turnout to watch in an unrelenting downpour as the pitch morphed into a pond. Deryk

Brown's *The Tottenham Hotspur Story* contains a lovely recollection of the occasion, 50 years on, by a reporter called F.H. Garside who was present. It was, remembered Garside, 'a traditional April day. For twenty minutes before the kick-off the sun shone and then the black clouds came over and the rain fell in torrents. There was no grass on the pitch and the king got bogged down in the mud as he sheltered under an umbrella and was introduced to the players.

'Neither side looked like scoring in the first half. Spurs were much the better team but the mud was a leveller – they couldn't make their skill tell.

'Just after half-time I remember seeing Dimmock get the ball although I don't know how he got it. He cut in straight from the wings with one of those diagonal runs which Joe Hulme and Cliff Bastin used to make in the Thirties. He didn't hit the ball hard – he couldn't because he had to lift it out of the mud. It kept low and crept underneath the goalkeeper's body at the far post. And that was the only goal.

'The crowd were pro-Tottenham with only a few gold rosettes for Wolves, and they went wild. But I've always thought Spurs might have won by a hatful. Wolves had no one to match Clay, Walters, Grimsdell and Dimmock.' Dimmock, Garside added, 'didn't look so handsome amid all that rain. He got the goal, though, and he was the hero'.

So Spurs had won the cup for the second time in 20 years. It was only the second time a southern club had had its name etched on the trophy, and that name was Tottenham Hotspur again.

The players travelled back in an open-top motorcoach to Tottenham where the streets were so crowded that the trams couldn't run. The cup, decorated with the blue-and-white ribbons preserved from 1901, was held by Billy Minter, now the trainer, because Grimsdell, having played a blinder, had done a 'reverse John Terry' and quietly slipped off home to Watford. It was Dimmock who the crowds were shouting for, but he'd also nipped away out of a side door. The celebration dinner was at the Holborn Restaurant, where McWilliam credited Grimsdell with being 'one of the finest captains I've ever known'.

The following season, Spurs came close to a consecutive cup win.

One-nil up at half-time against Preston in the semi-final, they conceded an equaliser soon after the restart. Bliss then got the ball into the net, but the goal was disallowed because, declared the referee, he had seen a Preston player lying injured and had stopped the game before Bliss's shot had landed.

Spurs lost their concentration and let Preston take the lead. That was how it finished. Back in the dressing-room, a disgusted Walden took off his boots. 'There goes my last chance of a cup medal,' he said. 'I'll never kick another ball.' (He wasn't quite right. Not long after, he left Spurs to end his playing days with Northampton. He'd always had a sideline as a county cricketer, and when he finished with football he went on to become a Test match umpire.)

It hadn't been a bad three years for McWilliam's Spurs. They'd won promotion from the Second Division in one season and won the cup the next, as well as finishing in sixth place in the league, three places above Arsenal. In the season that followed, 1921/22, they might have been knocked out of the cup in the semis, but they also finished runners-up to Liverpool in the First Division. Plus Arsenal finished sixth from bottom.

They might not have won a title, but in quality they compared to Rowe's push-and-run team and the one that won the Double for Bill Nicholson. Grimsdell, Seed, Walden, Clay, Smith and Dimmock all picked up England caps.

Maybe Walden was onto something, though. They weren't to know it that day in April 1922, but it was the beginning of the end of a great side.

CHAPTER EIGHT

SPURS SHOOT THEMSELVES IN THE FOOT

It was downhill all the way after the 1921/22 season. The board of directors had sunk the profits from the 1920/21 cup run into ground developments, buying the Red House restaurant by the club gates to convert into offices and adding Leitch-designed covered terraces at the Paxton Road end and the Park Lane End, increasing the ground capacity to 58,000. Unfortunately what all those people were watching wasn't so great, since McWilliam was being denied the funds he needed to build a new team.

Which should have been the imperative, as over the rest of the decade the side was breaking up. Bliss and Cantrell both lost track of how to score goals, with things getting so desperate that at one point Grimsdell was being used as a striker. Clay and Smith were spent forces. Dimmock managed to maintain his edge but, with Bliss and Cantrell out of form, Seed struggled to combine the roles of playmaker and goalscorer. Fresh legs were needed. With McWilliam under instruction to concentrate on bringing in local talent, preferably young, various candidates shuffled in and then out again. To add to the problems, Grimsdell then broke his leg and, towards the end of 1926,

Seed picked up an ankle injury and was sidelined for a couple of months.

He was replaced by an eager former groundstaff boy called Taffy O'Callaghan, who made such an impact on his debut in mid-January that Seed couldn't get his place back. A now-fit Seed moaned to McWilliam, whose response was brief and not altogether hopeful. 'If you were Taffy and you were playing as well as he is, would you expect to give up your place even to you?'

'I travelled as Spurs' 12th man to Liverpool,' recalled Seed, 'and after watching O'Callaghan give a skilled demonstration against Everton, I decided I had little future at Tottenham. I wanted to get out as a player before I boarded the soccer toboggan.'

By the time Seed got home from Liverpool, he'd succumbed to flu. Lying in bed with a temperature, he decided his best move would be to quit playing and go into management. His resolve hardened when Middlesbrough approached McWilliam in February 1927 with the offer of what was then a huge pay hike, one that would take him from £800 to £1500 a year, to take over the managerial reins. It would make him the highest-paid football manager in the country. Even so, McWilliam wanted to stay at White Hart Lane and would have done had the board upped his annual salary by £200 to £1000. They didn't, and off he headed to Teesside. 'I knew Tottenham would never be the same for me again without the man who had been my friend as well as manager,' said Seed.

Promoted to take McWilliam's place, Billy Minter opted to build his side around O'Callaghan. Seed, unsurprisingly, wasn't interested in playing in the stiffs, especially as Spurs cut his wages by a pound a week. He applied for the vacant managerial job at Leeds but got a knockback. Then he saw Aldershot had a job going. Aldershot wanted him, but the Spurs board blocked the move because they wouldn't get a transfer fee.

'Spurs have got something better in mind for you,' Minter told him. Unknown to Seed, Sheffield Wednesday had been making interested noises about him for 14 months. Now Spurs were willing to let him go as a makeweight in the transfer that would bring the wing-half

Darky Lowdell to Tottenham eight years after Peter McWilliam had gone to Mid-Rhondda to scout him and signed Seed instead.

After Minter persuaded Seed that he'd be better off going to Wednesday as a player than Aldershot as a manager, it was a done deal. Since Wednesday were looking copper-bottomed relegation fodder at the time, Spurs definitely thought they'd got the better half of the bargain.

By the end of February 1928, they were in their best position for seven years. They went to league leaders Everton and stuffed them 5-2. Four of the goals came from O'Callaghan. Two more from him in Spurs' 3-0 away win over Leicester put them in the FA Cup quarter-finals. With O'Callaghan being talked up as the new football genius, Minter's Spurs looked as though they were going to repeat the highs of 1921/22.

Then the season hit the wall and slid slowly down to the floor. Six-nil down at half-time, final score 6-1, in the cup quarter-final against Huddersfield on 3rd March. From seventh in the table to second from bottom, with 38 points, only three of which had come from their last seven games. Sheffield Wednesday, in contrast, with Seed as their captain, had taken 17 points from their last 10. Four were picked up from Tottenham over the Easter holiday. Worse, in both games, Seed, playing better than ever, was the scorer. Wednesday finished in a logjam of clubs with 39 points. One solitary point separated them from Spurs, who had 38, only six fewer than Derby County, who finished fourth. You'd have to hunt around for another case of a club getting relegated with that many points. This hatful of depressing statistics highlighted one killer fact – that by offloading Jimmy Seed to Wednesday Spurs had been the architects of their own downfall.

Even the fact that the club that went down with them was Middlesbrough, Peter McWilliam's new outfit, was very brief consolation. He got them promoted the following season. Spurs spent the best part of the next 10 years in the Second Division, with only short-lived appearances in the top flight. Wednesday, with Seed, went on to win a couple of league titles.

Out of his depth, Minter concertinaed under the pressure, and at the end of the 1929/30 season the board moved him sideways to the assistant secretary's job and brought in Percy Smith from Bury. Smith, a smart-witted, square-jawed 50-year-old who shared the playing philosophy of Peter McWilliam, addressed the outstanding problem straight away by finding a half-decent striker. Ted Harper, who arrived from Sheffield Wednesday, was never destined to be the Lionel Messi of his day but he was strong and quick enough to give the defences of the Second Division a torrid time. The 36 goals he scored in 30 league games in the 1930/31 season stayed a club record until Bobby Smith equalled it in 1957/58. They weren't enough to lift Spurs out of the Second Division, though. After that brilliant first season at White Hart Lane, Harper struggled with injury and in 1932/33, Tottenham's half-centenary season, he was replaced in the pantheon by George Hunt, whose wild-man reputation was hinted at in his nickname 'The Chesterfield Tough' but who went on to become England's first-choice centre-forward.

The press raved about him. 'There can never have been a more accomplished dribbler . . . not anyone more adept at recognising, or more fearless at seizing upon, anything remotely resembling a goalscoring chance.' It was a take-no-prisoners approach that produced the goals which hauled Spurs back to the First Division, abetted by the best forward line since the boys of 1921: the mobile Taffy O'Callaghan as playmaker, Willie Davies on the right and Willie Hall, a small, towheaded, brick outhouse of a man who was later to go down in history for scoring five for England against Northern Ireland, the first three of them in three-and-a-half minutes.

The brains of the side was Arthur Rowe, thinking man and attacking centre-half who had signed amateur forms for Spurs as a 15-year-old in 1923. With Rowe on board, Spurs didn't lose at home all season and a year later, back in the top flight, they were in third place by Christmas, just three points behind the leaders, Arsenal. Not for the first time, all the talk was of the championship coming to White Hart Lane at last.

The two rival teams maintained their first and second positions until the end of the season, though by the time Arsenal lifted the title the gap had widened to 10 points. And then, not for the first time either, it went all pear-shaped. Everyone seemed to get injured at once and the 1934/35 season featured a run of 22 defeats, one of the worst losing streaks in the club's history. They lost 6-0 at home to Arsenal, who also beat them 5-1 at Highbury. Smith used 36 players that season, 10 of them half-backs. Where the supporters were concerned every team sheet seemed to feature at least one mystery guest. Critically, in December 1934, Rowe's knee gave out and he was sidelined for most of the season. The brains and control room of the side had gone.

Meanwhile, behind the scenes, Smith had fallen out with the directors over team selection and the buying of players. The ghost of Peter McWilliam, who had left Middlesbrough to act as a scout for Arsenal, still strolled around the walkways at White Hart Lane. For months there had been strong rumours that Spurs wanted him back for real. At the same time, Wally Hardinge, better known as a one-time county cricketer and Arsenal inside-forward, was appointed reserve-team coach. Ostensibly there to knock a bit of shape into the stiffs, it was widely assumed that he was really caretaker-in-waiting for when Smith got the boot. With relegation a certainty, the board informed Smith that they proposed to make management changes. Smith didn't wait to be sacked. He walked out that April, leaving a somewhat reluctant Hardinge to take charge for the final three games of the season and keep the seat warm for McWilliam. Arsenal, though, declined to release McWilliam and Spurs were forced to advertise for a new manager.

So the man who replaced Percy Smith was the dapper, black-trilby-wearing Jack Tresadern, from Crystal Palace. Tresadern was a bit of a celebrity. A smart, terrier-like wing-half at West Ham, he had captained the side that lost to Bolton in the 1923 White Horse final, the first-ever FA Cup Final to be played at Wembley, and was famous for getting absorbed by the 200,000 crowd following Bolton's first goal and being unable to get back on the pitch.

With Tresadern, the cycle of boom and bust was repeated. Spurs started the 1935/36 season well and by the end of December they were second and looking good for getting back into the top flight. After that, they didn't win at home for three months. The promotion winners of 1933 were fading fast. There were some promising young-sters coming on at Northfleet, the nursery club that McWilliam had established at the start of the 1920s, but they weren't yet ready to shoulder the burden. Tresadern moaned later that he had 'inherited a legacy of bitterness and poor morale'. George Hunt, the best centre-forward in the game, was made the scapegoat for the barren run and dropped. Johnny Morrison, his replacement, was so off his game he couldn't hit a barn door with the back of a spade. Towards the end of the season, when Hunt got back in the side, it was too late.

Perversely, everything coincided with the completion of a breath-taking new double-decker stand along the east side of the ground. In 1934 Tottenham Hotspur, in an attempt to catch up Arsenal who were by now attracting twice the crowd, had demolished a row of terraced housing and put themselves in hock to Barclays Bank to develop the East Stand. This 'wedding cake stand shining with whiteness', as Simon Inglis later described it, had two levels of terraces for nearly 19,000 people, an upper tier seating nearly 5,000 supporters as well as the legendary 'Shelf', the only raised standing area in England. It was all topped off with a 'press box' designed to offer a bird's eye view of the action to up to 109 journalists (as it turned out, it was actually reserved for the use of staff).

Factoring in the cost of rehousing the former tenants of the levelled terraced houses – plus a new roof for the West Stand – spending on that year's construction work reached £60,000 and the total capacity of the ground rose to 80,000.

Now, from the undeniably beautiful new East Stand, another product of Leitch's soaring imagination, fans could watch Spurs again thrash about trying to get out of the Second Division.

A feat they would have to achieve without Hunt. Unable to get a regular place in the struggling Spurs side, he went to Arsenal in 1937, making him the first player to move there directly from Spurs since the club shifted to Highbury in 1913. The move paid off for him – he picked up a title-winner's medal in 1938. O'Callaghan went as well, to Leicester, Tottenham's fellow travellers in the drop into Division Two in 1935. Leicester were promoted back at the end of the 1936/37 season. Spurs weren't. Rumours surfaced again that Peter McWilliam had been sounded out about coming back to his old job. Like Smith, Tresadern declined to hang around for the sack. Grabbing at an offer from Plymouth Argyle, he walked out in April 1938.

Later on, Tresadern – member number seven of the Spurs ex-managers' club – told a journalist that his years at Spurs were his unhappiest in football and that he always kicked himself for giving up a job he enjoyed at Crystal Palace to move there. 'The players were set in their ways and did not want to take on new ideas, and the directors did not really need me there because they wanted to manage the team themselves. It was clear they were getting ready to sack me, so I saved them the trouble and resigned.' It wasn't, he concluded, 'a time I like to reflect on'.

This time, the rumours turned out to be true. Back for his second stint as manager, McWilliam found his old club in a mess. They'd taken on a huge debt to build the East Stand, they were back in the Second Division and not about to get out of it any time soon, and in O'Callagan and Hunt they'd got rid of two of their best men. Now was the time to bring in a group of players who would restore Tottenham to pre-eminence. And among them would be the one destined to define Tottenham Hotspur's identity for generations to come.

CHAPTER NINE

YOUNG, GIFTED AND SPURS

The town of Northfleet is 28 or so miles from Tottenham, part of the chain of dockyard towns on the edge of Kent. Its station is picturesquely old-fashioned, with a timber-clad ticket office that's been painted a silver-grey. You exit onto a new street of modern housing, curving below an old chapel with mullioned windows, one of the few remaining buildings that Bill Nicholson would have seen when he arrived more than 75 years ago to play for Northfleet United FC in the Kent Senior League on Saturdays.

Brown signs with a white football logo point you up, and then down, a hill: 'The Fleet 400 yards'. Northfleet United FC itself belongs in Wikipedia's category of Defunct Football Clubs. In 2007, it merged with Gravesend to become Ebbsfleet United, a Conference side, one that's doing okay and continues to play in Northfleet's old Stonebridge Road Stadium. Fixed on a wall next to one of the turnstiles is a plaque. It reads: 'THE FLEET FA Trophy Winners 2008' (they beat Torquay United 1-0 in the final at Wembley, becoming the first Kent club to win the competition). The stadium is on the fringe of the town in a hollow reached by a steep hill busy with speeding traffic even at midday. It's hard to distinguish the ground from the flat roofs of the commercial buildings that surround it. The hollow is dominated by pylons – the top of one floodlight pokes between the cables – and between the wooden fence and the corrugated iron back of the stand is a semi-wilderness sprouting a billboard advertising Specsavers. Then you round a corner, walk up a pitted driveway and see the wonderful intense green of a proper football pitch.

Which is almost certainly better than it would have looked in the rough old days of the 1920s and 1930s when Northfleet was Tottenham Hotspur's nursery club. The relationship with Northfleet began around 1922 when the Kent club wanted to take a Spurs player on a loan deal. That didn't work out but, soon after, Northfleet ran into financial problems and decided to cut their wage bill by getting rid of the senior players and using youngsters. Kids, after all, came cheap, and if they were Tottenham's they had to be good. In the close season of 1923, a more formal relationship began between the two clubs, one which entailed Spurs placing half a dozen youngsters with them. They'd hold a pre-season trial game at White Hart Lane in the close season and Northfleet would take their pick. At that point, Spurs were still loaning out youngsters to other clubs – they used Barnet and Cheshunt. Then, in the close season of 1931, the relationship between Spurs and Northfleet became formalised, and the two clubs shared staff.

Thirty-seven players on Tottenham's books made it to senior level – and nine became internationals – after going through Northfleet. Andy Porter, the Spurs historian, listed them all in the April 2012 issue of *Hotspur*, the club's official magazine – and the list included Arthur Rowe, who had five seasons there between 1925 and 1929, and Taffy O'Callaghan. Not all of them were galacticos in the making, as evidenced by the flops who were shunted in and out of Percy Smith's relegation-doomed side in the 1930s. But as well there was Vic Buckingham, who played as a defensive midfielder in Tottenham's pre-war side and later, as a manager, took what he'd learned of The Spurs Way to Ajax in Holland where he discovered Johan Cruyff. 'Vic Buckingham practically started "Total Football",' says *Guardian* journalist David Lacey. Also on the list were Bill Nicholson, Ronnie Burgess, Les Medley and Ted Ditchburn, who would go on to form the backbone of Rowe's title-winning side of 1951.

Nicholson was the son of a hansom cab driver who worked along the sea front in Scarborough. One of nine children, he was the only one to pass the scholarship into grammar school, where he excelled at geography and football before leaving at 16 to work in a local laundry, operating the drying machine. In his spare time he played in a local league run by a dentist called Nelson, a manic football fan who recommended him to Spurs. On 29th February, 1936, out of the blue, came a letter from Spurs' chief scout Ben Ives, inviting him for a trial. So, in the middle of March 1936, and having never in his life travelled beyond Scarborough, he took the steam train to King's Cross, had his first ride on the underground and made the final stage of his journey to White Hart Lane in a London bus. His arrival had been preceded by a small notice in the *Tottenham Weekly Herald*:

'On Trial – Spurs are giving a month's trial to an amateur, Wm. E. Nicholson, an inside-right of Scarborough Working Men's Club. He recently celebrated his 17th birthday. His height is 5ft 8in and weight 10st 12lb.'

The trial worked out and he was taken on as a groundstaff boy at £2 a week, on the same day as Ronnie Burgess, who had taken a less direct route to White Hart Lane. It was one that had begun in Cwm in the Rhondda valley, where he learnt to play on rough pitches next to the slagheaps. Cardiff City took him on in his mid-teens then dumped him, so he went down the pits and played inside-right for Cwm Villa. After a 59-goal season, Ives invited him to join Spurs as an unpaid junior. Burgess was fixed up with a job in a metal works in Chingford and he trained with the other juniors twice a week. Then, just before the end of the 1936/37 season, Spurs dumped him too.

Burgess was given a choice: he could carry on with the job at the metal works or accept his train fare back home. He chose the train fare, but on the way back to Wales stopped off to watch a Spurs junior game. They happened to be a man short, so Ives told him to get changed and stuck him at right-half, from where he still managed to score twice. The next day, he was summoned to speak to Jack Tresadern, who after unblushingly blaming his sacking on an oversight, invited him to join the Northfleet nursery.

Nicholson and Burgess lived in digs near White Hart Lane. During the week they clocked on at eight every morning and spent the next nine hours pulling the 6ft-wide roller over the pitch to flatten it after Saturday's game, or helping the groundsman re-seed it, or doing odd jobs. Nicholson was ordered to paint the girders of the newly-opened East Stand. He was terrified of heights. There was virtually no contact with the pros.

He and Burgess became mates, and they used to get a bit of prac-tice in by stuffing £5 money bags with paper, tying them with string and kicking them around the corridors at lunchtime. The only formal training was on Tuesday and Thursday evenings, when lamps were fixed at the corners of the ground so they could see where they were going as they ran round the track. They weren't allowed on the actual pitch, mind, let alone the dressing rooms.

The best glimpse of life as a Spurs ground-staff boy before the Second World War comes in Burgess's autobiography, *Football – My Life*. This is an innocently hearty little book in which everyone's a pal, even the trainer, George Hardy, a massive, wheezing martinet of a Northerner who kept Burgess back on his own after everyone else had packed up and made him do body-building exercises in the gym. 'George was a great believer in massage, but he did it all with those big hands of his – not forgetting gallons of olive oil. Some of us oozed with oil when George had finished with us . . .'

Every Saturday Nicholson and Burgess met up with the other ground-staff boys at the Lane and were taken by coach to London Bridge, where they caught the train to Northfleet or wherever in Kent the match was happening (Northfleet played in the Kent Senior League). The squad's average age was 19. It would have been even lower but for the weathered, shiny-scalped, veteran captain, Jack Coxford, who was there to keep them in line. On the way home from matches, they were given a lunch basket of hot pies, sausage rolls, sandwiches and cake.

The football they played with Northfleet was what Burgess described in his autobiography as 'robust', which was the standard euphemism for 'only just short of grievous bodily harm'. When they were promoted into the Spurs reserves side, which played its fixtures in the Combination League, it was even hairier. Burgess called it 'the toughest League in which I have ever played – yes, even tougher than the Kent Senior League, mainly, I think, because Combination sides have always been composed of youngsters striving to gain first-team promotion, and deposed first-teamers fighting for the chance to regain their senior places. I think I sustained more knocks in those reserve games than in the rest of my career . . .'

But the prize at the end of it all was first-team football. Nicholson was 19 when he made his Spurs debut during the 1938/39 season, filling in out of position at left-back for the injured Billy Whatley in the 3-1 defeat against Blackburn Rovers at Ewood Park. Nicholson strained a thigh muscle and had to play outside-right in the final minutes because substitutions were still decades away, a nightmare experience that afflicted him with a benign amnesia. 'I cannot really remember anything about the game,' he said. Burgess clinched his first-team place with an unbroken run in the last 17 games of the same season. He got his chance during the cup run, coming in for the injured Taffy Spelman against Norwich. Nicholson was in the side that day, too, along with four other Northfleet products in the form of Percy Hooper, George Ludford, Fred Sargent and Vic Buckingham.

There was a real feeling of optimism around White Hart Lane that Spurs might have a side destined for big things again. The *News Chronicle Football Annual* made Willie Hall one of their four Players of the Year. Savouring the prospect of a return to the First Division, making light of the probability of approaching war, the players reported back to White Hart Lane towards the end of summer 1939. 'We talked about the uncertainty of the future, of course, but the general opinion was that war would not come,' recalled Burgess. On 26th August, Spurs drew 1-1 at home to Birmingham. They got the same result the following Thursday away to Newport County. On 2nd September, 1939, they beat West Bromwich Albion 4-3 at The Hawthorns with a hat-trick from Johnny Morrison. They agreed that maybe luck was going to be with them that season, because West Brom's Cecil Shaw missed a penalty that would have made it 4-4. The next day, a Sunday morning, Nicholson and Burgess reported at White Hart Lane to prepare for Monday's game against Southampton. They never got to play it. Within 24 hours, Britain had declared war on Germany, and League football was suspended. It wouldn't restart for seven years.

Burgess threw himself into the new situation with characteristic enthusiasm. On the Monday morning, instead of getting ready to face Southampton, he led a posse of the lads round to the local constabulary where they enrolled as War Reserve police. Their new status lasted all of 10 days, when the authorities ruled that no one under 23 was allowed to do the job because they were all going to be called up.

Even then football didn't cease totally. On 14th September, the announcement came from on high that existing pre-war fixtures could go ahead as long as they were played as friendlies and not games in a competition. Substitute regional competitions were organised and Burgess, who fetched up in the RAF with Ted Ditchburn and Vic Buckingham, combined military service with playing for Spurs.

Or sometimes other clubs. Such was the dispersal of players among the various military bases that more often than not team sheets featured an eclectic selection picked from whoever happened to be around at the time. At one time or other during the war, Burgess turned out for Tottenham, Nottingham Forest, Notts County, the RAF and Wales. The midfielder Les Bennett, who had come to White Hart Lane as a junior not long before war broke out, made a handful of appearances for Spurs but his name also pops up in the records as a guest player for Torquay, along with Vic Woodley who under normal circumstances would have been in goal for Chelsea.

'One week, Bert Whittingham, who was a colleague of mine in several RAF teams, played for the Spurs,' recalled Burgess in his autobiography. 'A week later, when we met Bradford, Bert was playing against us! It was difficult sometimes to know who was friend or foe. On another occasion we went to Portsmouth and found, to our dismay, that our old pal Vic Buckingham had been chosen for Portsmouth.'

On another Saturday, Burgess and three other Spurs – Arthur Willis, Sonny Walters and George Ludford – turned out for Millwall. 'Anything for a game,' said Burgess.

Mind you, whether you were a player or a fan, life around White Hart Lane was less than relaxing. On 15th September, 1940, a day when the Tottenham programme featured 10 changes, among them a 16-year-old local lad roped in at centre-forward, the gigantic aerial ding-dong that was the Battle of Britain started raging over the south of England. The game was halted after a quarter of an hour, and a 1,622-strong crowd of die-hards waited until it restarted an hour and 15 minutes later. True to form, Spurs won 3-2. Another time a doodlebug buzzed low over the Lane, then cut out. Everyone threw themselves to the floor quicker than a Jürgen Klinsmann goal celebration. Nothing happened, so after a bit they got up and carried on with the match.

Things got even nearer to Armageddon the day Spurs played away to West Ham. They were 4-1 up with 10 minutes to go when the air raid sirens sounded around Upton Park, which was vulnerably close to London's docks. 'We carried on for a time,' recalled Burgess, 'and then we heard the drone of enemy aircraft – and the sound of bombs dropping not far away. We left the field to take shelter in the tunnel under the stand . . . The game was called off owing to the fact that there was considerable bomb damage not far from the ground.'

These were strange times all round at White Hart Lane. An air raid shelter went up at the ground, conveniently positioned just in front of the Directors' Box. Meanwhile, the top of the East Stand became a mortuary for Blitz victims. Which was nowhere near as creepy as another of Tottenham's wartime arrangements; Arsenal moved in.

The reason was that Highbury had been requisitioned as a First Aid Post and Air Raid Precautions centre. That left them without anywhere to play, so the Spurs directors offered them a ground-share. It was, said one director, 'time to bury the hatchet for a while'.

The relationship went on to get even cosier. Before the war started Spurs had been in the Second Division, but with the supply of young lions honed at Northfleet, with Burgess already shaping up as a future captain, with Peter McWilliam coaching and chivvying them into the next great Spurs side, they looked near-certainties for promotion if not that season, then the next. No one expected that the fighting would go on for five years or that halfway through it the ageing McWilliam would retire and return to his adopted home of the north east. The second of Tottenham's great managers, the man who brought them the 1921 FA Cup and established the imprint of The Spurs Way for all time, strolled out of White Hart Lane for good.

Arthur Turner, the club secretary who had filled in 30 years back after the departure of Fred Kirkham, obliged again. He took over for a couple of years while the board got around to hiring a permanent replacement. They didn't look very far. In the new mellow atmosphere of the groundshare with Arsenal, they had taken on a former Highbury man, Joe Hulme, as chief scout early in 1944. By October 1945, during the transitional post-war season of 1945/46, Hulme was assistant manager, and three months later he had his feet under the desk in the manager's office.

While all this was going on, Nicholson's war had taken a different course from Burgess's. His call-up had come more or less straight away and he spent the best part of six years in the Durham Light Infantry at Brancepeth, barking orders at troops, first in infantry training – 'which I didn't know much about' – and then as a PE instructor. Although occasionally he got to turn out for Newcastle and Darlington, there wasn't much time for football; he was processing several hundred troops on 16-week courses. It was, he said, punishing work. But Nicholson thrived on it. Later, he was sent to join the HQ of the Central Mediterranean Forces in Udini, Italy, where he carried on in the same role, operating alongside Geoff Dyson, who went on to become the first national athletics coach. 'Geoff was a fantastic organiser and lecturer and probably had more to do with my becoming a coach than anyone,' Nicholson said later. 'My experience as a PE instructor proved invaluable because one of the prime requisites in coaching is being able to put your ideas over and I was used to addressing a large number of men.'

So by the time Nicholson was back at Tottenham after the war, he knew exactly what he wanted to do with his life. And he was about to meet the man who, in sharing his ambitions, would become his greatest rival.

CHAPTER TEN

IT'S ALL ABOUT TRIANGLES

In the spring of 1949, in a desperate attempt to lift a side that was lodged stubbornly in the Second Division despite possessing the talents of Eddie Baily, Ted Ditchburn and Ron Burgess, Joe Hulme tried and failed to buy Alf Ramsey from Southampton before the transfer deadline on 16th March.

Two months later, Hulme was sacked, and the first thing Arthur Rowe did when he took over as manager was revive the offer by telegram. This time, Spurs got their man.

At Southampton, Ramsey's qualities as a full-back had stood out sufficiently for him to be an automatic pick for England, even though Southampton were a Second Division side. Raven-haired, solidly built, concealing his shyness behind a defensive snootiness, Ramsey was calm under intense pressure, demonstrated natural leadership and was a brilliant user of the ball and reader of the game. He was not exactly under-endowed with confidence on the pitch, either – he even bossed Stanley Matthews about in one international. In the words of Billy Wright, then England captain: 'Ramsey's expressed aim was to play constructive football. I soon learned that nothing could disturb this footballer with the perfect balance and poise, no situation, however desperate, could force him into abandoning his immaculate style.'

You couldn't, in fact, force Ramsey into anything. In July 1949, Tottenham Hotspur's new manager called the squad up before pre-season training, so as to get to know them. They met at Chingford, back then a byword for rustic tranquility, rather than at the ground. The only no-show was Ramsey. He'd written to Rowe saying he'd already arranged his holidays and didn't anticipate reporting to Tottenham a week early.

Rowe didn't rise to the snub. 'Fine,' he wrote back. 'We'll see you when you get back. PS: This is the last Second Division training you'll do.'

In telling the story of the rivalry between Nicholson and Ramsey, and how it impacted on Spurs' destiny, it's necessary to start with Arthur Rowe, the man from whom both learned how titles were won. Before Rowe took over, the squad lacked direction, the defence was apparently made of wool and the closest Hulme had taken them to silverware was the 1948 FA Cup semi-final. The fans had never really accepted Hulme because he was an Arsenal man.

Rowe, in contrast, was Tottenham through and through. He was born only 10 minutes walk from White Hart Lane and, as soon as he showed promise, Spurs inevitably became his club. He joined as a schoolboy in 1921, did his time at the Northfleet nursery then signed for the seniors in 1929. Playing at centre-half he stood out for several reasons – he was small, his hair was turning prematurely silver and, unusually for a defender back then, he was a thinker and he liked to attack. He was also a popular captain – 'Cockney, with a great sense of humour', according to journalist Brian Scovell. 'He was very good with one-liners.'

But at the age of 32, after eight seasons and 210 appearances, a knee injury and subsequent unsuccessful cartilage operation finished his career and in May 1939 he was appointed the Hungarian government's official instructor to their soccer coaches and moved to Budapest.

The players he found in Hungary were skilful and intelligent, the kind Rowe found easy to coach in the radical ideas he was developing about positional play and free-moving football.

According to Deryk Brown in his 1971 history *The Tottenham*

Hotspur Story, the origin of these ideas had a time and a place: ' . . . on 15th November 1932 at Valley Parade, Bradford, a ground not noted for its inspirational qualities. Tottenham were playing a Second Division match there and the score was 0-0 with only a minute to go. Rowe played a one-two with Felton on the edge of his penalty area and when he took the return Tottenham had a numerical advantage which they quickly made use of. Four more short passes and the ball was with McCormick on the right wing. He centred and Hunt scored. The team talked about little else on the way back to London. They analysed the goal back to Rowe's original pass. It had been simple and quick. It was the germ of an idea.'

It was push and run, the complete opposite of the hairy-chested mud-encrusted English game of the time. 'Barcelona are only doing the same thing now,' says David Lacey. 'It's all about triangles. If you've got someone to pass to, you pass it. Happy to receive the ball even if you've got opponents round you. Back then everyone was geared to numbers. Nine was the centre-forward. Eleven was the left-winger. They all stayed in the places dictated by their numbers. But if you look at a photo of Spurs from 1951 you see all the players are out of position. Les Medley is at outside-right. Bill Nicholson is at inside-left.'

'I can't see a more simple way to play than in triangles; get the ball, give it, and then support the man you've given it to,' said Rowe. 'There just aren't that many people who can put a 40-yard pass into the path of another man who's had to run 30 yards to get there. So you just do simple things and do them accurately. Now if you've got players whose skills transcend that, you don't tell them how to play. You say, "Go out there and get on with it."'

Back in Hungary in 1939, Rowe was offered the job of national coach but he was thwarted by the start of the war. So just two months after his arrival, he was obliged to return home and join the army.

Fourteen years later, on a dank afternoon at Wembley, England's unbeaten home record and assumed pre-eminence against continental opposition ended in a humiliating 6-3 defeat by the 'Magical Magyars'. The Hungary team of 1953, playing a fast, short-passing game, had left England standing around like table-football players.

It's said that Rowe based his methods on Hungary's, but it should be remembered that he was the one coaching their coaches. 'The Hungarians did not "invent" the beautiful version of the game,' Rowe's son Graham wrote in a letter to the sports section of *The Financial Times* in 2006. 'If anyone invented it, it was my father. In Budapest were sown the seeds of the "push and run" approach, which for the next 13 years, incubated and ultimately manifested itself in that great Hungarian team. But it was a style that was first played by the glorious Spurs team of 1949-53.'

Maybe, maybe not. But there are more than enough extraordinary elements among Rowe's acknowledged achievements to make the Hungarian aspect unessential. Arthur Rowe is the only manager apart from Bill Nicholson to have taken Spurs to the league title. He was mentor to Nicholson and Ramsey, two alpha managers who between them dominated the English game. He was the man who brought Danny Blanchflower to Tottenham Hotspur.

After the war, Rowe spent four years managing Chelmsford, where the ideas he put in place led them to a Southern League and cup double. Then, when he was informed that Hulme had left Spurs, he applied in writing for the job, clearly after being tapped up. Early in 1949, Spurs had played a testimonial at Chelmsford and Rowe's wife said later that the Tottenham directors present kept asking her if he was happy at Chelmsford.

At Spurs, he posted mottos on the dressing room walls: 'A rolling ball gathers no moss.' 'The team makes the stars, not the stars the team.' 'Make it simple, make it quick.' It must have been like living inside a Christmas cracker. But Rowe was not like the then England manager Walter Winterbottom whose high-flown schoolmasterly manner was way above most people's heads. Rowe was down-to-earth and quick-witted. He'd been a player and he spoke their language. One of the fashionable coaching slogans of the time was 'peripheral vision', a term which attracted Rowe's derision. 'You know what that means? It means seeing out of your arse,' said Rowe, as recounted by Leo McKinstry in *Sir Alf*.

And at Tottenham Hotspur in 1949, there were a lot of sphincters with 20-20 vision. 'Ramsey and Nicholson – there was an intelligence there,' says Lacey. 'Eddie Baily was crucial to how things worked, too. What Rowe realised was the importance of movement. What does a player do when he hasn't got the ball. Tottenham have always had a player who links defence to attack and uses his loaf. Modric reminded me of Ossie Ardiles in that whenever the defence was under pressure he offered himself as an outlet. And Ossie did the same things that Eddie Baily used to do.'

Baily was the local hero, a cheeky chappie, a prodigy – at 10 he scored all nine goals in a schools match. Every side he was in seemed to win. To Rowe, he was almost superhuman in the way he could play a moving ball either way and with either foot. Nicholson described him as 'the best first-time passer of the ball at that particular time'. The great journalist and broadcaster John Arlott was inevitably more lyrical: 'Eddie Baily, neat as a trivet, busy as a one-man band, alert as a boarding house cat, elusive as a dog in a fair . . . no other forward can stand comparison with him,' was his description.

Then there was Burgess. 'Brilliant, a great player,' said Rowe. Burgess was skipper and midfield inspiration, an immensely strong, toil-until-he-dropped man who, Nicholson said later, played like Bryan Robson. Only better. 'He had everything: good feet, ability in the air, strength in the tackle and was a beautiful passer of the ball. He was my favourite player in all my years at Tottenham.'

But the side wasn't only about Ramsey and Ditchburn, Burgess and Baily. It was about Len Duquemin, centre-forward and determined, tireless team man. It was about Les Medley, a truculent, pacy, unpredictable greyhound at outside-left. And Les Bennett, a kind of licensed loose cannon, the one individualist, his wall-passes with Baily zigzagging through an entire defence. Sonny Walters was in charge of keeping possession and nudging things forward. He wasn't above a bit of diving, either, if a penalty was up for grabs. Harry Clarke was the rock-solid, diamond-hard core of defence. 'A lovely person to have on your side,' commented Nicholson approvingly. 'He was so straightforward. He was tall and wore those baggy shorts . . . a formidable character, good in the air and absolutely fearless.'

Charlie Withers and Arthur Willis battled for the number 3 shirt and Withers, veteran of the Normandy landings on D-Day, came off best, a hard man of few words and many crunching tackles.

And they had Ted Ditchburn, a shovel-handed lad from Kent who had a pro boxer for a father and nearly went into the family trade himself – he had the physique, the agility and the giant fists, the mobility and timing. But these were qualities that also suited him for what he did instead. In goal for Spurs, he was destined to become a colossus. Best Spurs keeper of all time? Ted Ditchburn v Pat Jennings; it's still an argument. Often Ditchburn would get things going with a throw from the penalty area, his own innovation in an era when goalies just thumped the ball hopefully upfield. He was so strong and accurate he could reach the halfway line easily. Plus, he said, he started doing it because he was 'a bloody awful kicker of a dead ball'. And from his vantage point in goal, he could see everything that made the others so good. 'It was a beautiful, machine-like movement,' he recalled. 'The way the ball flew from one end of the park to the other was fantastic. Once we hit that rhythm, nothing could stop us. After a while we became so confident we could lay the ball off without looking.'

Rowe didn't saddle them with dogma, coming in with a system and telling them exactly what to do. 'He encouraged us in certain directions, got us thinking, trying things,' said Eddie Baily, 'and then, when it all came together, he'd say: "That's it, that's the way to play."'

And it was.

When Arthur Rowe told Ramsey it was the last Second Division training he would ever do, it was no empty promise. Before Rowe took over, Spurs seemed to owe their survival to draws. Rowe gave the fans the experience of supporting a team that actually won on a regular basis.

It was a team later described by Rowe as 'two or three great performers and a lot who were not'. Where he succeeded was by using a system that made them all look like great players. And they had the confidence that came from being winners. This was a whole new style of playing. That 1949/50 season, they went 23 games unbeaten, knocked out Sunderland – then First Division giants – 5-1 in the fourth round of the cup (they were being tipped for a promotion and cup double until Everton knocked them out in the next round), and headed the table for virtually the whole season.

All the forwards could score. By the end of the season, the tally of league and cup goals went like this: Medley (19), Duquemin (18), Bennett and Walters (both 16). Even Nicholson got on the scoresheet.

They had Ramsey, the nerveless spot-kick king. They had luck – the dubious penalty decisions went their way. They could play badly and win. They clinched promotion on the last Saturday in March, with a 4-1 victory at the Lane over West Bromwich Albion. Then on 1st April, they won 2-0 at Brentford. Baily made the first for Medley and scored the second himself. That victory sent them up as champions. After 15 years, four changes of manager and an intervening war, Tottenham Hotspur had made it back into the First Division with a kind of football that no one in England had ever seen before.

And things, as nineties pop band D-Ream would have put it, could only get better.

The 1950/51 season, however, took off like a concrete kite. In the opening game, Blackpool and Stanley Matthews came to White Hart Lane and left with the points. A 4-1 beating cued newspaper headlines: 'Are Spurs Good Enough?'

But the defining answer to that question came on the last day of September 1950, when they beat Aston Villa 3-2 on a pitch that 12 hours of rain had turned into a paddling pool. That launched a run of eight straight wins, including a 7-0 hammering of Jackie Milburn's Newcastle, second in the table that morning and the side who would go on to win that season's FA Cup. Even though Ron Burgess was out injured, the game went down in history as one of the masterclasses in winning football.

They lost away to Huddersfield after that (and went out to them in the cup too) but then launched themselves on an unbeaten run of seven. Over the Christmas period, three wins and one draw took them level on top with Middlesbrough, who they finally managed to shake off on 3rd March when they beat Chelsea 2-1 at home. From there, they didn't look back. By 14th April they only had to beat Huddersfield at White Hart Lane to clinch the title. With Ramsey at Wembley playing for England against Scotland, Spurs lost 1-0. Which left them four points clear of Manchester United at the top with three left to play. On 21st April, they drew 1-1 away to Middlesbrough while Manchester United won away at Newcastle. On 28th April, Manchester United beat Huddersfield 6-0 at Old Trafford. Tottenham, in their turn, had to beat Sheffield Wednesday. It was looking very much like the kind of game when they outplayed the opposition without scoring. Then a Len Duquemin goal just before half-time brought Tottenham Hotspur their first-ever league title.

'The crowd went crazy, and I don't think many of the players were too sane at that particular moment,' said Ron Burgess.

A 3-1 win over Liverpool in their final game brought the season to a fitting conclusion. After Arthur Drewry, president of the Football League, handed the trophy to Burgess, he congratulated Spurs for 'not only on having won it, but also in the manner in which they did so'.

Two days on, a 'Grand Celebration Dance' was laid on for players and staff at The Royal on Tottenham Court Road. Supporters willing to fork out 10 shillings 6 pence for a ticket could rub shoulders with their heroes to the strains of Ivor Kirchin and his Ballroom Orchestra.

At least one passionate fan missed out on the fun, though. 'All my life I'd waited for Tottenham to win the title and I missed it because I was in the army in Egypt,' notes Morris Keston ruefully.

In all, Tottenham Hotspur had lost only seven times. Before the start of the season, people had been predicting that once they were in the top division they would be found out. Now they were being called the 'Team of the Century', expected to dominate for years to come with their push–and–run football.

Instead, the sound of celebration began to grow faint. The decline was slow enough for no one to notice at first. The 1951/52 season featured a three-month unbeaten spell that had the Lilywhites finishing runners-up to Manchester United. But apart from Withers and Willis alternating at left-back, the same XI played together throughout, getting longer and longer in the tooth. They had been far from young guns when they won the title. Burgess had been well over 30. New players like George Robb, Johnny Brooks, Mel Hopkins and Tony Marchi were starting to arrive but lacked the experience and confidence to make an impact. Winger Tommy Harmer, a local boy, was a brilliantly gifted individualist who didn't fit in with the push-and-run ethos.

Plus the surprise factor had gone as other managers wised up to Rowe's tactics. In the 1952/53 season, the team that had surged so unstoppably to the title two years back started talking about saving the season with a cup run. Twenty seconds before the end of their semi-final against Stanley Matthews's Blackpool, with the score 1-1 and Spurs looking by far the better bet for extra-time, Ramsey mishit a backpass meant for Ditchburn. It went, instead, to Blackpool's Jackie Mudie for the winning goal.

Having lost a game that had taken on so much importance, Spurs seemed to fall apart. By the end of the season they had slumped to 10th, and the next campaign began badly. The gap between what Rowe's men had achieved and what they had come down to was now starkly obvious. By Christmas 1954, the idea of Spurs renewing a title challenge was far-fetched. With 15 points from 20 games, the rest of the season threatened to be all about avoiding relegation. Meanwhile, Rowe was going from feted to slated.

'He had one weakness, which was that he was too loyal to his players,' said Ron Reynolds, Ditchburn's understudy, in *The Life of a 1950s Footballer*. 'He ignored the fact that they were all getting old together, especially the half-back line of Burgess and Nicholson. Alf Ramsey relied on them, especially Bill, who gave him the freedom to go forward by slotting back.'

It was Ramsey's reliance on Nicholson during Spurs games that trickled petrol on the flames. In spite of being one of the best in the country at wing-half – busy, hard-tackling but constructive too – and regularly being called up to the England squad, Nicholson had to sit and watch as an unused reserve for England on 22 occasions. For Tottenham, his masterly sizing up of situations and ability to read the whole picture on the pitch had largely been dedicated to Ramsey's cause because Ramsey, outstanding full-back though he was, possessed one flaw – he had all the turning speed of a container ship.

According to Ron Reynolds, it was frequently 'out-and-out war' in the dressing room between the two. 'I can remember some absolutely enormous, blazing rows between Alf Ramsey and Bill Nicholson, which was odd really because both didn't have much to say most of the time. Alf was terrible like that – he didn't suffer what he saw to be fools gladly and he would quickly chew you out if he disagreed with you – but Bill could give as good as he got. Typically dour Yorkshireman, very blunt.

'He got fed up that Alf would cut him out of the game, he'd bypass him and go straight on to the forwards, he'd race upfield and just expect Bill to slot in behind him. Bill only got the one England cap whereas Alf got dozens and I think Bill sometimes thought he was winning them for Alf and not getting noticed himself.'

In a winning side, strife between the two big thinkers at the heart of the team wasn't a problem. As far as Rowe was concerned, it showed they cared. Once they started losing, though, the frequent arguments corroded the spirit that had bonded the team in the glory seasons.

'And with Alf and Bill there was a very strong rivalry because I think they both had come to the conclusion that they were going to stay in the game after they'd finished playing,' said Reynolds, 'and I think they both had designs on staying at Tottenham. But there was no way both of them could have stayed on as coaches there. First, you didn't have a whole staff of coaches in a club in those days, but also, it was clear they could never work together as coaches, especially with one senior to the other. And with both coming closer to retiring from playing, that meant there was a real rivalry between them.'

There's a telling, almost throwaway comment that Alan Mullery makes about Nicholson in his autobiography: 'There was,' he said, 'a stealth to everything he did.' So, towards the end of the 1953/54 season, when Nicholson recognised he was a spent force as a player, he told Rowe it was time someone else was put in his place.

'By speaking up, I was making it easier for him,' Nicholson explained.

'It was unusual, I suppose, for a player to say such a thing to his manager. Most players resent it when the time comes to drop down to a lower team or be sold to an inferior club, but I felt it was an honest way of going about it.'

And, to be fair, one which suited him. 'I think Bill had in mind that if he wanted to stay at Tottenham as a coach, he had to get in before Alf Ramsey did,' said Ron Reynolds. 'With Bill being that bit older, it meant he could retire earlier.'

So Nicholson was appointed to the coaching staff in 1954, initially with a playing contract. Meanwhile, Rowe threw someone else into the mix. Someone who in due course would embody the glory and glamour of Tottenham Hotspur. Someone who just at that moment would bring a fresh bout of turmoil.

CHAPTER ELEVEN

ONE OF THE GOOD GUYS

It was close to the end of Arthur Rowe's career as Spurs manager when he landed Danny Blanchflower. But Rowe had been tracking him for well over two years, ever since they had met after a Northern Ireland v Wales international in the spring of 1952. Northern Ireland got beaten 3-0 but when Rowe congratulated him on his performance at wing-half Blanchflower had thanked him so nicely that Rowe fell under his spell. 'I'll never forget,' he said later, 'as we stood sizing each other up, as people do when meeting for the first time, the way Danny looked at me out of those big, sparkling Irish eyes. I instinctively thought, here is a good guy . . . He made other people play. He protected the players behind and supported those in front. I wanted him as captain.'

'Good guy' probably wouldn't have been the two words Blanchflower's first three bosses would have chosen to describe him. He had run-ins with managers and directors wherever he went, from Glentoran, his first club in Northern Ireland, to Barnsley, the club that brought him to England, to Aston Villa, where he rattled the cage before joining Spurs. They fell out over training methods, they fell out over tactics, they had flaming rows over money and over the stuff he wrote in newspapers and said on radio (and if, later, the Spurs directors thought they might be able to control Blanchflower, they were quickly disabused of the idea. On one occasion, when they demanded to see what he'd written before it went in the paper he told them: 'If you pay me more than the *Daily Mail* do, that'll be fine. Otherwise you'll have to buy the paper like everyone else').

Already in his late twenties, Rowe's 'Chosen One', the natural leader with what Rowe spoke of as 'a commanding personality' with 'a tremendous ego, which every great captain needs', had reached the peak of his frustration with life at Villa. It was a club that seemed happy to rest on past laurels, just surviving in the First Division, with the occasional cup run. Blanchflower wanted serious silverware, he enjoyed the trappings – fast cars, money, girls – that his parallel career as a journalist was starting to bring him, but most of all he was a romantic. He wanted glory.

Cultivated, ambitious, sparklingly witty and literate, Blanchflower was a young man of intriguing contradictions. He combined tub-thumping enthusiasm for players' rights with staunch devotion to capitalism. At Barnsley he studied accountancy in his spare time. He did not, in short, conform to that era's expectations of a footballer at all. 'He was always dressed well, very smart,' said George Robb, an early team-mate at Spurs, 'and the lads didn't earn much in those days, so he stood out a little because of that.'

And because of the way he was built. In an era of strapping centre-forwards and huge-hammed defenders, Blanchflower was physically slight. Except, that is, for his feet. The Barnsley inside-right, Steve Griffiths, claims he nearly fainted one time when Blanchflower took off his shoes. 'He must have had feet as large as I had ever seen.'

Griffiths's instant reaction was to wonder how somebody endowed with such gargantuan plates of meat could play football. He soon found out. Everybody did. The *Barnsley Chronicle* wrote of him: 'Blanchflower is cast in the mould of soccer giants' and noted his 'ice-cool defence-splitting constructions'.

'There was no physical presence about Danny whatsoever,' explained the *Daily Mirror* journalist Ken Jones. 'He didn't look as though he could have won a ball in a raffle. But he was a cerebral player, always a thought ahead, and he kept things in his mind to use later on. He would do things that other people wouldn't attempt. The kind that would persuade others that anything was possible.'

So Blanchflower was the player Rowe had wanted at the heart of Spurs, someone he could pair up with Tommy Harmer to replace the Ramsey and Nicholson duo who had made the team so powerful on the right flank. It wouldn't be push and run – other teams had worked out how to counter that. He was going to draw a line and start all over again.

Perish the thought that Rowe had already tapped him up. Tottenham Hotspur would never stoop to that kind of thing. But by summer 1954, Blanchflower was already telling team-mates on the golf course that he was headed for White Hart Lane. That said, by October he had heard rumours that Rowe's job at Tottenham wasn't safe, and after Villa agreed to his transfer request and put him on the market for a record £40,000, Arsenal looked a better proposition.

With both Tottenham and Arsenal bidding an identical £28,500, Blanchflower opted for the latter, who promised him they would outbid anyone else who came in for him. Twenty-four hours later, Arthur Rowe turned up at Villa and attempted to change his mind.

'I like Tottenham's style better than any other club in the country, I respect you and I'd like to work for you,' Blanchflower said. 'But how strong are you at the club? Is your job safe?'

'If you join us, I'll be stronger.'

Weakening slightly, Blanchflower agreed to think about it. He had seen the push-and-run side fall apart and he knew there would be the chance to put his own imprint on a new team. He admired Rowe, too, as an individual who cared about the game, who wasn't afraid to take chances and try new ideas. Plus, he said later, 'I liked Tottenham's traditions and style of football and there was a strange appeal in their name for me.' Even then he was still intending to sign for Arsenal until the moment that Tottenham upped their bid to £30,000 and Arsenal refused to match it.

So Danny Blanchflower became a Spur. He made his debut on 11th December, 1954, away to Manchester City. The result was a goalless draw which, given the state they'd been in, was worth celebrating. 'It was the first time for weeks,' Rowe said afterwards, 'that I was able to sit back with confidence and enjoy the match.'

The Blanchflower effect lasted two months, during which Spurs played 11 and lost one, but was terminated abruptly in February by an FA Cup fifth-round beating at snow-bound York City, a not very good Third Division side.

The defeat had a dramatic effect on Rowe, who promptly suffered a complete psychological collapse. 'Arthur was a lovely man, a very emotional person,' says Brian Scovell. 'He cared so deeply about the game. He wasn't a hard taskmaster like Bill. He didn't have Alf's steel. He was almost fragile. Towards the end, if things went wrong there'd be tears in his eyes. Today you'd call it depression, and you'd be prescribed anti-depressants and be back to work in weeks but then they didn't have a word for it.'

Rowe was given time off and his assistant, Jimmy Anderson, put in temporary charge. He, and Spurs, limped to the end of the season, only a run of three straight wins at the end lifting them clear of relegation. Rowe's contract was due to expire in January 1956. Rather than letting him move sideways into some less-demanding role, the board informed him they would honour his contract until January. After that, they didn't want to know. So Rowe decided to make a dignified exit under his own control, and resigned in July 1955.

'There's no doubt that as Arthur's health deteriorated, people around the club were putting daggers in his back,' said Ron Reynolds, 'which was really terrible to see, given the man he was and everything that he had done for Tottenham over his time there.'

Anderson, a 62-year-old who had joined the club as boot boy in 1908, was named as the new Spurs manager. Known as 'The Man In Plus Fours', in his 46 years at Tottenham he had risen without trace through various jobs such as gofer, youth coach at Northfleet and scout. He had excelled at the last of these, bringing in youngsters such as Terry Dyson, Ron Henry, Peter Baker and Tony Marchi. In *Spurs: The Double*, Julian Holland described him as 'a cheery, jolly football of a man. Red of face, approachable and friendly . . . [he] never impressed as one of the great thinkers of the game.' Managing Spurs, it followed, was a promotion too far. No one survives at the same company for that long without being a good politician, though. Anderson appointed his one-time Northfleet protégé Nicholson as his assistant and quickly got rid of the main threat to his new (and future) position.

It was turning out to be a bad season for Ramsey, who had always been Rowe's man. Now 35, his hopes of becoming Rowe's assistant had gone and Blanchflower's arrival meant he was finished as a Spurs player. Blanchflower, who matched him effortlessly for size of ego, would not have been prepared to cover for him the way Nicholson had done. Anderson, meanwhile, had no intention of letting Ramsey hang around pontificating on tactics and waiting to pounce as his successor. 'He was no great lover of Alf,' said Eddie Baily.

In March, Ramsey was given the runaround at Leicester by a jour-neyman winger called Derek Hogg. Anderson dropped him for the rest of the season and then underscored the message by leaving Ramsey's name off the list of players going on the close-season tour of Hungary. A devastated Ramsey spent the summer of 1955 coaching in Rhodesia and then left to become Ipswich manager. 'But I don't think that had ever been his intention,' said Reynolds. 'I'm sure he had intended to continue playing for Spurs for at least another season. I think it was simply the case that Anderson didn't want any threat to his position at the club because he knew that he wasn't really good enough to take over from Arthur.'

Meanwhile, in an attempt to keep him onside, Anderson installed Blanchflower as captain. But it was never going to be the Jimmy and Danny show. Blanchflower had come to the club expecting to work with a man he respected for his original thinking and high football principles, not a company man promoted beyond his level of compe-tence and with a policy of whatever pragmatic, workmanlike football it took to ensure survival. Anderson's efforts to impress everyone with what he thought were Rowe-type innovations made things worse. One of the bizarre ideas he introduced was inviting boys from the local school to join the team in their training sessions. 'We'd finish up with the youngsters in among us in five-a-sides, which was ludicrous,' said Reynolds. 'On one occasion I got a real kick on the shin from one of the kids – you couldn't blame them, they were just so enthusiastic – and I had this great egg come up on my shin right away.'

'The players weren't impressed,' says Terry Dyson. 'They'd rather listen to Danny Blanchflower than Jimmy Anderson. When I signed, I was put in digs with a family in Ponders End and they treated me like an eldest son. I had my own room, no responsibilities, £3 a week, bacon-and-egg breakfast and evening meal part of the deal. But I didn't really need a meal in the evening at first because every day when we came off training we all ate together at White Hart Lane – reserves, A team, first team, everyone. It was a good idea, that, because we all mixed in. Then Jimmy Anderson stopped it, to save money. It was a big mistake. They were getting stacks of money at the time, paying players peanuts and earning a fortune with big crowds. But that's what he was like – kowtowing to the directors.'

In his first season in charge, Anderson's desire to look good in front of the board triggered a permanent stand-off between him and Blanchflower. The catalyst was Maurice Norman, the giant, good-natured gardener's son from East Anglia (he was quickly christened 'The Norfolk Swede') who signed in November 1955, a month before Bobby Smith arrived from a Yorkshire mining village via Chelsea. Spurs, who had been courting relegation more or less from the start of the season, began to pick up momentum.

'Bringing Maurice in was very important,' said Reynolds, 'because he was such a good player on the ball, not just a defensive tackler, but a real footballer, which was the way Spurs liked to play, bringing it out from the back. From there, the season was very like the one before: we started to pull away from the bottom of the table, though not as far as we wanted, and we went on a very good run in the cup.'

For the semi-final against Manchester City at Villa Park, Anderson somewhat quixotically changed the line-up, leaving out Blanchflower's successful partner in attack, Harmer, in favour of the mercurial centre-forward Dave Dunmore.

'We were one down and just didn't look like scoring,' said Robb. 'Danny switched Maurice up front to create something and brought one of the forwards, Johnny Brooks, back. Then a few moments later he sent Johnny back into the forward line too.'

Deploying Norman as a massive, looming loose cannon at corner kicks had proved successful in the past and with 15 minutes to go it seemed the best hope of cancelling out the deficit. This time it was unsuccessful and in the dressing room afterwards, Anderson went bonkers.

'You were happy enough when it worked against West Ham,' Blanchflower pointed out.

'I'm the manager here and I'll make the changes,' said Anderson. 'It made me look silly in front of the directors.

The Spurs revival immediately spluttered and died. The rest of the season turned into another relegation struggle, while Blanchflower's relationship with Anderson deteriorated further. Having ensured they were safe (they finished in 18th place, two points clear of the drop), Blanchflower resigned as captain.

But in the following two seasons, with Nicholson now master-minding as coach, with the team freshened and strengthened by Bobby Smith at centre-forward, Terry Medwin on the right and a 23-year-old Welshman, Cliff Jones, making his debut on the wing, and with the Blanchflower-Harmer partnership working spectacularly well, Spurs chalked up second- and third-place finishes. Then the 1958/59 season started with Jones breaking his leg in training, and continued with three defeats on the spin including a 5-0 hammering by Blackburn Rovers. With nine points from 11 games and the Blanchflower problem still not resolved, Anderson was quietly encouraged to retire.

At White Hart Lane, the longest chapter in Tottenham's story was about to begin.

CHAPTER TWELVE

GOING UP, UP, UP

In 2003, a Russian billionaire called Roman Abramovich, a major shareholder in the giant oil company Sibneft, became the owner of Chelsea Football Club in a deal worth £140 million. Shortly after that he sacked the incumbent manager, Claudio Ranieri, and recruited Jose Mourinho, who had just won the Champions League with Porto, at a salary of £4.2 million a year. In the press conference that followed, Mourinho said, 'Please don't call me arrogant, but I'm European champion and I think I'm a special one.'

On 11th October 1958, Bill Nicholson went to see Fred Wale, the vice-chairman of Tottenham Hotspur, at Brown's of Tottenham, the Wale family's nut and bolt company. 'He told me: "Jimmy Anderson isn't going to carry on as manager and would you like the job?" I had been coaching at the club for four years and I felt I could do it, so I accepted. He didn't mention a contract or pay increase, so I didn't either.' Nicholson didn't even tell his wife, Darkie, about the job. The first she heard of her husband's promotion was when she was listening to the radio.

Still, the new regime was under way. And it had a deceptively promising beginning. The way things stood on the morning Nicholson took over, Spurs had managed just nine points from their 11 opening games and sat a point clear of the relegation zone. The three bottom-feeders included that afternoon's opponents, Everton. By the end of the afternoon, with Blanchflower and Harmer back, Spurs had beaten

Everton 10-4. 'We don't score 10 every game,' Harmer joked to Nicholson as they walked off the pitch. Blanchflower added the rider. 'It can only get worse from here,' he said.

He wasn't exaggerating. In no time at all, the new manager was made aware of the size of the job in front of him. As coach, working under Jimmy Anderson, he had been in his comfort zone. Being out there on the training ground, in his tracksuit, was the part of the job he would always love best. Now he was having to get to grips with man-management, and the first confrontation was with the most popular, influential, challenging player at White Hart Lane.

The Nicholson effect had lasted all of a week. After Spurs followed up their crushing of Everton by beating Leicester 4-3, they embarked on a run of one win in 11 games and spent the next three months in the bottom third of the table. Blanchflower may have been the 1950s poster boy for Spurs – he was writing for the *Daily Mail*, he was on the radio, he was about to publish his first book, a Weetabix advert ('Pass the hot milk, please') was looming on the horizon – but on the pitch his attacking zeal was proving a recipe for disaster. In January 1959, Nicholson axed him in favour of a young, aggressive defender called Bill Dodge. Blanchflower was, said Nicholson, 'an expensive luxury in a poor side'.

Blanchflower countered with one of his classic retorts. 'It's the bad players in a bad team who are the luxury. The poorest of families needs some luxury, it gives them hope.' Maybe that was true. But Nicholson was determined to shore up the defence before the team slid any further towards relegation. With another attack-minded wing-half, the 24-year-old Jim Iley, coming into the side, Blanchflower and his instinctive creativity were surplus to requirements.

'You're taking too many liberties,' Nicholson told him. 'When the ball is played into our box, you're often on your way out looking for a throw from the keeper. You should be in that box marking someone and doing your defensive job.'

Blanchflower was now in the stiffs, a month off his 33rd birthday. He wasn't even playing at wing-half but at inside-right, a position he hadn't occupied since his early days at Barnsley. Without him, the team won four in a row. The rumours started. It was the end for Blanchflower at Tottenham – maybe it was the end for him, full stop. Everyone thought that except Blanchflower. After a month he demanded a meeting with Nicholson and asked for a transfer.

That, said Nicholson, wasn't an option. If he wanted to ask for a move, he could, but the directors would be told the manager was dead against it. The club couldn't afford to let him go, considering the position they were in. Even though Blanchflower was no longer guaranteed a first-team place, Nicholson still wanted to keep his options open.

On the face of it, the meeting changed nothing. But Nicholson had spoken to him as an equal and the man's candour and firmness had won Blanchflower's respect. What was more, the captaincy issue hadn't been resolved. Nobody doing the job since Blanchflower handed back the armband had been a blazing success. The team lacked vision, cohesion and leadership. It needed Blanchflower. Perhaps both of them figured all that out while they were talking. But Blanchflower was the one who blinked first. Within a week he decided to forget the transfer request, just as the team started losing again. Nicholson brought him back for the relegation struggle against Portsmouth at White Hart Lane, though he made the point that he still didn't trust Blanchflower as a defender. Blanchflower was slotted in at inside-right in place of Tommy Harmer.

'We were struggling and Danny always wanted to play football, and Bill felt something more straightforward was needed to get us out of trouble,' says Cliff Jones. 'But if you've got Danny at the club, you've got to play him, and Bill soon recognised that.'

Bobby Smith had been Jimmy Anderson's latest choice of captain, but had never fancied the job. In any case, Nicholson was dead against having a front-line man as captain. Strikers were out of touch with what was going on around them, he believed, and any captain of his had to be a midfield player. Fate played a hand when Smith picked up an injury. That Monday, they were going to have to do without him when they went up to Molineux to play Wolves, the champions and league leaders. In *The Double and Before*, Blanchflower recalled: 'About six o'clock that evening, Bill Nicholson addressed us in a private room in our Wolverhampton hotel. He told us the team: Hollowbread; Baker, Hopkins; myself, Norman, Ryden; Harmer, Brooks, Medwin, Dunmore, Jones. He also said that he had decided to appoint me as club captain and that the players would respect my position.'

That night, with Blanchflower back in the number 4 shirt, Spurs took a point off Wolves and followed it up the following Saturday by putting six past Leicester, rivals in the relegation struggle. 'There was no acrimony,' Nicholson said later. 'He was one player you could have a rational discussion with and still remain friends.'

Results still weren't consistent enough to lift Spurs out of danger, but in the spring of 1959 Nicholson gave the world its first demonstration of the stealth tactics he used to sign all his significant players. He'd already made a wish list. The Welsh international Mel Charles had figured high on it but opted for Arsenal instead, which turned out to be the bit of luck Nicholson needed. Charles spent a lot of the next three seasons nursing injuries on the Arsenal treatment table. Spurs got Dave Mackay.

The deal that brought Mackay from Hearts to Tottenham was the outcome of a tip-off from a small, fat, Scottish journalist called Jim Rodger, who effectively acted as an agent. His reward wasn't a cut of the transfer fee but exclusives for his newspaper, *The Daily Record*. Rodger, who later achieved the distinction of being the man who tapped up young striker Alex Ferguson when he moved from Dunfermline to Rangers, was one of Nicholson's closest friends in the game. In March 1958, he informed Nicholson that Hearts needed to build a new stand and were steeling themselves to part with their rampantly competitive 24-year-old captain, Dave Mackay. Manchester United, painfully rebuilding after the Munich air crash of 1958, were in need of just the sort of qualities that Mackay would bring to a side and Nicholson had to act quickly. Nicholson caught a night train to Edinburgh and agreed a £32,000 deal before the midnight transfer deadline.

Nicholson always thought Mackay was the best signing he ever made: 'If he had served in a war, he would have been the first man into action. He would have won the Victoria Cross.' Captain of Hearts at 20, barrel-chested, gimlet-eyed, he combined delicacy of touch with an air of only just restrained violence, and of all the players Nicholson ever put in his side, more than Jimmy Greaves and Alan Gilzean, even, he was probably the one he loved most. According to Alan Mullery, the bond between them was very strong. 'They saw the world through the same eyes.'

Mackay settled in straight away, even though a foot injury stopped him playing all the remaining games. Grafting, fetching and carrying, extinguishing threats from opponents, he set up an instant rapport with Blanchflower. The other players approved of him too. 'Danny was the inspiration,' says the former *Daily Mail* journalist Brian James, 'but when players did something you would catch them glance quickly, looking for Dave's approbation. They wouldn't want that glare of his.'

'He made all the difference between a good side and a very good side,' says Cliff Jones. 'He was the type of player we were missing, someone competitive and with great energy, someone who drove the team on. He had to win, at everything. If you were playing Dave at five-a-side, it would be, "We might be mates but not today, laddie. Not today."'

'You'd have to go in the gym with body armour,' said Bobby Smith. 'Dave would smash you against a wall.'

One week before the end of the season, a 5-0 home win against West Bromwich Albion (Smith scored four) guaranteed Spurs would stay in the First Division. Nicholson wanted more than that, though. Much more. During the summer, he carried on shopping. The first essential was a keeper to replace Ron Reynolds and his stand-in, John Hollowbread. 'Neither was good enough, in my opinion,' he said. 'I wanted an international-class goalkeeper who was going to win us the championship.'

Jim Rodger pointed him in the direction of Dundee's Bill Brown. 'Who smoked 50 fags a day,' says Cliff Jones. 'But he was very agile, confident, quiet and a great shot-stopper. And a terrific golfer – he played off a one handicap and it was touch and go at one time whether he was going to be a golfer or a footballer.'

A bit of a Brad Friedel in style, Brown was a calm, quietly efficient keeper who preferred to stay on his line. He didn't even look much like a goalie, according to Ivan Ponting in *Tottenham Hotspur: Player-by-player*. 'He was tall, sure enough, but where the majority of top custodians boasted immense, muscular frames suggestive of barrier-like impregnability, Bill was lean and stringy and seemingly insubstantial; every line of the Brown figure was angular, an effect heightened by his aquiline features.'

In September, through another Jim Rodger tip-off, Nicholson found himself in a draughty stand at Brockville watching Falkirk's John White, a wiry, insignificant-looking 22-year-old playmaker, who moved around the pitch with the unpredictable energy of some force of nature. Falkirk, newly relegated from the Scottish First Division, had put White up for sale with a £20,000 price tag but his washed-out appearance had already deterred a bunch of big clubs from snapping him up. This was in spite of White's success as a cross-country runner in the army and his fledgling career as a Scotland inside-right. Nicholson waited until the start of October, when Blanchflower and Mackay came back from a Northern Ireland v Scotland fixture in Belfast. 'What do you think of John White?' he asked them. Blanchflower was unequivocal. 'Fly up and get him straight away.'

At White Hart Lane, it took White a while to settle. Part of the trouble was that he was still on National Service and had to commute to matches from Berwick. More than that, his best position was inside-right, a position already occupied by Harmer, who wasn't about to vacate it any time soon. White, in consequence, found himself the uneasy occupant of the inside-left position while an underwhelmed crowd got on his back and Nicholson tried to decide whom he preferred in the number 8 shirt. Another decision, though, was made for him. In November, the left-back Mel Hopkins broke his nose colliding with Ian St John in a Wales-Scotland international. 'It was horrible,' recalls Terry Dyson. 'His nose was completely flat. Two holes in his face for his nostrils.' Over a period of months Hopkins's features were restored but what he never got back was his place in the side. The suave-looking understudy Ron Henry took it over on a permanent basis. 'He was stronger in the tackle than Mel, good in the air and possibly more composed on the ball,' Nicholson said.

December 1959 brought the final piece in the jigsaw. Hollowbread and Reynolds weren't the only relics of the Anderson years shown the exit door. Late on in 1959, Johnny Brooks, a skilful but inconsistent striker, found himself on the way out. He was, said Nicholson devastatingly, 'a better player in a winning side than in a losing one'. Not that that put off Ted Drake, manager of a Chelsea side already giving relegation the come-on signs.

'Billy, I need Johnny Brooks.'

'What do you want him for?' said Nicholson. 'He's not the kind of player who'll get you out of a hole.' Having done his best to discourage Drake, he then arranged a straight swap with Les Allen, a youngster whom he'd been keeping track of in the Chelsea reserves. On the slow side, was his verdict, but good at sniffing out goals and a reliable finisher.

'I went training as normal,' says Allen, 'and got called in. "I'd like you to go to Tottenham," Ted Drake said. "Why?" I said. Ted said, "I'm doing a deal with them and they've asked for you." I was surprised. I didn't know what to think. Tottenham were a bigger club than Chelsea. We met Bill Nick in Ilford where my dad used to work. He was a very clever man, Bill. He picked John White out, Dave, Bill Brown. "You're the last piece in the jigsaw," Bill said. "I've been watching you. I admired the way you scored against us." That was it. Johnny went that way and I went this way. The next day I was training with Tottenham.'

'I felt,' said Nicholson, with massive understatement, 'we were building a side that could win a trophy.'

And then some. I've still got a cutting from *The Guardian* preserved from four years back. In it David Lacey chooses the Tottenham Hotspur side of 1959/60 as one of his 'Six Beautiful Teams Of The Last 50 Years': 'The pre-Double side stick in the mind because of the impact they had on an era dominated by the breathless, long-passing style of Stan Cullis's Wolves. The subtler, more thoughtful football of Bill Nicholson's team gave the English game a new learning.'

'I first watched them at the end of the 1950s when I was doing my National Service,' Lacey tells me. 'That season I reckon I saw the two matches which saw the sea change – the two games against Wolves. Home in autumn 1959. I was standing on the terraces at White Hart Lane and Bobby Smith scored a hat-trick.'

Then in April 1960, Lacey watched the return fixture at Molineux and recalls Blanchflower holding a team meeting on the pitch an hour before kick-off with the players in their suits and coats and the crowd offering their tuppence worth from the terraces.

'You felt you were watching something different, something superior,' he says. 'The way the ball effortlessly moved around the pitch, the expertise, it was quite a revelation.'

Spurs had looked capable of winning the Double that season – for a long time they occupied top place in the table – but there were too many slip-ups in the run-in. After back-to-back league wins over Arsenal and Manchester United in January, and a 13-2 crushing of Crewe Alexandra in a fourth-round FA Cup replay (which remains the club's record win), their form fell into a crater. Smith and Allen stopped scoring – Allen to the extent that he didn't figure on the team sheet for the rest of the season – and Blackburn knocked them out of the cup in the fifth round. There was also the unresolved battle between Harmer and White for the number 8 shirt. Misled by the unobtrusiveness that was part of White's genius, the fans much preferred Harmer and his whole fancy repertoire of ball-juggling and mazy dribbling. Then Harmer picked up an injury. In his absence, White tried on the number 8 shirt. It fitted him well.

But Spurs' loss of form had turned the title race into a three-way fight with Wolves and Burnley, and by the time that spring day at Molineux came around, by the time Blanchflower held the team meeting before kick-off, it was too late to do anything except play brilliantly. Wolves were crushed 3-1, with goals from Smith, Mackay and Jones. Blanchflower was in dazzling form and White played a blinder as the link man in midfield. Meanwhile, Wolves won the cup and Burnley scraped through to be champions.

For impartial observers, there was only one conclusion. And it was a depressing one. Spurs might have been one of the six most beautiful teams. But they just didn't have the bottle.

CHAPTER THIRTEEN

WHAT'S THE STORY, ETERNAL GLORY?

The easiest way of explaining how Spurs did the Double is to tell two anecdotes, one from the beginning of the season and one from the end.

The first is the story of what happened when the troops gathered at Cheshunt for pre-season training, when Blanchflower promised Fred Bearman, the chairman, that they were going to do it. Then there's the moment after Spurs beat Leicester in the cup final, when Henry shook Nicholson's hand and said, 'Well done, Bill, we've done it.' Nicholson made a face. 'Yes, but we were bloody awful. That wasn't like our team.' Nicholson was so dissatisfied with their performance in the final that it was more important to him than the fact they'd just won the FA Cup. In a nutshell, it was Blanchflower's belief and Nicholson's perfectionism that brought the Double to Tottenham Hotspur.

There were other, not exactly secondary, factors. Nicholson brought Terry Dyson in on the left wing. In the 1959/60 season, Spurs had been dismissed as psychologically brittle, a side that cracked under pressure. Dyson, the red–haired pocket rocket who would run for the whole 90 minutes, had attitude. He was enthusiastic and a trier. He brought resolve.

Then there was the growing confidence of White. At last he had won acceptance from the crowd. The press were starting to create his myth, calling him the 'Ghost of White Hart Lane' not just because of his pale complexion but also the way he drifted into space undetected. No longer sapped by the commute to matches from his army base in Berwick, living in London, able to train with the team, he had taken over permanently from Harmer in the number 8 shirt and his presence was decisive. 'He could ping 'em in,' says Allen. 'He was accurate. He used to do it all the time.' 'He was always looking for the open space and the alternative position that can mean so much to the man in possession,' says Jones. 'When he was there I always knew there was going to be an extra man waiting for my pass. He did so much intelligent running that he seemed to cover the whole width of the field.'

Jones must have covered nearly as much. Short, dark and aquiline like an ancient Roman, as athletic and skilful as his fellow Welshman Gareth Bale, he was also blessed with the certainty of genius. The first game of the Double season, he got smacked across the ankle by Everton's Alex Parker and was out for the next six games. 'I wasn't worried,' he says. 'I could play outside-right or outside-left. I just understood it – that I wouldn't lose my place. I was Bill's number one winger.'

That confidence came through in Mackay's mind games, too. Running out onto the pitch, he had started throwing the ball high in the air in front of the opposition. 'Have a kick now, you won't get one when the game starts,' he'd invite them before killing it stone dead as it dropped. Now the defence, once so flimsy, was similarly assured. In front of the lean, prowling but metaphorically rock-solid figure of Brown, Baker and Henry formed one of the sturdiest full-back pairings of the era. Norman, a bit of a rustic lost soul when he joined Spurs, had become a linchpin.

They also had a happy dressing room. When they scored, they hugged each other, in displays of man-love that didn't go down well with the British press who pronounced them 'Un-British, effeminate and childish'. It was the kind of thing that was banned at Turf Moor, home of the reigning champions, Burnley, and their pop-eyed, red-faced diminutive chairman Bob Lord. 'At Chelsea, the players didn't seem to mix,' said Smith, whose playing career had started at Stamford Bridge. 'They had a snooker hall but everyone just went home after training. Tottenham were like a family. You never got into a row. No one ever got in a mood. It only got out of order once when Peter Baker and one of the reserves had a fight at Cheshunt. We broke it up and the next day John put one chair in one corner of the dressing room and one chair in another corner for them. Bill couldn't work out what was going on.'

Away from the pitch as well as on it, White was turning out to be a definite asset, his friendship with Jones resulting in a series of spectacularly barmy pranks like putting pebbles in the wheel hubs of Smith's car. They dressed up as waiters on the train back from Birmingham and served Henry with a box of Trill bird food (he was at the time a devoted member of the budgerigar fancy). They re-enacted Errol Flynn swordfights dressed in tablecloths. White was also an enthusiastic subscriber to the post-match drinking school that usually assembled in a small back room set aside for them by the landlord of the Bell and Hare on Tottenham High Road, where Mackay was in charge of admissions and White once took a chrysanthemum from a vase and casually ate it. (The only non-attender was Blanchflower, who was teetotal and whom Mel Hopkins likened to Grandad, the character in *Only Fools and Horses*, sitting amused as the madness unfolded around him.)

Then there was the run of 11 wins at the start of the season. It started on 20th August, when they beat Everton 2-0 at White Hart Lane. On 31st August, Blackpool came to the Lane to be beaten 3-1 by a Bobby Smith hat-trick which broke the club scoring record previously held by George Hunt: 138 in the league and the cup between 1930 and 1937 back in the day. Not bad for someone who, when he arrived in London as a schoolboy player with Chelsea, fled back to Yorkshire within days. Now the scared 14-year-old had turned into a massive physical presence, a swarthy, thick-thighed, ruddy-faced tormentor who combined artistry and thuggery ('Smithy didn't think he was in the game until he had hammered into the goalkeeper in the earliest possible moment in a match,' said Jimmy Greaves).

Just over halfway through the winning run came the first defining moment of the Double season. It was at Highbury on 10th September, the day of the first-ever league match to be screened live on TV and the day of one of the greatest demonstrations of football skill and resilience ever shown. And the cameras, hundreds of miles up country filming Blackpool v Bolton, missed it. Now, when it mattered most, Spurs proved they could fight. Sparkling, brilliant, they were two up within 23 minutes through the reserve Frank Saul and Dyson. And then they let Arsenal draw level. They were overwhelmed by red shirts. The fans knew it had to be the end. It always was, this sudden, inexplicable folding up against their great rivals. But this time the collapse never happened. Instead Spurs rode out the spell of Arsenal pressure and began to play composed, skilful football again. A long, devastating free-kick from Blanchflower in the second half picked out Allen to lob the winner over the Arsenal keeper. It was a record-breaking performance, the best-ever start by any club in the First Division. It was the day the myth was debunked that Spurs had no bottle.

On 1st October, they handed out a four-goal, almost casually brutal beating to a reputedly impregnable Wolves defence at Molineux – the scorers were Jones, Blanchflower, Allen and Dyson. Interrupted by a 1-1 draw on 10th October, at home to Manchester City, the run restarted with four more wins taking them into November.

Finally, though, one team got the better of them. At Hillsborough, Sheffield Wednesday, their closest challengers for the title, won 2-1 to go five points behind them with a game in hand, cueing the predictable question in the next day's papers: Were Spurs about to crack?

There's nothing like scepticism in the media to breathe fresh fire into tired hearts and legs. Spurs went on to beat Birmingham 6-0 the following Saturday, overwhelming them with a three-in-15-minutes goal rush. They were unstoppable and unplayable, they piled up the points. In eight games they dropped just one, against Burnley at White Hart Lane. From 4-0 in front, they had to settle for 4-4, a result that so disgusted Mackay that he raged to the press: 'A great game and a classic? I'll believe that when we've won the championship. No team on earth should catch us after we've taken that sort of lead.' Two weeks later, away to Everton, they scored three times in thick fog, the *coup de grace* being a 35-yarder from Mackay's left foot. They took all the points in back-to-back fixtures with West Ham United over Christmas. The last match of 1960, in brilliant sunshine, was at home to Blackburn. A goal down in 15 minutes, no Mackay, no Jones, and Marchi playing with his back killing him, the final score of 5-2 said it all. 'What a team, what fighters,' said Nicholson. 'This bunch deserve nothing but the best.'

Early in January, the FA Cup run started. Charlton Athletic came to White Hart Lane. The season before, Spurs had been top of the league at the same stage. In just the same way, all talk had centred round the Double. They'd got through to the fifth round, but then they'd gone out 3-1 to Blackburn in the White Hart Lane mud. Losing at home to Manchester City and Chelsea over Easter killed their title hopes. They'd won a lot of admirers that season but finished up with nothing. You can't put applause in a trophy cabinet.

This time it was different. Driven by Mackay and Blanchflower, Spurs got a two-goal start through Allen within the first half hour before Charlton pulled a goal back in the 33rd minute. Dyson, already limping and vaguely onside, made it 3-1 nine minutes before the half-time break. Immediately after the restart, Charlton pulled another back. One heroic save from Brown, and a bit of luck when Charlton missed a sitter, kept the score at 3-2. It had been close, said Blanchflower, but it was enough.

But in the league, the momentum was slowing. Spurs lost 2-0 at Old Trafford in the Monday night game, though they were still way ahead at the top of the table. On 21st January came the second victory of the season over Arsenal: 4-2 at White Hart Lane. A week later, in the fourth round of the cup, 7,000 Crewe Alexandra fans plus a 2ft home-made plaster robin (well, that was one way to fill those long, dark northern evenings) descended on White Hart Lane to see their side beaten 5-1 in the mud. Mackay was inspirational.

Then, early in February, Spurs lost at the Lane for the first time that season, 3-2 to Leicester. It was only the third defeat, but the fans were agitated. This was the point where Spurs had started to fall apart a year back. Was their huge lead in the title race about to fade away?

Not just then. A week later, in what was billed as the match of the season – a rehearsal for the fifth-round cup tie against Aston Villa to be played the following Saturday at Villa Park – Spurs clocked up a convincing 2-1 victory, with Blanchflower, Mackay and Norman magnificent.

The second meeting with Villa was an anti-climax, with Spurs two goals up by half-time and coasting to the final. But it led to the season's second defining moment, the sixth-round cup-tie against Sunderland. In the first match, Spurs let a 1-0 lead get wiped out by an 18-year-old called Willie McPheat, the cue for hundreds of delirious Mackems to invade the pitch. It was Blanchflower who held the players together. 'Now keep your heads,' he told them, 'and let's get going after a goal. We don't want that business down in our goalmouth again.'

'Everyone had had enough excitement for one day,' he wrote later. 'We should have won the game in the first half,' commented an unimpressed Nicholson.

Four days later, in the replay at White Hart Lane, where 150,000 fans queued for 65,000 tickets and the gates were stormed, Spurs delivered an awesome reclamation of supremacy with goals from Allen, Smith, Dyson (he got two) and Mackay as Sunderland were crushed 5-0.

Now there was just Burnley to beat in the semi-final and they'd have their place at Wembley. They were going to have to do it at Villa Park, which as they'd lost there in three semis since the war, each time through a very late goal, was something of a bogey ground. In the last league game before the semi-final, they lost to Cardiff, not exactly the Barcelona of their day. But against Burnley, Norman held it together for them until Blanchflower's thoughtful passing started to click in and swing the game. Spurs began to look like their real selves. At which point the Burnley keeper failed to trap a speculative Allen lob, and the ball spun on. Smith, completely shut out until then, slammed the ball home. Fast forward to the second half, and a sensational restart in which, within four minutes, Burnley had a goal disallowed, Spurs had two near misses, then Smith struck again after Jones was felled. Mackay's free kick was charged down but he pushed it back again and Smith scored with a dipping pot shot from the edge of the area.

Burnley were spirited in recovery but Norman remained supreme at centre-half, his head work and giant frame withstanding everything Burnley threw at him. And in the final minute came the knockout blow: a White left-foot flick inside and Jones left-footer. 3-0. When the final whistle blew, Spurs fans rushed the field to carry Smith to the dressing room entrance. Norman was maybe just too big to lift.

Then, suddenly, around Easter, something went wrong. Since the beginning of the year, they'd been averaging a point a game. By the evening of 18th March, Sheffield Wednesday had reduced Spurs' lead to four points. It was not difficult to come up with an explanation – White, now a key man, was enduring a temporary loss of form and Jones, a player so recklessly brave and goal-hungry he would dive head-first into a sea of boots to get at the ball, had been out injured through Christmas and the early part of January. But what haunted everyone was the recollection that in 1954, on FA Cup semi-final night, West Bromwich Albion, then managed by the former Spur Vic Buckingham, had needed only seven points from the last seven league matches and to beat Preston North End at Wembley to clinch the Double. They won the cup but took only three more league points. Wolves had overtaken them to win the title.

On 22nd March, Newcastle took both points away from White Hart Lane. It was a game Spurs should have won 10-0, but they did everything except score and Blanchflower missed a penalty. In front of goal, they had suddenly started to play with a panicky, impotent desperation.

Three days later, they dropped a point at Fulham. Feeling the breath of Wednesday down their necks where once the Yorkshire team had been 10 points behind, Spurs were a flagging team, their hopes of the Double squeezing the air out of them. They hadn't won in the league since 25th February. They had picked up just eight points from the last nine games in a featureless stretch of low-energy football. Meanwhile, up at Hillsborough, Wednesday were busy thumping Manchester United 5-0.

Then came the third defining moment. And it belonged to Jones. On Good Friday, at home to Chelsea, Spurs were completely dominant in the first half with nothing to show for it. Then, five minutes into the second half, following a movement on the right inevitably initiated by a tireless Blanchflower, a final cross found Jones alone in front of an open goal. Maybe as a precaution, he didn't shoot. Instead, he ran the ball into the net.

That single goal flipped Spurs back into all their old swagger and mastery. A kind of madness set in. They added three more before conceding a couple back. By the next day, they'd calmed down a bit. Four up at half-time against Preston, they won 5-0. On Easter Monday, they completed the double over Chelsea. The title was virtually assured. Then they knocked three past Birmingham while Wednesday could only draw at home to Leicester.

Even so, Wednesday were still arguably in with a chance as they arrived at White Hart Lane on 15th April for what was nominally the title decider. A goal down after 29 minutes through Wednesday's Don Megson, Spurs were neither fluent nor stylish. Some terrifying tackles flew in; Mackay picked up a booking and Jones had to have stitches in his knee. But the title was clinched in the space of two minutes of brilliant mayhem. Three minutes before half-time, Dyson beat Wednesday's Swan, a man practically twice his height, in the air and directed a header back to Smith. Smith pulled it down as if he had magnets for boots, turned and volleyed past Springett, the Wednesday keeper. One minute later, Norman headed a free kick down to Allen. The player Nicholson had swapped almost casually for the unloved Johnny Brooks scored the goal that won the title.

For the statisticians, there were a few more bits and pieces to be tied up. Spurs, now eight points up with three more fixtures to play, needed only three more points for the all-time First Division record. But for the most part the fans had lost interest in numbers. Spurs had won the title. Now for the cup, the other half of the Double, the half that would make them immortal.

Spurs' simple participation in an FA Cup Final gave Morris Keston his greatest thrill in an historic season: 'The League Championship doesn't mean anything to me – you win it, it's over. But to get to Wembley . . . It was the first time we'd got to a final for a long time. Weeks before, the local shops put the bunting out. Then there was walking down Wembley Way, the song sheets, *Abide with Me* – it was a wonderful thing.'

No matter that the quality of play in the final left a lot to be desired. If you look at the DVD of the 1961 FA Cup Final now, you'll see Nicholson had a point when he said that Spurs were bloody awful. Even in the eyes of those who love them unconditionally, they don't look great, that's for sure. The most entertaining part was before kick-off, when Blanchflower was introducing his team to the Duchess of Kent.

'All the Leicester players have their names on their tracksuits,' said the Duchess. 'You don't.'

'Yes, Ma'am,' said Blanchflower, 'but we all know each other.'

The rest was mundane, really. It's hard to see how it could have been otherwise. So much was at stake. Anyway, as Blanchflower pointed out afterwards, there is more to winning the cup than getting it right at Wembley. Much more.

The weather was chilly, with a blustery wind. Spurs found the Leicester defence hard to crack. White shot over the bar from eight yards. Then, with 19 minutes gone, the Leicester right-back Len Chalmers didn't see Allen coming into the tackle and turned; trying to block the ball, Allen caught his leg. From then on, Chalmers was a mere passenger, hobbling on the wing. Ten-man Leicester made few breakaways. Nothing much was happening in either goalmouth because both defences were on top. Henry, masterful in his tackling, interception and use of the ball, was Spurs' best player.

Coming up to 40 minutes, Jones had a goal disallowed. The real thing didn't happen until the second half when Smith collected a Dyson pass, saw Gordon Banks move one way so directed his shot the other. Then he fell over. It was only when his mates started snogging him that he realised he'd scored.

The goal knocked the stuffing out of Leicester. With 77 minutes on the clock, Dyson headed the second from a mighty centre from

Smith. Two minutes later, as if to symbolise Leicester's acceptance of defeat, Chalmers hobbled off the pitch.

And that was that. The final whistle blew. Barbara Wallace, Nicholson's assistant and for a long time Spurs' only female employee, attached the blue and white ribbons to the cup, 60 years after Morton Cadman's wife, Wallace's grandmother, had first done so. The original ribbons of 1901 and 1921 had been lost, and the redoubtable Wallace would be entrusted with the safe keeping of the new set for years to come. Blanchflower's lovely smile as he raised the cup is imprinted on my childhood memory. Spurs did their lap of honour while *McNamara's Band* boomed out from the terraces. Leicester's 10 remaining rubber-legged players waited at the entrance to the tunnel, generously applauding them off.

There's not much argument about who were the true greats in the Double side. Blanchflower, Mackay, Jones and White are the usual names put forward, though you could make a case for the mighty Smith. But though Spurs were the money club of the era, only the genius that was Nicholson could have spent the money that well. Along with Blanchflower's inspired, vocal, life-affirming captaincy, White's magical ubiquity, Jones's speed and courage, Mackay's huge physicality, his almost terrifying commitment and hardness and energy, were the contributions of relatively unsung but still outstanding players: Brown, Baker, Henry, Norman, Allen, Dyson – any club would have thrown open its gates to welcome them.

Spurs did the Double using just 17 players. The only changes in the first-choice team were made through injuries. Four went through the 49 league and cup games without missing a match – Blanchflower, Henry, White and Allen. Smith was the top scorer with 33 goals in 43 games, followed by Allen with 27 goals in 49 games. In total, the tally was higher than in any championship since the war. The only two names which didn't get on the scoresheet were Brown and Henry. They did not need to have scored to be seen as magnificent. Even the reserves would have made it into any other club's first team: Hopkins, Terry Medwin, Marchi, and 17-year-old Frank Saul.

Henry and Baker were at the front of the open-top bus, holding the trophies as it crawled two and three-quarter miles between the Town Halls of Edmonton and Tottenham. Both sides of the road were crowded all the way. Banners and blue-and-white bunting spilt down the sides of the Fore Street tower block, every shop window had tribute displays, there were brass bands, motorbike outriders, bugles, rattles, streamers and flowers. The bus stopped outside the ground so the directors could wave decorously from the boardroom. As it rolled past the Royal dance hall, the resident band launched into *McNamara's Band*. Thousands broke through the police cordon by the War Memorial onto the approach road to the Town Hall. TV cameras whirled and flash-lamps popped. Finally Blanchflower appeared on the Town Hall balcony and spoke to the thousands below; 'I never really realised before how important football is or what it really means till today.'

One at a time, the players took their bows on the balcony. No one was left out. The stiffs and the magic sponge man received their due acclaim: John Hollowbread, Terry Medwin, Mel Hopkins, Tony Marchi, Frank Saul, Ken Barton, John Smith, Cecil Poynton.

Tottenham Hotspur had turned a seemingly impossible task into reality. It's tempting to write a lot of high-flown stuff, but words aren't enough to put across just how marvellous it was to have been there in the world the season that Spurs won the Double. Perhaps the best way is to end how it started, with Blanchflower, whose quest for glory and belief in the unattainable provided the motivation and inspiration, and whose wit and grace will never be forgotten. He was, unsurprisingly, that season's Player of the Year. As he said in his acceptance speech at the Football Writers' Association dinner, 'It's not been a bad year for Tottenham, as Bill Nicholson might admit in one of his more passionate moments.'

CHAPTER FOURTEEN

CONQUERING EUROPE, FIRST

Thered was no question of Nicholson hitching up his knifepoint-creased trousers and sitting back on his laurels. On the agenda for the 1961/62 season was the Treble. This time it was going to be the title, the FA Cup *and* the pinnacle of success in Europe.

The European Cup had not been a happy hunting ground for English teams in Europe, ever since its inaugural season in 1955 when Chelsea were strong-armed into withdrawing by the portly, grim-faced Football League chairman Alan Hardaker, who believed it was not in the best interests of English football and the game in general. Instead, the first five years of the competition were dominated by Real Madrid, although Manchester United reached the semi-finals in 1957. The whole world knows what happened one year later when they set off home from their successful quarter-final second leg against Red Star Belgrade in Munich. In the two years that followed, neither Wolves nor Burnley could get beyond the quarter-finals.

In the first-round first leg, Spurs were due to play Gornik Zabrze in Katowice in the Polish coalfields. Late in the summer of 1961, there being no airport at Katowice, Nicholson flew to Warsaw and took the night train from there to inspect hotels and watch Gornik play a league match. Met by a scene from *The Spy Who Came in*

From the Cold, he was directed by club officials to a hotel with grimy coal-stained curtains, bug-infested beds and carpets so filthy that he demanded to look at alternatives, at which he discovered it was the best in Katowice.

And on the night of the match, Gornik played the best football in Katowice. Spurs were 4-0 down within an hour, though Jones and Dyson scored near the end to make it 4-2. Smith and Mackay threw themselves into the fray so robustly that afterwards the Polish coach observed that Spurs were 'no angels'. In consequence, three Spurs fans dressed as angels (creative use of bedsheets was involved) for the return leg, when they paraded around the touchline with placards saying: 'Rejoice This Is The Night of Vengeance'; 'Glory Be To Shining White Hart Lane'; 'Who Heard of Dirty Spurs?'; and 'And It Came To Pass: Jones to White to Smudger: Goal.'

'After the first leg, Bill wasn't very happy, big time.' says Jones. 'Giving us a lot of stick. Words at training. But in the home leg we'd never experienced anything like it. We were really up for it and so were the crowd. Sixty-five thousand people all craving for us to really take this team.'

They did. Myth has it that Gornik scored first to put Spurs 2-5 down on aggregate; the slightly less compelling reality is that Spurs went 3-0 up (5-4 on aggregate) before Gornik scored to make it 3-1 on the night and 5-5 on aggregate. The final tally that night was 8-1 – Blanchflower [pen], Jones 3, Smith 2, Dyson, White – and 10-5 on aggregate. That night in September was the first of the glory nights of European football at White Hart Lane, the birth of 'Glory Glory Hallelujah' as the fans, inspired by the angelic demonstration, burst spontaneously into song. The fans made the biggest noise in the south. It became the Tottenham hymn.

'At Gornik's ground, the pitch was within a running track and a ditch,' says Jones. 'At Tottenham, the crowd is right on top of you. The atmosphere was indescribable. We could see the Gornik players thinking, "What the hell is this?" Right away we broke away, Les Allen hit the bar and the crowd went mad. Gornik were intimidated. The supporters just picked that up. We tore into Gornik – they never stood a chance. For 90 minutes it was a continuous roar. We'd have taken anybody apart that night.'

For Morris Keston, it stands out as his greatest Spurs memory. 'I stood behind the goal. We were 4-2 down from the first leg. The Poles scored and we thought that was it. Then we scored again to make it 4-1 and then it got better and better. Afterwards, everyone was dancing up and down our street.'

A few weeks later Spurs went to Rotterdam for the second-round first leg against Feyenoord. Two goals from the 18-year-old Frank Saul, standing in for the injured Smith, and one more from Dyson brought a 3-1 victory. 'We muddled our way through,' said Nicholson, from whom words of praise were about as rare as ornamental ponds in the Sahara. The return leg at White Hart Lane finished 1-1 and was a dreary and patchy performance that stood out mainly for a demonstration of courage exceptional even by Mackay's standards when, after being stretchered off concussed and blood-spattered, he sat up 10 minutes later with the enquiry, 'What am I doing here?' and got back on the field. He was later discovered to have a fractured skull.

The same inconsistent form was keeping Spurs in fourth place in the league, a position Nicholson intended to remedy with the sensational signing of Jimmy Greaves from AC Milan. Four years earlier at Chelsea, Greaves had been the wonderkid, the 17-year-old who announced his arrival in the first team with a goal against Spurs in August 1957. It was the kind of goal that was going to become his trademark, beating three defenders before stroking the ball into the net. 'It had all the hallmarks of his game, improvisation and genius,' said Nicholson. 'I had to have him.' Greaves inspired that kind of passion in everyone who saw him. One of White Hart Lane's most celebrated touts, a devoted Spurs fan called 'Johnny The Stick', whom Greaves kept supplied with cup tickets, used to sleep in one of his old Spurs shirts. Without question, he was the best young striker in Europe, putting away 132 goals in 169 league games. 'I was just amazed by him,' says Steve Perryman. 'His balance. His off-the-mark sharpness. His eye for goal. He glided, just glided past people. I saw him score some amazing goals, in five-a-side, in hockey-sized goals. He scored unbelievable goals. That bit of Messi when he's on a run, flicking through people – that's how Jimmy was.'

For Greaves himself, it was quite simple. 'I was born with an instinctive, natural gift for sticking the ball in the net. I just get in as close as I can and let rip.'

When Milan came in for Greaves, life had just delivered him and his wife a wrecking ball in the shape of the death from pneumonia of their four-month-old son, Jimmy Jnr. Greaves admits he was attracted by the Italian money as well as the chance to put as many miles as possible between himself and the pain. Whereas English football still had a maximum wage, Torino were about to sign Denis Law for £100,000. It was no contest. Milan signed him for £80,000 and he continued to play for Chelsea until Italy's embargo on foreign players was lifted.

But while he was waiting, Jimmy Hill and the Players Union got the maximum wage abolished, suddenly Johnny Haynes was earning £100 a week at Fulham and Greaves realised he was committed to going out to Italy when he could be earning a fortune in England, where he wouldn't have to expand his knowledge of Italian beyond 'spaghetti bolognese'.

He tried everything and everyone – lawyers, agents, the England manager, Jimmy Hill – to get out of the agreement with Milan, who promised him they would get him banned from ever kicking a ball again if he reneged on the contract. Then they gave him more money. Off he went to Italy, where the manager decided what he was going to eat and sat watching until he ate it, he was fined for going outside city limits and allowed no more than two cigarettes a day which meant he took every opportunity to snatch a covert smoke. They owned him. Plus he hated the kind of defence-choked football they played, even though he proceeded to reduce it to fragments, becoming Milan's top scorer with nine goals in 14 games.

Greaves instigated a policy of non-cooperation that cost him more in fines than he was getting in wages. Inevitably word had got out about his unhappiness and when, in the summer of 1961, he travelled back to England for a function at the Café Royal, Nicholson alerted him to Spurs' interest while standing alongside him in the gentlemen's toilets. With Milan lining up a Brazilian to replace him and Chelsea getting ready to receive him back, Nicholson stepped in with a cheque for £99,999 (he was unwilling to saddle Greaves with the label of England's first £100,000 player). Nicholson felt sorry for Les Allen, whose place Greaves had taken, but as he observed: 'A football manager can't afford sentiment.' That, he said, was why his old mate Ron Burgess hadn't succeeded as a manager. 'He was too nice.'

Greaves made his first appearance for Spurs in a reserve match at Plymouth in front of a record crowd for a stiffs game of 13,000. A week later, in mid-December, he launched himself in the first team with a hat-trick in the 5-2 defeat of Blackpool at White Hart Lane. Ten days later, he scored again in the 2-0 win at Chelsea.

A new era had begun at Spurs, the era of Jimmy, and it coincided with a fixture pile-up. Competing on three fronts, Spurs lost 3-1 at Molineux at the beginning of February and from leading the table for much of the season they dropped to third behind Burnley and Ipswich. In the middle of the month, the European Cup took them to Czechoslovakia, where on a snow-bound pitch they resisted Dukla Prague in a highly uncharacteristic bus-parking performance that featured White as their first line of defence. In the end, they lost 1-0. 'It was an Irish victory,' said Blanchflower. From there they flew direct to the Midlands for an FA Cup fifth-round tie against West Bromwich Albion, which they won 4-2. Two of the goals were from Smith, two belonged to Greaves.

Spurs were now starting to have to blow the dust off the reserves – Brown, Blanchflower, Baker, Mackay and Jones were all inhabiting the treatment room. Even so, at the end of February 1962, they beat Dukla Prague 4-1 in the European Cup return leg at White Hart Lane. Now in the semis, they had to face the holders, Benfica, a side that included a youngster with the same kind of magic talent that Greaves had at 17. Eusebio would go on to be one of the stand-out performers at the 1966 World Cup and one of the greatest players of all time.

In the first leg at the Estadio de Luz, Spurs were two behind within 10 minutes and the final score was 3-1, with Smith their solitary scorer.

Mackay was unfazed. 'We'll do them at Tottenham, just wait and see,' he promised. Nicholson, too, was bullish, predicting that Spurs would draw level in the return leg at White Hart Lane. Neither proved to be much cop as clairvoyants. Spurs were one down within 15 minutes and then Greaves had a goal – which looked radiantly okay to everyone except a linesman – disallowed.

'The referee . . . seemed satisfied,' wrote Ian Wooldridge in the *Daily Mail*. 'As 65,000 hysterical Londoners unleashed the greatest roar of this ear-shattering night, he went striding back to the centre spot.

'But Hensen, a slim, erect, isolated figure on the far touchlines, had his magenta flag pointed skywards. This was fortune's vengeance on Spurs.'

Then, with 35 minutes gone, Smith equalised. Needing three more for an outright win and two to earn a replay, Blanchflower scored from the penalty spot to make it 2-1, but in spite of the best efforts of the crowd and the Tottenham angels, whose placards now read 'Lisbon Greaves Tonight', that was how it finished.

'Everyone felt sick,' recalls Morris Keston. 'I went to the first leg and coming back to The Lane we thought, "Yeah, we're going to beat them." Then the goal gets disallowed. It was one of the worst decisions of our time. We just felt cheated, but once you're beat, you're beat. In our minds, we did win though.'

A quarter of a century on, the perceived injustice of his disallowed goal still festered with Greaves. 'I was sure then that it was a good goal,' he said. 'I don't think anyone will ever be able to change my view of that. There were defenders all around me. Bobby [Smith] slotted the ball through and I went between at least two defenders before shooting past Costa Pereiera, the Benfica goalkeeper. I really thought that goal would be the one that put us through to the final.'

Out of the European Cup, the Double was about to slip out of reach. The turning point was in March, when they lost 6-2 away to Manchester City and went down 3-1 to Alf Ramsey's Ipswich Town at White Hart Lane, having already lost to them at Portman Road earlier in the season. According to Brian Scovell, Nicholson's biographer, Nicholson went against his own instincts and instead took the advice of Mackay and Blanchflower not to change the tactics to counter Ramsey's style of playing withdrawn wingers. Had they picked up two of those four points, Spurs, with their goal average boosted by Greaves, would have been champions.

The title race went down to the wire, mind. Tottenham Hotspur, though, weren't contesting it. Ipswich had to beat Aston Villa at Portman Road, while Burnley had to be held at home by Chelsea. It was Ipswich – provincial, newly promoted Ipswich – who got the right result.

At the little East Anglian club, the crowd invaded the pitch, the trainer was thrown into the bath, the chairman cracked open the champagne. Only Ramsey remained impassive in the spillage of joy that washed over Portman Road. Until everyone had gone home, that was. Once he was on his own, he walked down to the pitch and did a lap of honour, the sides of his suit jacket flapping, in front of the empty terraces. He had beaten Bill Nicholson's Tottenham, spoiled their chance of a second Double in successive seasons. Winning the title was marvellous. Payback for all that went on at Tottenham six years earlier made it all the sweeter.

It became imperative that Spurs took something from a season that had begun with such colossal hope. A 3-1 semi-final victory over Manchester United at Hillsborough earned Spurs another trip to Wembley, with the FA Cup their last chance of glory. The same went for their cup final opponents, Burnley, a side of four internationals and, in Jimmy Adamson, a captain who almost rivalled Blanchflower for sage-like blatherings.

Greaves pledged he would score a goal in five minutes. It actually took him three to roll the ball into Burnley's net. Burnley equalised five minutes after the restart. A minute later, White floated in a ball for Smith to put Spurs ahead again. That was really the match-winner, though for Spurs fans 2-1 was never going to be a comfortable lead and it was an edgy half hour or so until Burnley's Cummings kept out a Medwin shot with his hand. Blanchflower's penalty kick sent Blacklaw, the Burnley keeper, the wrong way. The FA Cup returned to White Hart Lane and Spurs had another chance to become the first English club to conquer Europe, via the European Cup Winners' Cup.

Pausing only to destroy Ipswich 5-1 in the Charity Shield, the curtain raiser to the 1962/63 season, Spurs set off on another bid for the title, a campaign that had them leading the table in October but started skidding early in the new year when White and Blanchflower were both hospitalised – White for back pains and exhaustion, Blanchflower for knee surgery.

The Cup Winners' Cup campaign began with a 5-2 home-leg win against Rangers and in the away leg, Spurs beat them 3-2. Then Spurs were knocked out of the FA Cup third round by Burnley and the competition assumed increased importance. Early in March, they played their quarter-final first leg away to Slovan Bratislava and in the snow were lucky to depart with a deficit of only 2-0. As the players left the pitch, Viliam Schroif, Slovan's goalie, encountered the clenched fist of Smith under his nose. 'Londres,' Smith growled. 'Londres . . . Londres . . . You'll get yours in Londres . . .' This was no empty threat. A week later, in the second leg at White Hart Lane, Smith hammered into him in the first minute and, in a performance brilliantly orchestrated by White, Spurs put six past him.

So Spurs were into the semi-finals of the European Cup Winners' Cup, for the purposes of which they travelled to Yugoslavia. Where it all got rather tasty.

OFK Belgrade 1 Spurs 2. 'Greaves Sent Off – But Spurs Storm On' was a sample of the next day's headlines after Greaves did the walk of shame for what the referee called 'not acting like a gentleman'. 'The goalkeeper, he spat in my face for 80 minutes,' said Smith. 'It got wilder and wilder. I got the centre-half in the stomach with an elbow and he went down. Then this other geezer went at Greavsie, came round his back and tried to punch him so Greavsie tried to punch him back. Dave kicked him, Greavsie came to congratulate Dave and got sent off because the ref thought it was him that done it. Never stopped. Never stopped. Over dinner I said to a reporter, "Tell that geezer to have pneumonia when they come to London because I'll have him." And I did. I bowled him in the back of the net, I tormented him to death. "If you want to start, I'm here," I said, giving him a fucking kick.'

So having beaten OFK Belgrade 3-1 in the second leg, a game in which, commented the ref afterwards, 'the players seemed to be more interested in each other than the ball', Spurs headed for Rotterdam and a final against the cup holders Atletico Madrid. They already knew one bit of the bad news – Mackay wouldn't be fit. It was touch and go whether Blanchflower would make it, too.

His knee operation hadn't worked out, but he had gone back to playing anyway. 'I was too old to sit around waiting for recovery,' he said. 'I had to keep in motion to have a chance at all.' The morning of the second-leg tie against OFK Belgrade, someone caught the knee in training but he opted to play on rather than jeopardise his place in the final. In the two league games that followed, he played through the pain, with the result that every time he extended his knee the torn ligament started bleeding. By the day of the final in Rotterdam, the knee was the size of a small tax haven. According to Blanchflower, Nicholson's choice was down to 'me on one leg or John Smith on two.'

Nicholson chose Blanchflower. The man's presence was worth it for the half hour before kick-off alone. That night Nicholson's team talk was one of the most spirit-crushing in the history of football. 'Dave Mackay failed a fitness test shortly before the final and this really shook Bill, who like everybody else believed in the miracle that was Mackay,' recalled Greaves in *This One's on Me*. 'He was thoroughly miserable at the pre-match team talk and built Atletico Madrid up as the greatest team he had ever seen . . . I knew Bill was trying to avoid complacency among us but he had overplayed it. He had frightened us to death!'

It was Blanchflower who lifted them up again. Later, in his *Sunday Express* column, he wrote: '"Let's respect these Atletico fellows," I said, "but let's not get carried away with all we say and read about them. They are probably having a team meeting at this very moment and somebody is saying, "They've got this big six-foot-three-inch white fellow . . . " They've got quick players? Cliff Jones can catch pigeons. They've got hard men? When Maurice Norman takes his teeth out, he frightens me. Jimmy Greaves invents ways of scoring goals.'

'We needed him to remind us that we were a good side and we went out thinking they weren't in our class,' says Jones.

They also walked out to the cheers of at least 4,000 Spurs fans courtesy of what newspapers called 'Operation Rotterdam'.

Aubrey Morris, Spurs fan and owner of the Riviera Holidays travel agency, had begun handing out leaflets at home games advertising trips to Tottenham's away ties during the club's first season in the European Cup. By the semi-final against Benfica, he was offering a five-night ferry package to Portugal, and demand remained high through the Cup Winners' Cup campaign, but the final took numbers to another level. The company eventually took 2,500 people on 33 aircrafts. 'We had a real mix of people,' Morris recalled in *The Tottenham Hotspur Opus*, 'Kids queuing up with the money, £8 10s, old-time Spurs supporters.'

Morris said that he could have sold twice as many seats if sufficient planes had been available, and at least 1,500 more people made their way to the match. The Spurs Supporters Club took 65 coachloads and an extra ship was laid on to supplement the normal two night ferries from Harwich to Holland. Hundreds of British troops based in mainland Europe also travelled to Rotterdam, adding to the sense of national pride at Spurs reaching the final. 'The Berlin airlift had nothing on this,' reported the *Tottenham and Edmonton Weekly Herald*. 'Never before has an English team had so much fantastic support on the Continent.'

But all the passion from the Spurs travelling army couldn't shield the players from the dubious tactics of Atletico once the game got under way. Minutes after the start, Smith was left doubled-up twice by Griffa, Atletico's brutish centre-half. White, Jones and Greaves all got clattered. The violence of the welcome goaded Spurs into defiant action and with 16 minutes gone Greaves plucked a Jones cross out of the air to put them into the lead. Not much more than a quarter of an hour had passed before White rammed a shot in off the crossbar from a Dyson cross.

Emerging for the second half, Spurs felt the beginnings of a certainty that proved short-lived when Henry conceded a penalty, punching a shot from the unmarked Adelardo away from goal. Still 2-1 up, the Spurs defence went through a torrid 15 minutes that ended with Dyson throwing himself into the path of a shot from Rivilla that met his foot with the force of a cannonball, all but crippling himself in the process. From thereon in, it was Dyson's final. In an extraordinary transformation, he followed up at the other end with a curling cross from the left that was somehow caught by the wind, the ball looping between the keeper's head and the crossbar into goal. Then, from his centre, Greaves made it 4-1. Finally, limping now, Dyson set off upfield on a wounded-animal run and scored with a belter from 25 yards. On the terraces, joyous Spurs fans were singing any English songs that came to mind from *Land of Hope and Glory* to *Knees Up Mother Brown*.

Tottenham Hotspur 5 Atletico Madrid 1. Thousands packed the streets of Tottenham to greet their heroes home. Three fans dressed as angels carrying banners with the slogans 'Hallowed be thy names' and 'Praise them for they are glorious'. Only the local vicar countered the prevailing mood of veneration, sending a telegram to the Home Secretary urging that the club be prosecuted for blasphemy.

Not that anyone cared about that. Spurs had become the first British club to win in Europe. Eight years from the day that Hardaker had blocked Chelsea from contesting the European Cup for not being in the national game's best interests, they had demonstrated English football at its finest and bravest. This was more than compensation for two years of missing out on the title; this was an emphatic underlining that the Double side had still got it. As an elated Blanchflower had told anyone who would listen in the dressing room after the match, 'We're going to be the [FA] Cup winners next year as well', and as a gutted Mackay sobbed his eyes out because he hadn't been part of it, Smith had bellowed across the floor: 'Dyson! Dyson! You'd better retire now, Dyson, because there's no way on God's earth you'll ever play that well again.'

In a sense, Smith was right. Except it was the whole team he should have been shouting at.

CHAPTER FIFTEEN

EVERYBODY HURTS

One of the worst-ever periods in Tottenham Hotspur's history has a timeline, and it goes like this.

On 24th August, 1963, Spurs lost away to newly-promoted Stoke. Nicholson changed to a 4-2-4 formation, with Blanchflower alongside Norman in the centre of defence and White dropping back deeper in midfield. At first the changes worked, with Spurs clocking up a lavish amount of points. On 7th September they lost 7-2 to Blackburn Rovers but on 16th September, when Phil Beal made his debut in place of the injured Danny Blanchflower, they won 4-2 away to Aston Villa. On 21st September, they beat Chelsea 3-0. As the month drew to an end, Spurs were one of five clubs separated from the leaders, Nottingham Forest, by a single point. On 2nd October, at White Hart Lane, they beat Birmingham 6-1 to go top of the table. Then Manchester United drew 3-3 away at Sheffield United and went a point above them.

The two teams were in the same position when they met on 9th November. The match possessed added significance because they were drawn to play each other again in the European Cup Winners' Cup the following month. Manchester United beat Spurs 4-1. The next day's papers barely required reading beyond the headlines. 'March Of Time Catches Up On Tottenham; Spurs Put To The Sword' said all it was necessary to know about the state of Tottenham Hotspur. The problem was that while against average forward lines Nicholson's changed formation held out, it could effortlessly be exposed by a Law or a Charlton. After the final whistle, Matt Busby told journalists his game plan had been simple. 'I told the players to run at Danny.'

The conversation that followed between Nicholson and Blanchflower was brief and merciless. 'I'm thinking of leaving you out this Saturday and bringing in Tony Marchi,' Nicholson told him.

'Well, that's up to you,' replied Blanchflower. While he took himself off to play in the stiffs, with the expressed intention of staying fit in case he was needed again, Spurs recorded two wins and a draw in the league without him. Without him, too, Mackay and Dyson were the scorers in their 2-0 win over Manchester United in the second-round first leg of the European Cup Winners' Cup at White Hart Lane at the start of December. 'It will be an awfully hard job for United to get three goals in the second leg,' said Nicholson afterwards.

On 7th December, Jimmy Greaves scored his 200th goal for Spurs in their 3-1 away win at Bolton to put them third in the table behind Liverpool and Blackburn.

Confident, they returned to Old Trafford for the second leg of the Cup Winners' Cup tie, where Mackay and United's Noel Cantwell went for a 50-50 ball. Cantwell went over the top and broke Mackay's leg.

In spite of the fact that the lower half of his leg was skewed towards his face, Mackay sat, rather than lay down, on the stretcher, as if signalling to the team that his departure was only temporary, that if they hung on for 10 minutes he would be back mixing it on the pitch. As the game went into extra-time, he listened to it on the radio in hospital while having the break set. Manchester United 4 Spurs 1, 4-3 on aggregate. Spurs were out of the Cup Winners' Cup. In less than a month they had seen the loss of two of the linchpins of the Double side. Two-thirds of the greatest midfield in the country. Looking back, Greaves said later, the heart of Tottenham Hotspur went on the stretcher with Dave Mackay. It was as if the team died overnight.

That said, White coped with the heavier workload as playmaker and Greaves's goals kept Spurs in contention. On 11th January, 1964, his hat-trick against Blackburn took them to the top of the league.

Nicholson, meanwhile, set about finding a replacement for Blanchflower. And across the other side of London was someone he thought might just be the man.

'About three days after Dave Mackay broke his leg I picked up the *Evening Standard* on the way home from training and read that Tottenham were after Alan Mullery or Bobby Moore,' said Alan Mullery. 'The following day I went in to see Frank Osborne, Fulham's general manager who did all the dealings with the players, and said, "What's all this about?"

'He had his cigarette in the side of his mouth, his trilby hat on, and he said, "Don't believe it, son, it's paper talk, they want Mooro. I've got it on good information." And that was it. I forgot all about it.

'Three weeks later, Friday night, we were due to play Liverpool the next day, and I'm in the house. I lived in Worcester Park then and Frank Osborne lived in Epsom, which was only 10 minutes away. It was about eight o'clock. We'd just had dinner, my wife and I, when the phone went and it was Frank. He said, "Get in your car and come over, I've got to talk to you." I said, "Can't it wait till tomorrow?" and he said, "*No*, you've got to do it tonight.:

'"So I drove over to his house and rang the doorbell. His wife answered it. She looked as though she'd been crying, so I said, "He's not been beating you up again, has he?" He was sitting in his armchair with his trilby hat and jacket on – he never took his jacket off either. Glass of Scotch by his side because he drank a bottle of Scotch a day as well as smoking 60 fags. "Have a sherry," he said.

'I said, "I don't drink sherry and it's getting late, I've got to be back in bed because we've got Liverpool tomorrow. What have you got me over here for?" And then he started reminiscing about when I first went to Fulham as a kid, when I was 15. He said, "I remember when you used to clean my Sunbeam Rapier, I was never satisfied with the way you cleaned it, and when it came down to signing your contract when you were 17 you wanted this and you wanted that, I nearly had a heart attack."

'"Frank, why am I here?" I said.

'"Bill Nicholson is coming over," he said. "He wants to sign you for Tottenham."

'"I thought you told me he was after Bobby Moore," I said.

'He said, "No, he wanted you and the chairman's agreed to let you go."

'"But I don't want to go, I'm enjoying myself," I said. "I live 20 minutes down the road from the training ground. I live half an hour from Fulham. We're in the First Division. What do I want to go to Tottenham for?"

'"The chairman needs the money," he said.

'The doorbell rang and in came Bill and Eddie Baily, his assistant. "I want to ask you a question," said Bill. "Can you play full-back?"

'I said I'd never played full-back in my life.

'"If you play full-back we've got another midfield player we can get," Bill said. "That'll make us even stronger."

'"I'm not interested," I said. "I'm telling you now, I don't want to come. I'm being forced out of Fulham Football Club by Tommy Trinder and his board. You either take me as a midfield player or you don't take me at all."

'"Okay, fine, then," he said. "Can you play for Fulham against Liverpool tomorrow? Because if they beat Liverpool it will do us a favour. You can tell your wife, but I don't want anyone else to know till seven o'clock tomorrow night when I'll come over to your house and we'll get the forms signed."

'Frank's wife started crying again and Frank was choked, so I just went, left them to it. I got home and told my wife I had just got transferred to Tottenham Hotspur. "Where's Tottenham Hotspur?" she said.

'"North London."

'"Oh blimey," she said.'

After a sleepless night, during which Mullery wrestled with his vow of silence, he went off to Fulham to face Liverpool.

'We were winning 1-0 at half-time, sat down in the dressing room. Johnny Haynes was sitting next to me, he said, "What are you doing after the game?" And I couldn't hold it in any more, I said, "I'm going to Tottenham."

133

'"What are you going to do over there?" he said. "Is there a dance?"

'I said, "No, I'm being transferred. I'm signing straight after the game."

'Haynesy grabbed hold of Bedford Jezzard, the manager, and said, "Do you know he's going to Tottenham?"

'"The board don't want me, they want the money," I explained.

'So Bedford Jezzard stormed out, left the door open, crashed through the door of the board room along the corridor, screamed and shouted at Tommy Trinder and Frank Osborne, came out again, walked straight past us, walked out of the ground and never came back again. So we didn't have a manager after half-time. We won 1-0, I took my boots and that was that. I was a Tottenham Hotspur player.'

On 21st March, at White Hart Lane against Manchester United, Mullery made his debut. And it was not a triumphant one. Signed for a then record fee of £72,500 for a wing-half, bigged up as the first of Nicholson's rebuilding buys, he felt the antipathy of the crowd straight away. 'It was bloody awful taking over from Danny Blanchflower. The expectations were impossible. I was nothing like Danny Blanchflower.'

Be that as it may, on 30th March at Anfield, he scored his first goal for Spurs. The trouble was, Liverpool scored three. In the three weeks that followed, Spurs' hopes of the title petered out. A week before the end of the season, Liverpool were crowned champions.

On 26th April, the last day of the season, White scored the only goal of the 1-0 away win against Leicester. In June, Nicholson called him into his office, gave him a pay rise and informed him he was going to build the new Spurs side around him. White then went off on holiday with wife, toddler daughter and baby son to Fisherrow, Musselburgh, his home town in Scotland. While they were there they paid a visit to nearby Whitecraigs, the village where Mackay's wife Isobel had grown up and to which she had returned to await the imminent birth of a fourth child. All Mackay's children had to be born north of the border, so that if they were boys they would qualify to play for Scotland. 'John told me he couldn't wait until pre-season training started,' she says. 'He said, "Bill Nick's took me in and says he's giving me a rise. Imagine, him building a team around *me*."'

On 21st July, the weather was typical for a British mid-summer – boiling hot, then humid. As the morning sun half-melted the tarmac on the roads around Tottenham, the players gathered at White Hart Lane for the pre-season photocall. After it was done, White headed for the ball court. Nicholson handed White a tennis racket and told him to hit a few balls with Terry Medwin, who was trying to get his fitness back after breaking his leg the year before during a close-season tour of South Africa. 'John stripped down to his underpants and we started a knock-about against the wall,' says Medwin. 'Then Cliff came in.'

Jones turned down White's invitation to play a round of golf and left, sneaking off with White's trousers as a prank.

The sky was beginning to look threatening when Jimmy Robertson, the speedy right-winger newly signed from St Mirren, made a vague arrangement with White to meet him at the golf club. Later Robertson said that once he'd noticed the weather he decided against it.

It was coming up to lunchtime when Jones drove away from White Hart Lane, slowing only when a group of female fans crowded round his car. 'I've got John's trousers in the boot,' he said. 'Don't tell him.'

White hunted for his trousers everywhere then drove home in his training kit, changed there and set off for Crews Hill golf course.

Tony Marchi hadn't been needed for the first-team photoshoot. Instead, he went to Crews Hill to hit a few practice balls on his own. 'I finished around lunchtime and went into the locker room and there was John. I said, "Hello, John. Who are you playing with?" and he said, "I'm going to play a round with some friends." We sat having a chat. I packed up: "See you then – I'm off."'

Marchi left White in the locker room and drove home. 'I remember the old dark clouds coming over and I thought, John's going to be lucky.'

The storm still hadn't broken. The lady members were out on the course, about to play a trophy match. Robertson hadn't shown up so White bought three golf balls from the pro shop and decided to get going on his own before the ladies teed off.

Sandra, White's wife, had taken the children round to Linda Baker's. When it was time to set off to pick White up from the golf club,

Mandy, his daughter, hadn't wanted to leave so Sandra left her with Linda and set off with Rob, the baby.

Arriving there, she found the car park 'full of police'. They took her into an office where they told her, 'Your husband's had an accident.'

White's body had been found in a hollow alongside the oak tree he had been sheltering under when the storm broke. He had been sitting with his hands clasped and the force of the lightning strike had sent him there. It had been so powerful that the two rings he wore on the fourth finger of either hand had fused together.

When the Tottenham police called Nicholson, he thought it was a hoax at first. He had been getting similar calls claiming that Greaves had been killed in a car crash. When he demanded to know the number they were calling from and rang them back, he realised all too well that the call was genuine. With Sandra too shocked to identify the body, he was asked to go to the morgue and perform the duty. He asked Cecil Poynton, the trainer, to go with him for moral support. The two men looked at the body and both had the same thought. Bill wrote in his autobiography:

'Outside, I said to Cec: "From the expression on his face, you'd think he was up to one of his skylarks."

'"I know," said Cec. "I felt the same way." John liked a practical joke.'

Even though Nicholson had seen the body, he struggled to accept what had happened. 'It seemed such a brief, almost wasted life. He had so much more to give.'

'I don't mind admitting I cried,' said Greaves. 'We'd lost a wonderful, humorous, mischievous, lovable human being. It was a senseless death, beyond a tragedy.'

Jones, White's best mate, visited the funeral parlour with White's younger brother Tom. 'John looked like there was nothing wrong with him. He almost seemed to be smiling.' Jones admits he was 'in bits'. They'd been soulmates, they'd got on so well together. They were like a couple of schoolkids the way they got into mischief. 'Coming back from the funeral parlour was the first time I cried,' he said later. 'And I'm not ashamed to say it because we were so close. I just broke down from seeing him. He was my pal, and he was no more.'

Mel Hopkins remembered: 'When we all gathered at the club, Bill called everyone into the changing room and started to talk about what kind of bloke John was. Then he broke down and ran into the toilets.'

'It was quite shocking,' said Terry Dyson. 'Bill wasn't that sort of bloke.' They went out on the pitch and held three minutes silence for White. 'All the staff, everybody came out. It was the most eerie thing I'd ever seen in my life. John was so well liked. Lots of lads were crying and Dave Mackay was the worst of the lot.'

Early on in the summer of 2012, a small group led by Pipe Major Willie Cochrane made their way to a tree beside the ninth hole of Crews Hill golf course to witness the ceremonial instalment of a plaque. Jones was there, with Allen, Dyson, Baker and Pat Jennings, along with White's son Rob.

The plaque is unshowy and hard to spot. In that, it seems in character with the elusive, modest man it commemorates. The words engraved on it read:

In Memory of The Ghost of White Hart Lane
John Anderson White, 1937-1964
Struck by lightning, whilst playing this hole
Spurs and Scotland
All glory comes from daring to begin

Rob chose the inscription because, once again, it was in character. 'I thought it chimed in with him daring to leave Fisherrow, daring to keep going when people didn't think he was good enough.'

The inscription had been typed out and checked by several people before it went for engraving. The last to see it was Rob, who noticed something everyone else had missed. 'There was an "n" missing. It said, "struck by lighting".' He thought his dad, who had such a highly-developed sense of mischief, would have liked the image it conjured up, of being brained by a standard lamp.

CHAPTER SIXTEEN

BRAVEHEART COMES BACK

There was a symmetry about the 67-year-old Pat Jennings's presence at the Crews Hill ceremony. His first day at Tottenham Hotspur, aged 19, had been spent attending White's funeral.

Part of Nicholson's rebuilding, Jennings had just arrived from Watford to replace Bill Brown. No one could have claimed he was the finished article, this raw, mumbling 19-year-old with hands the size of fireguards. Few of the fans, the ones who got on his back that season with such passionate disaffection that Nicholson tried appealing to their better natures to give the boy a chance, would have predicted a subsequent Spurs career of 13 years, of more than 600 appearances and countless world-class saves (many featuring the raising of just one, not the statutory two, of those giant hands to pluck a cross from the air). They would never have forecast that majestic domination of the six-yard box. The humongous upfield punt in the 1967 Charity Shield that bounced home over the head of Manchester United's Alex Stepney would have been beyond their wildest imaginings. Back then in August 1964, on the first day of the new season, Jennings's main value was the distraction his nervous, unconfident handling afforded the fans as an alternative to the bitter reflection that in just one season everything had changed.

Blanchflower was gone for good, in his place the unfamiliar figure of Phil Beal. Mackay would surely, even if he recovered from his broken leg, never be the player he had been. There was no Smith – he had left, acrimoniously, for Brighton. Another 19-year-old stranger was at right-back where Baker had once been. All anyone knew about him was that his name was Cyril Knowles and it had cost Nicholson £45,000 to spring him from Middlesbrough. Most gut-wrenchingly of all, it was the first game without White. This realisation was continuously underlined by the sight of Greaves in the number 8 shirt, which Nicholson had asked if he minded wearing and which Greaves adopted as an almost sacred responsibility and privilege for the rest of his Spurs career.

That first game was the hardest, and they survived it, beating Sheffield United comfortably. But the fates had not yet finished with Spurs. The second week in September, Mackay's longed-for comeback ended the day it started, on a pitch in a reserve game against Shrewsbury while the first team were losing to West Ham at Upton Park. As he went to play the ball, a Shrewsbury player came down on the back of his left leg and broke it again. Mackay's first words were: 'Don't tell Bill till the West Ham game's over.'

But in spite of headlines like 'Spurs Without Glory', 'Spurs Are Not Yet Good Enough For Honours' and 'Struggling Spurs A Sad Sight', things weren't as hopeless as the hand-wringers in the press made out. By October, the back-page headline said: 'Spurs Crush Spiritless, Disjointed Arsenal.' Spurs were fourth in the table. They were pulling themselves back from the edge of the canyon.

But in a sense it was White's testimonial game in November that drew the line between the recent past and the future. Here, playing for a Scotland XI that beat a Tottenham Hotspur XI 6-2, in the shape of a tall, bashful Scottish forward with a rapidly backtracking hairline, was the new Spurs.

There was something old-fashioned, almost unworldly about Alan Gilzean. 'He came from a place called Coupar Angus, somewhere in the back end of Scotland,' said Greaves. 'As soon as he arrived I showed him all those new sights of London which would seem strange to him – electric lights, carpets, that kind of thing.'

'We called him the Scottish soldier,' says Jones. 'We were playing a pre-season tournament in Amsterdam and there was a military tattoo on at the same time. One day we were sitting outside at a bar and this Scottish regiment came marching back to camp. They saw Gilly and shouted over, 'Gilzean, it's Gilzean.' The next thing we know, Gilly's over there talking to them and then he's marching off with them to the barracks with the sergeant's sash draped over his shoulder. It was another 24 hours before we saw him again.'

Nicholson had been watching Gilzean for some months before he got him that December, beating Sunderland and Torino to his signature. Seventy-two thousand five hundred pounds and some intense haggling bought a player whose nine goals had taken Dundee to a European Cup semi-final, a player of whom Miljan Miljanic, the manager of Red Star Belgrade, said: 'If ever a Football University is founded Alan Gilzean should be appointed as the first professor to lecture on how to use one's head and to play with one's head.'

It would have been some lecture. It was almost weird the way Gilzean seemed to be able to hover and change direction in the air, seemed to make a judgement while he was up there whether to try a header on goal for himself or nod it down for someone running in. And even then it wasn't a straight nod. Nicholson described it like this: 'He didn't head the ball full on like Smith. He preferred to glance it as he turned his head.'

Which was what made Gilzean a football writer's joy. In 1973 I described him in a match report as 'tossing his head like a shampoo advertisement', a line I was proud of at the time. It wouldn't have been a very convincing ad. He was 35 years old by then and very bare on top. It just added to his misleading demeanour. He didn't look like a centre-forward at all, more like a middle-ranking civil servant. He didn't play much like a conventional centre-forward, either. He seemed to be able to pinpoint a pass as precisely from his head as from his foot.

Listen to the stories about him, read James Morgan's cracking biography *In Search of Alan Gilzean*, and you get the impression of a quirky, mysterious, slightly anarchic character. There's the tale of how a supporter phoned Nicholson to complain that he had seen Gilzean leaving a club at two o'clock in the morning. The Spurs players pointed out that he was actually going *into* the club. There's the story that he would go to his favourite restaurant, say he wanted his usual, and get presented with a bottle of Bacardi and four glasses of Coke. His team-mates used to call him Cuba Libre. As Jones puts it: 'He had quite an interesting lifestyle.'

But the fans adored him. Shortly after he arrived, the terraces were resounding with: 'Gilzean, Gilzean, Born is the king of White Hart Lane.' In the words of Steve Perryman, 'You just felt the love for Gilly. Someone said he could sit in the middle of the pitch and have a crap and he'd be applauded.'

The biggest love-in of all, though, was between him and Greaves. As a second terrace song had it: 'We've got the G-men, In Greaves and Gilzean, They're the world's best goalscoring machine.'

'We were like blood brothers,' said Greaves. 'Right from the word go, we just had this incredible telepathy on a football pitch, like nothing I experienced before or since.'

'It was a relationship,' agreed Mullery. 'As soon as they went on the field they reacted in the way you would if you'd been living with your wife for 50 years. You know exactly what she's going to do. It was like that with Greavsie and Gilly.'

Over the rest of that season, the G-men took Spurs to a sixth-place finish behind Leeds United, Manchester United, Chelsea, Everton and Nottingham Forest. It was over. They hadn't fallen apart. The season was done. The next one, everything would be back to normal. All that was left was to watch Mackay's dogged attempt at a second resurrection, and marvel at the man's will.

It was unheard of in those days for a player to recover from two broken legs. But Mackay, burning fierce flames of willpower and fortitude, imposing on himself a strict diet to avoid weight gain, daily forcing himself up and down the stairs on a now wishbone-shaped pair of legs at White Hart Lane again, wasn't just any player.

On 25th August, 1965, having not played a first team game since December 1963, he came back. Spurs beat Leicester 4-2 that day, and Nicholson made him club captain.

Some two months later, he was supplying the ball for a Greaves wonder goal in Tottenham's 5-1 defeat of Manchester United at White Hart Lane. Greaves, 35 yards out with his back to goal at the time, sold two dummies, changed direction and darted past three converging tackles. Then he drew out Dunne, the keeper, darted past him and tapped the ball into an empty net. True genius. True Greaves. True Spurs.

But with Spurs heading for an eighth-place finish, in danger of becoming just another mid-table side, Nicholson went to work on the team again. In the closing weeks of the 1965/66 season, he gave a debut to a 19-year-old right-back called Joe Kinnear, who after being turned down by Watford was playing for an amateur side, St Albans, when Spurs spotted him. Then, in May, Nicholson took on board Terry Venables, who had been the star turn at Chelsea but who was clearly required to prove himself anew at White Hart Lane. His first day in the gym featured a special Spurs welcome from Dave Mackay. 'As I tried to go past him, Dave hit me right in the balls with his fist,' Venables recalled.

Mackay repeated the performance the next time Venables tried to go past him, so Venables punched him in the face, in the process slicing Mackay's cheek open with the ring on his middle finger. 'Things,' said Venables economically, 'remained a little strained between us for a couple of days.'

Meanwhile, Nicholson's rebuilding was nearly done. One more signing completed it. He had been trying to replace Norman for more than two years but his first attempt, bringing Laurie Brown over from Arsenal, had been a flop. Then Norman broke his leg in a friendly in November 1965 and never played competitive football again. Now in urgent need of reliability in the middle of defence, Nicholson moved in on Mike England, signing him from Blackburn Rovers in August 1966 for what was then, for a defender, a record fee of £95,000.

England was acknowledged to be class, especially for a centre-half. He could turn on the pace and at set pieces he was a menace. For Nicholson, who beat Manchester United to his signature, he ticked all the boxes: ball control, accurate passing, strength in the air. Plus he was hard case when circumstances dictated despite his deceptively easy-going manner.

Straight away, too, a long-standing problem was solved. 'When Pat Jennings first played, it was behind Laurie Brown,' says David Lacey. 'Jennings was very dodgy, nervous. Then Bill signed Mike England and Jennings became the goalkeeper we all remember.'

Mullery sums up that Spurs side of the 1966/67 season thus. 'Mike England was as good as any centre-half in the country. Huge, tall man, good feet, fantastic in the air, really dominant. He loved it in London, it was a big wide world to him, coming there from Blackburn. Cyril Knowles – beautiful left foot and a very good tackler. Joe Kinnear was very good on the ball and an excellent reader of a situation. Alan Gilzean – a tremendous header of the ball. Him and Greavsie were the two best forwards in the country. You had people like Denis Law and Bestie playing in those days, but as a pair Gilly and Greavsie were fantastic.'

You get the picture. The Spurs side that would go on to win the 1967 FA Cup was packed with all the traditional style and pedigree. To a large extent it was a hybrid of two great sides. From the European Cup Winners' Cup team there was Mackay, Greaves, Jones and Saul. From what would become the great side of the early 1970s, there was Mullery, Knowles, Kinnear, Jennings, Beal and Gilzean. The only two who belonged to that 1966/67 side alone were Venables and Jimmy Robertson.

In the case of Venables, essentially this was Nicholson's attempt to replace like with like. That brought problems. Not everybody on the terraces was enthusiastic about him. As with Mullery, who as Blanchflower's intended successor took a long and miserable time to be accepted, Venables was standing in for someone who had already passed into myth. 'I had been brought in to replace John White . . . and the fans may have been heckling me just for not being John White, although I was never a similar style of player anyway.'

There was one who, by common consent, could never be replaced. There would never be another Mackay. Some had his skill. No one had his attitude, his furious competitiveness, his aura of self-belief. In his autobiography, Venables recalls: 'Looking back on the Spurs–Chelsea final now, what stands out was the absolute confidence of Dave Mackay; there was no question in his mind about the result . . . he kept saying we would slaughter them, there was not a chance that we would lose. Nor was he saying it just to give the rest of us confidence, he was genuinely convinced we would win. As usual, he was right.'

At the start of the cup run, Nicholson had not shared his conviction. 'Oh dear, that's not so brilliant,' he said on hearing the third-round draw in January. Spurs had drawn Millwall, who had not lost at home in the league for 32 months during which time they'd gone from Division Four to Division Two. Back then, Millwall played at Cold Blow Lane, a dystopian construction in the badlands of South London that perfectly embodied the supporters' reputation for a certain lack of gentility. As the Spurs players gathered in the centre-circle before kick-off, two fans ran on to the pitch with a cockerel and a set of gallows from which they proceeded to hang the unfortunate fowl.

There was a 0–0 draw that day, but the replay was won with a second-half goal from Gilzean. After that, Spurs had it almost easy. In every round until the semi-finals, they faced Second Division opponents – Millwall, Portsmouth, Bristol City and Birmingham. They met Nottingham Forest in the semi-final at Hillsborough, went two up through Jimmy Greaves and Frank Saul and survived a late Forest goal. Five years after the final against Burnley, they were back at Wembley. Chelsea v Tottenham Hotspur was one for the record books – the first all-London final.

In a fit of inexplicable naivety, Chelsea's normally needle-witted manager Tommy Docherty revealed to the press the shape he was going to use against Nicholson's Spurs. Docherty had been using Marvin Hinton as a sweeper, a system that at Stamford Bridge had nobbled the threat of Gilzean and brought about Spurs' heaviest defeat of the season. Now he was abandoning the idea. For the cup final, Chelsea would be fielding an orthodox defence.

The knowledge cheered Nicholson enormously. Chelsea had done Spurs a favour. At Wembley, without a sweeper to shackle him, Gilzean won almost total mastery in the air and led the forward line brilliantly.

There was a superlative performance from Mullery in defence and attack, and Robertson delivered Chelsea a psychologically crushing blow with his volleyed goal a minute before half-time. Saul's second-half goal clinched Spurs' 2-1 victory. Afterwards Mackay, who admitted to a wee tear in his eye when he lifted the cup, claimed Tommy Docherty had made his day. 'He said we were a fine, young side. As a 32-year-old, I hasten to agree.'

They were a nearly side, though. They ended that season with 56 points in the league, more than any other Spurs side since 1961, but had to settle for finishing third behind Manchester United and Nottingham Forest. There were reasons, of course there were – a bad run of injuries to key players at vital times, casual errors that cost them three home defeats. They were unbeaten in their last 16 league games, and if they had shown that kind of form at the start of the season they could have had the second Double Nicholson desired. But they didn't, and it soon became clear that they wouldn't get another chance. The following season, Liverpool knocked them out of the FA Cup in the fifth round, and the European Cup Winners' Cup campaign petered out in the second round, after a violent first leg away to Olympique Lyonnais in which Mullery was sent off. By the end of the 1967/68 season they were in seventh place.

Taking responsibility for the decline, Mackay told Nicholson he was finished and the two of them made discreet preparations for him to return to Hearts as player-manager. Then Brian Clough, the young manager of Second Division Derby County, came in for him, rolling up at the Cheshunt training ground. 'I've come to buy Dave Mackay,' he announced. Mackay thought he was bonkers, but Clough persisted. Twenty-four hours later, he had his man. After 12 years, a League Championship, three FA Cup winners medals and two broken legs, 'Braveheart' was leaving.

'He came towards me, hand outstretched,' Clough recalled in his autobiography. 'I was only three or four years younger than him, but I remember thinking, "Christ, he looks 10 years older than me."'

The suspicion is that Nicholson might have been misled by Mackay's battered appearance too. Because The Man had more to give. Much more. All that will, that fire, that refusal to crack under pressure, that winners' mindset that had transformed Spurs from a pretty but brittle side into a team of immortals was unleashed on an unsung Midlands club built of journeymen. By the end of his first season at Derby, Mackay had lifted them into the First Division as champions of Division Two. Then, during their first season in the top rank, Spurs travelled to the Baseball Ground.

'It was a mud heap of a pitch,' recalled Mullery in his autobiography, 'and, as Spurs skipper, I walked up to the centre of the ground to spin the coin. Mackay was the Derby captain and, as I shook hands with him, I said, "Dave, it's really lovely to see you." He snapped back at me: "We're going to stuff you this afternoon. I mean, *stuff you*."'

Derby played Spurs off the park. It was 5-0, and Mackay was man of the match.

'The most amazing thing,' said Mullery, 'was that after winning the cup in 1967, the following season Dave Mackay was on his way and between then and 1970 we didn't win a cup. Then we won the League Cup in 1971 and the UEFA Cup in 1972, so it took another three years to build a side without Mackay as the captain.'

But what a side it was.

CHAPTER SEVENTEEN

PARK LANE ROARS

Six weeks after Frank Saul's cup-clinching goal, Nicholson summoned him to his office. 'That's never usually a good sign,' said Saul. 'He told me that he'd had an offer from Southampton for me, and that he was keen on a young lad there.'

Some young lad. 'My first hero was Martin Chivers,' says Danny Keene. 'Centre-forward, big, strong, scored the goals. I was seven years old. Buying that little programme and lying in the bath reading it, cover to cover, every single word over and over again. Looking at the stats, how many Chivers had scored. I still remember the terrace chant: "Chi-vers, Chi-vers. Jennings kicks, Gilzean flicks, Chivers scores, Park Lane roars."'

Except there wasn't much roaring at first. Chivers arrived in January 1968, £125,000-worth of blond centre-forward, 22 years old, six feet tall with fierce dark eyebrows and a talent for striking a ball with the power and delicacy of Bobby Charlton in his prime. At Southampton he'd been a first-team regular since the age of 17, scoring 97 goals in 175 appearances and winning 12 England Under-23 caps.

'Marvellous,' Nicholson wrote of him later in his autobiography, though that may not have been the adjective that tripped quickest off his lips at the time. The awkward, moody, haughty young man was like no player Nicholson had ever dealt with before. For a start, he seemed to possess none of the fierce tough-mindedness that characterised Nicholson's teams in the 1960s – the Double side and the 1967 FA Cup-winning side. He was no Bobby Smith, merrily dishing it out before it got dished out to him, a player of whom Nicholson said approvingly, 'I have seen him come into the dressing room after a match with swollen ankles and bruised legs and he never complained . . . he seemed to enjoy taking physical punishment and handing it out.'

Which Chivers didn't. 'I'd always been a timid player,' he admitted.

But to fully explain the tumult that Chivers's presence regularly caused in the dressing room entails the introduction of another character into the drama. Eddie Baily, the player who could land a ball on a beer mat from 35 yards, had been one of the stars of Rowe's title-winning side of 1951. In 1956 he went to Port Vale, where he lasted seven months before he was offloaded for being 'too much of an individualist' who left the other players 'confused'. Nottingham Forest signed him, and he helped them win promotion before moving on to the coaching staff at Leyton Orient.

Up until then, the job of Spurs' assistant manager had been done by Harry Evans, John White's father-in-law, a placid, kindly man who organised all the backroom stuff while Nicholson got on with his first love, coaching. It was Evans's sudden death at the end of 1962 that brought Baily back to Tottenham. He was the complete opposite of Evans – sergeant-majorish, waspish, and in-yer-face. The cheeky chappie of the push-and-run years was no more. This was another Baily, at full volume in the dugout, cussing every mistake, screaming orders. 'What Eddie could do on the field was better than the players he was working with,' says Brian Scovell. 'He had that bitter and twisted approach to life, but he talked a lot of common sense. As well as a lot of effing and blinding. Baily was a hate figure for a lot of the players. Everybody said he was a tyrant, but his values were right, about playing the game the proper way, not cheating. A lot of footballers don't give their maximum and need a kick up the backside. But he expressed it in a harsh way all the time; he didn't start off with a smile.'

'He was just someone whose role in life was to say it how it was,' says Steve Perryman. 'The underlying thing at Tottenham was that Bill didn't want anyone to get above himself. Eddie was the one who delivered that to you. In his own way.'

Perryman recalls his years as a schoolboy, the target of several clubs, most of whom were prepared to offer blandishments for the services of this aggressively skilful midfield prodigy. 'Eddie's attitude was, "He'll never fucking sign for us. You're kidding yourself if you think that. Why wouldn't yer take the money? Why wouldn't yer?" So he was as surprised as anyone when I signed for Tottenham for no money. "So. You've decided to join us, Perryman. I suppose we should be honoured, should we?" They've signed me in front of all these other clubs. I think he gave me slightly more of an even break because I made the decision football-based rather than money-based.

'When I stepped up from being an apprentice, Eddie was in charge of the reserves. Late fixture, early evening, end of April. As I'm walking off the pitch at the end, Eddie says: "'Ere, Perryman, I think you need to look on the board before you go home."

'"Why's that, Eddie?"

'"Someone's telling me your name's on the list of possibles to go on tour to America."

'That's like someone else saying, "Well done, you deserve it." It was well done, by default. What he meant was, this doesn't mean to say you're a great player. It doesn't even mean you're going to be a good player. It just means you're on the list. It was a way of keeping your feet on the floor so you didn't get above yourself.'

'I played for the reserves, Saturday afternoon at Bristol City. Coming in at half-time, we were winning 2-0. He points at me: "You, you little toe-rag, you let your player get in the box, he could have scored. If you do that again, you're coming off." He was the deliverer of the obvious. What you needed to know. The things a parent would say to a grown-up son.'

Nicholson himself described Baily thus: 'He is a typical East Ender – amusing, sometimes barbed in his comments, but a loyal friend. He was the man who geed up the players before matches, employing a wide range of similies, most of which were related to his time in the services during the war. "Fixing bayonets and going over the top was one of them . . . "' Unfortunately, for all the impact it had on Chivers it might as well have been delivered in Mandarin Chinese.

The problem was intensified by the fact that Nicholson himself wasn't the type to hand out the sweeties. Making a player feel loved was never going to be high up in his priorities.

'You rarely got praise out of Bill,' said Kinnear. 'Being picked – that was the most praise you got.' And Roger Morgan, who arrived from QPR in 1969, had this story to tell. 'We'd just beaten Blackpool, who at the time were a good side. I'd had possibly my best game and was feeling really pleased about myself. In the changing room after, Bill was going around the players, doing what Bill would do, and I was waiting for him to tell me how well I'd played. I'd been up against Jimmy Armfield, who was an ex-England full-back, and as experienced a defender as you could find. I'd given him a right torrid time. I waited, but the expected praise never came, so I thought I'd ask him. "Bill," I said, pleased as punch with myself. "What do you reckon on today? I had Jimmy Armfield in my pocket." "I should bloody well hope you would," he replied. "Jimmy's an old man."'

It didn't help Chivers that he suffered a bad knee injury at home to Nottingham Forest early in 1969 and that was him out for the rest of that season. As the young centre-forward plunged into misery and self-doubt, Nicholson and Baily didn't exactly reach for the kid gloves. 'He had an impressive physique but he seemed reluctant to use it to his advantage,' said Nicholson later. 'We asked Mike England and Peter Collins to play hard against him in training to goad him into a more physical approach. On one occasion, Chivers was so angry when England tackled him that it led to a scrap – they had to be pulled apart.'

At least it made a change from the regular Baily-Chivers stand-offs. 'Eddie loathed him,' said Nicholson. 'He would storm into my office, shouting and swearing about him. "How can you have so much patience with him? I don't know how you put up with it."' Not a fan, then. But Nicholson found his star striker troubling, too. 'Chivers was probably the only player I found it almost impossible to get along with because of his moods. He was the sort of player whose behaviour drains the enthusiasm out of a manager.'

S.T.DADD.

An illustration depicting the 1901 FA Cup Final between Tottenham Hotspur and Sheffield United at Crystal Palace. The match finished 2-2 but Spurs won the replay to become the first and only non-league team to lift the cup

The Spurs team leave Stamford Bridge with the FA Cup, having beaten Wolverhampton Wanderers there in the 1921 FA Cup Final

Legendary Tottenham manager Arthur Rowe talks to his players at White Hart Lane before the start of the 1950/51 season, at the end of which Spurs clinched their first-ever league title

Bill Nicholson, playing here for Spurs in 1954, went on to become the club's manager and the greatest figure in Tottenham's history

Nicholson's team included football legends Dave Mackay (left) and Danny Blanchflower (right), seen here in training

Victory over Leicester in the 1961 FA Cup Final gave Spurs the first-ever league and cup Double of modern times, an incredible achievement, and the team paraded the trophies down the Tottenham High Road from an open top bus

The Double was won, incredibly, using a total of just 17 players (three of whom only played once each) during the course of the whole season

The European Cup Winners' Cup is paraded around White Hart Lane in August 1963, Spurs having beaten Atletico Madrid 5–1 to become the first British team to win a European trophy

Martin Chivers and Alan Mullery parade the 1971 League Cup with manager Bill Nicholson. Spurs won the trophy again in 1973, but it proved to be Nicholson's final trophy with the club which he served for his entire life. His ashes are buried under the White Hart Lane pitch

'Spurs Scoop the World!' So ran the headline in the *Daily Express* when Tottenham manager Keith Burkinshaw signed Argentinian World Cup-winning duo Ossie Ardiles and Ricky Villa in 1978

The pair would inspire the club to new glories, including the 1981 FA Cup Final in which Villa famously scored the greatest Wembley goal ever

Eighties star Glenn Hoddle is one of the greatest players ever to pull on the Spurs shirt, or in this case a QPR one, after the 1982 FA Cup win

Tony Parks and stand-in skipper Graham Roberts celebrate the dramatic penalty shoot-out win in the 1984 UEFA Cup Final

Paul Gascoigne celebrates the famous victory over Arsenal at Wembley in the 1991 FA Cup semi-final. Gazza may have been 'daft as a brush' but he was some player

An unlikely couple. Alan Sugar and Terry Venables, who jointly took over the club in 1991, with the FA Cup of the same year

Jürgen Klinsmann's signing in 1994 had a huge impact on Spurs, and English football in general

Ex-Arsenal manager George Graham took over in 1998 and, despite winning the League Cup in 1999, was always known as the 'man in the raincoat' by most Spurs fans

The emergence of Ledley King, pictured here during the 2002 Worthington Cup semi-final victory against Chelsea, was one of the few bright features of the early 2000s

The 2008 Carling Cup triumph over Chelsea, under the management of Juande Ramos, was celebrated jubilantly at the new Wembley

By 2010 Harry Redknapp had guided Spurs into the Champions League, where Gareth Bale demolished Inter Milan's Brazilian full-back Maicon (twice!)

Jermain Defoe is chaired from the pitch by his teammates, as the club's record scorer in European competition bids farewell to White Hart Lane in February 2014

Spurs fans' new idol Harry Kane, one of a new generation of home-grown players, celebrates after scoring in the North London derby in February 2015. He netted both goals in the 2-1 win

In between, Chivers went out on the pitch and scored superlative goals. That didn't prevent Nicholson and Baily getting on his case.

'I got so many problems fighting Martin's corner,' says Mullery. 'He should have been fighting mine, the size of him. The arguments I used to get in with Bill over him. He used to think Martin was lazy. I didn't care how lazy he was as long as he won us football matches. He was a fantastic goalscorer.'

Which was just as well. Spurs in 1969/70 were a team sliding down the table to midfield anonymity. Though neither Nicholson nor his team-mates realised, Greaves was sliding too, into the alcoholism that nearly destroyed him before he conquered it to emerge as a TV personality of wit and charm. The fans had no idea, either. For them, he was still the Greaves of two years back, the Greaves who, after being stuck on 299 for three weeks, headed home Chivers's cross to score his 300th league goal in Spurs' 5-0 defeat of Burnley at White Hart Lane. Before the final whistle went, he increased the tally to 301. And a season later came his final Tottenham goal ever. 5th October, 1968. Tottenham Hotspur 3 Leicester City 2. Jennings booted the ball out to the wing where Greaves killed it instantly, spun round and abandoned his marker. He then left four defenders on their backsides, danced around the referee, drew Peter Shilton and stroked the ball into the net.

Now all the fans could see that the goals weren't flying in. When Spurs caved in limply to a Gerry Queen goal at Crystal Palace in a fourth-round FA Cup replay – the headline in the next day's *Observer* was 'Queen King At The Palace' – it was Greaves who felt the sharp edge of the axe.

The choice Nicholson gave him was bleak. Move, retire or stick out the last 18 months of your contract. Then he was kept in the reserves until transfer deadline day, when Greaves got a phone call from him. 'I've got Martin Peters with me and he's agreed to sign.' The price West Ham was asking was £200,000, but they would accept Greaves as a makeweight. Tottenham's greatest ever striker was valued at £54,000.

Greaves's last appearance in a Spurs strip was in a reserves game against Arsenal. He was still such a magical and compelling presence that the *Match of the Day* cameras turned up at Highbury to record the highlights.

With Greaves gone, Spurs looked to Chivers more than ever to come up with the goals. He and Gilzean quickly reproduced the successful partnership the Scot had enjoyed with his fellow G-man. In this they were supplied by the trademark blindside runs of Peters, now with the burden of being the nation's first £200,000 player along with the one Ramsey had lumped on him of being '10 years ahead of his time'. Which was one way of putting it, even so. Twenty-seven years old, Peters had the lot: pace, industry, creativity and exquisite timing on the run in addition to being a free-kick specialist.

The problem was that Peters had replaced the legend that was Greaves. Having been part of the furniture at Upton Park for 10 years didn't help, either. Moore, Hurst, Peters – heroes of the 1966 World Cup, the trio were as firmly bracketed in the public consciousness as Compo, Foggy and Clegg of *Last of the Summer Wine* would become in the seventies.

In consequence, even though he scored on his debut against Coventry (for the record, it was in a 2-1 home defeat), the fans weren't too sure about him at first. He didn't look as though he was putting in the effort, either. 'Martin Peters was very long striding,' says the former *Daily Mail* journalist Brian James. 'He'd cover the ground in great, big, inverted bracket-shapes and you were never conscious of any urgency about him. Other players bustle – draw the eye. But Martin looked almost casual, and that was why. He made no fuss about getting there.'

So this was how things were at the start of the 1970/71 season – Peters working his way in, Chivers alternating between making Baily blow gaskets in the dressing room and breaking goalkeepers' spirits on the pitch, and Nicholson's last great Spurs side starting to gel. There was Mullery, providing the voltage, one of the greats among Spurs captains. There was Perryman, a captain in waiting, as vocal as Mullery, as dynamic as Burgess. 'He was one of those players whose importance you realised when he wasn't playing,' says David Lacey. 'One of the players you take for granted.' Then there was John Pratt, a grafter in midfield, the unappreciated workhorse and unabashed target of the fans' derision. 'He was one of Eddie's soldiers,' comments Perryman. 'He had front. He'd run upfield and hit the ball over the bar. Then he'd run upfield again and hit the ball over the bar. Then he'd run upfield *again* and hit the ball over the bar.' The story goes that when he asked for a pay rise, Nicholson said, 'There's just one thing that stops me giving you more money. You lack skill.'

Ramsey's England had dispensed with wingers. But the wide men were part of the Spurs tradition and Nicholson had three to choose from: Morgan and the two Jimmys, Pierce and Neighbour. The defence was settled, with England's skill and physicality and Beal's unshowy reliability at its heart, a young Kinnear returning from a broken leg to stake ownership of the right-back position, and the fierce and committed Knowles on the left.

Plus, in Jennings, they had the best keeper in the league. 'In the dressing room he'd mumble,' says Perryman. 'But if you were in front of 65,000 people at Old Trafford, if he wanted to move you, you'd hear him. "This is serious. This is real life. This is now. Game on. Moment on." He was correct. He did it right. In lots of ways he wasn't the textbook goalkeeper. No one could teach him to come out and catch left-handed. But the way he lives his life is driven by niceness, kindness. That makes him sound soft, which he wasn't by any means. Good man, Pat. Good man. One of my favourite people in the world.'

The night Jennings made a double save in the League Cup semi-final second leg against Bristol City, he was everyone's favourite. In extra-time at White Hart Lane, Spurs went on to win 2-0 and returned to Wembley for the first time since 1967. There they met Aston Villa, then a Third Division side, but no pushovers. In the first 20 minutes, Gilzean, Peters and Chivers all wasted opportunities and, as a result, Spurs were put on the back foot to the extent that moments into the second half Jennings would have been beaten had Chico Hamilton's shot not kissed the bar and gone over. Things got even scarier – on the hour mark, they had Perryman to thank for a goal-line clearance as Andy Lochhead's shot headed towards an empty net. Then, 12 minutes from time, John Dunn, the Villa keeper, parried a shot from Neighbour only for Chivers to bang it home. Three minutes later, Mullery chipped with precision to find Chivers among the goalmouth throng, and he sent the Villa defence the wrong way and won the cup with a rasping drive.

To the impartial observer, that 1970/71 season, if not great, was a good one for Tottenham Hotspur as they went on to finish third in the league. However, for the fans, any satisfaction was wiped out by Arsenal becoming the second club that century to do the League Championship and FA Cup Double. Worse, the 1-0 victory that saw them clinch the league title was at White Hart Lane.

'We were warned by Bill that the ground was going to be full up,' recalls Martin Chivers. 'It wasn't all-ticket and there were 14,000 fans outside blocking the High Road. Alan Mullery only got there 15 minutes before the kick-off.

'We bunked off school at about 2pm and the ground was heaving,' remembers fan Ian Katz. 'Kids that left school at 4.30pm couldn't get in.' Morris Keston also has vivid memories of a tumultuous evening: 'We had to go through the players' entrance to get in because there were so many people there. There'd been people there from 1.30 for a 7.30 kick-off. A 0-0 draw would have suited Arsenal, it would have put them in position to win the title. When they scored we weren't unhappy because we only had to get one back and 1-1 was going to be worse for them. So it was a game of extremes.'

Ray Kennedy said the wait for the final whistle after he scored Arsenal's decisive goal was 'the longest three minutes I have ever known' as Tottenham steamed forward in search of an equaliser. 'I remember thinking that perhaps it might have been better had my header not gone in.'

'We tried so hard during the game to stop them from scoring,' says Chivers, 'but Arsenal weren't at the top for nothing.'

'I remember Ray Kennedy heading that winning goal and all the Arsenal fans running onto the pitch,' says Katz. 'It took until Gazza scored that goal in 1991 at Wembley to erase that pain.'

Mike England later said that Nicholson wore his anguish on his face. He'd managed the team that alone had done the Double, and now here it was almost in the hands of their biggest rivals. But even then Nicholson was magnanimous enough to swallow his hurt, walk into the Arsenal dressing room and congratulate them.

So that piece of silverware called the League Cup was a highly welcome and compensatory addition to the trophy cabinet. And it meant another season in Europe, one that would bring with it a story of despair, struggle and success against the odds. A story with one of the most life-affirming, triumphant endings in the life of Tottenham Hotspur.

CHAPTER EIGHTEEN

THE MULLERY FINAL

On the evening of 27th March, 1964, Alan Mullery drove away from his home debut for Spurs an unhappy man. Spurs had lost to Liverpool and an underwhelmed crowd had made him the focus of their dissatisfaction. It wasn't hard to see why. He was taking over from Blanchflower, who had spent 10 years delighting them with sweetly accurate passes in between raising various pieces of silverware. Mullery's strengths were more primal – hard tackles and limitless energy. 'The crowd wanted Blanchflower and Mackay rolled into one,' he said later. 'I couldn't live up to their expectations.'

Over the weeks that followed, it was only admiration for Mackay's struggle to get back after his broken leg that stopped him asking for a transfer. That helped him deal with the abuse in the street and the letters telling him how useless he was. The turning point came that October, when Spurs were at home to Chelsea. Nicholson had told him to get stuck early into their young winger, Albert Murray, who was, said Mullery, 'quite useful'. 'That was always the way in those days,' Mullery recalled in his autobiography. 'You tried to get heavy tackles in early. The referees nearly always let them go. So, when Murray got the ball on the wing, I slid in on my backside and took the ball and man.'

Mullery wired into him so hard that Murray flew into the crowd like a can into a waste bin. In the awed silence that followed he heard someone shout, 'Come on, "The Tank"!' He acknowledged it and got stuck in. That had been a special moment. The crowd had conceded he was neither Blanchflower nor Mackay. He was accepted for who he was – Alan Mullery, The Tank.

In the years that followed, Mullery was a vital part of the side. He helped them win the 1967 FA Cup, succeeded Mackay as captain and would go on to lift the 1972 League Cup and become an essential force for Ramsey's England.

As the 1971/72 season got under way, things were still looking good for Spurs. Back in Europe again, in the UEFA Cup, they had coasted through their first-round tie against Keyflavik of Iceland, winning 15-1 on aggregate. He had provided two of the first-leg goals.

Then, in October 1971, the lights started going off. Whenever he tried to run, he would suffer excruciating pain in his groin. 'If you pull a muscle you know what it is, but with this groin problem, if I got out of a car and threw one leg out first – oh, it was like a shooting pain. And it was both sides.'

At first, nobody seemed to know what the problem was. He told Nicholson, knowing what he'd say: 'Mackay had it and it went.'

'Cecil Poynton, the trainer, said, "What we did with Dave Mackay was to get him a corset, a ladies' corset, which held the stomach muscles in." So I started wearing this corset for matches, like the tight underpants which they now wear under their shorts.'

Naturally, everybody teased him. When he put the corset on, they'd ask him when he was going to start wearing suspenders. But for a time it wasn't too bad. Then, after a month, he'd take the corset off after games and have trouble walking. He'd stuck it out, though, going with Spurs to Nantes just after the middle of October for the second-round first-leg UEFA Cup tie and still capable of looking after himself. One of his most celebrated skirmishes had been in Europe in 1967, against Olympique Lyonnais, when he and the French forward Andre Guy were both ordered off after exchanging pleasantries. Moments later, the half-time whistle blew. Nicholson was first into the tunnel and was rewarded with a smack in the face from Guy, who had mistaken him for Mullery. Nicholson responded in kind and Mullery and Gilzean joined in. Against Nantes, the fighting went on behind closed doors; no one from either side was ordered off, but Nicholson and Chivers had a furious row in the dressing room at half-time.

The match ended in a 0-0 draw and a Peters goal won the home leg at the start of November. By then, though, Mullery was out of the side. It hadn't been the sending off that did for him. The crisis had come at Stoke at the end of October. Trying to run back to tackle a defender, he'd been in so much pain he couldn't move. He'd stuck it out until the 76th minute when Pratt took his place. It was his last first-team game for five months.

In his absence, Pratt took his place in the UEFA Cup third-round tie against Rapid Bucharest and had a brilliant game in midfield at White Hart Lane, scoring one and laying on the assist for one of Chivers's two. Pratt was also there for the away leg, won with goals from Jimmy Pearce and Chivers but a game contested with such violence by the opposition – Gilzean was punched in the kidneys, Chivers brutally kicked and Perryman sidelined with a dislocated shoulder incurred when falling after a vicious tackle – that Nicholson called Rapid 'the dirtiest team I've seen in 30 years', adding, 'If this is European football, I'd rather have the Combination League.'

By this time, Mullery had been diagnosed by a Harley Street specialist. He was suffering from a syndrome that affected a lot of American Football players because of the heavy knocks they took. 'In the pubic bone there's a gap between the two parts, and with me that gap was all jagged down each side. He said, "That's an arthritic condition, so basically the only thing you can do is rest. It won't go away unless you do that for at least three months." He told me not to climb stairs. We moved the bed downstairs. No sexual relations with my wife, nothing at all. That's what I did, I stuck to it.'

After three months, he was allowed to train again. Within weeks he was playing for the reserves and feeling good enough to return to the first team for the away leg of the UEFA Cup quarter-final against a second Romanian side, UT Arad. Nicholson, though, didn't even consider including him, and without him Spurs won in style with goals from England and Morgan.

He went to see Nicholson, who told him the side was doing well so he couldn't change it. But reserve football wasn't any good to Mullery. He wanted to play in the first team. Anybody's first team. 'If I can't get in the side now after getting fit I want to go out on loan somewhere,' he said. So by the time Spurs took themselves into the semi-finals with a laboured 1-1 draw at home, he was playing for Second Division Fulham, the club where he'd started out.

Hardly anybody thought he'd ever go back to Spurs. He was over 30. He'd see the season out with Fulham, then in the summer Spurs would transfer him. Then Spurs picked up only two points out of three games at Easter and Pratt broke his nose in a collision. Finally, Mullers got his chance.

'The phone rang on Sunday morning, it was Bill Nick. He said, "How are you doing?"

'I said, "Not bad."

'"I've had Charlie Faulkner watching you every game," he said. "He says you're the best player Fulham's got, you look fit, so Monday morning get your boots and get back here. John Pratt's broken his nose, Phil Beal's injured, and we're playing AC Milan in the semi-final of the UEFA Cup."

'It was a bit strange coming in after being away for a month, especially as I hadn't trained with the first team for four months before that. A bit like coming back again after being sold. There was Eddie Baily as large as life in the dressing room, there must have been about half an hour to go. Bill, who used to go round and talk individually to players before a game, was sitting with Stevie Perryman, and Eddie Baily said, "Well, Bill, who's going to take the captain's armband today?" And Bill looked across at me and said, "When he's here, we've only got one captain." And Baily gave me the armband.'

Naturally, the fans gave him a standing ovation when he led Spurs out at White Hart Lane. Boosted by being given the armband, Mullery inspired Spurs to victory after the Italians took the lead, with Perryman scoring both the equaliser and then the winner. Two weeks later they went out to Milan, Mullery scored early with a spectacular bender from 25 yards to give Spurs a 3-1 aggregate lead and, though Milan pulled one back in the second half from the penalty spot, his goal was enough to see them through to the final.

But it wasn't just the goal against Milan, it was what he added to the side elsewhere. After Mullery returned, Spurs won pretty much everything they turned up for. He played 11 games at the end of the season, Spurs were undefeated and when they beat Arsenal at Highbury he scored one of the goals. 'It was a terrific volley, even though I say it myself.'

An even better goal was to come. The UEFA Cup Final was against Wolves and Spurs held a 2-1 advantage from the away leg, with Chivers the double scorer, the second a 35-yard strike from the touchline that remains one of *the* Chivers goals. But at White Hart Lane, on 17th May, it was Mullery's diving header from a Peters free kick that put them into the lead. The force of the header knocked him out and when he got back onto the pitch after receiving treatment, it was to see David Wagstaffe give Wolves some hope with an equaliser just before half-time.

The last 20 minutes were frantic, with Jennings so busy and the tension so relentless as Wolves threw everything into reducing the deficit that for the fans it was almost impossible to watch. But Mullery kept the side together, inspired them to hold on. Tottenham Hotspur 1 Wolverhampton Wanderers 1. Spurs had won the UEFA Cup. Nicholson had won his seventh trophy.

And it was Mullery's goal that had won it. When it came to the lap of honour, he found himself carried shoulder-high around the pitch by the fans, holding the cup as though he'd just become betrothed to it, still dazed, with the fallout from the diving header, with exhaustion, with joy. It was his last game at White Hart Lane. A week before the start of the 1972/73 season, he was transferred to Fulham. But if anyone had ever questioned what he had brought to Spurs, questioned his right to be up there in the pantheon of Tottenham

Hotspur's great captains, there were no doubts about it on that glory night. Or whose glory night it was.

If the 1971/72 season belonged to Mullery, '72/73 was the property of Ralph Coates. He'd come to Spurs in the summer of 1971 for £192,000, the highest fee ever paid for a British player if you discount the £200,000 for Peters that included Greaves along with hard cash. Coates was from Burnley's post-relegation clear-out and couldn't have chosen a better season to join Spurs. In eight years with Burnley, he'd won nothing.

Nicholson had been tracking him for a while. In 1967, managing an England Under-23 tour of Greece, Bulgaria and Turkey, he had been impressed by a goal he'd scored. Coates still had a full head of hair back then. By the time he got to White Hart Lane, still in his mid-twenties, he was up there with Bobby Charlton and Howard Kendall as one of the great names of the comb-over era. With Coates it took the form of a kind of intricately woven hair beret until he started running, when the construction rapidly dismantled and a clump of maverick tresses followed a few beats behind the rest of him.

According to Hunter Davies's masterwork *The Glory Game*, Coates had been Darkie Nicholson's favourite footballer, long before he signed for Spurs. She kept a little drawing of him pinned above a door in the Nicholson household at Creighton Road. It was, she said, because he was so full of what Baily called 'G and T' – guts and tenacity. The question was, though, whether that was enough. When Coates arrived at Tottenham, the jury was out as to whether he was worth the outlay and for a while he was the butt of the others' mickey-taking.

'He was hard-working and earnest,' commented Nicholson, 'but his skills were inferior to some of the more experienced players and his shooting wasn't up to the standard I had been led to expect after seeing him strike that shot in Turkey.' Nicholson himself wasn't above the odd jibe. After Coates scored in a practice match, he asked, 'Who were you trying to pass to?'

That first season, played as a forward, he didn't quite fit in. His speciality seemed to be long, effortful runs that ended in his being dispossessed by a defender or losing control of the ball. But though it was taking him a long time to click into his Burnley form the fans, like Darkie, warmed to him because he was a trier. And in his second season, brought back into midfield, he came good.

Not so much in the league, mind. The outstanding player for Spurs that season was Jennings, whose goalkeeping in the 1-1 draw at Anfield in March, when he saved two Liverpool penalties, earned him a standing ovation from the Kop the night Spurs returned at the start of December for a fifth-round League Cup tie and a 1-1 draw. At Upton Park on Boxing Day, when Spurs drew 2-2 with West Ham, the *Daily Telegraph* wrote: 'Only the sure-fingered genius of Jennings, surely the best goalkeeper in the land, kept Moore, Brooking and Robson from victory.' Goalkeeping like that earned him the Football Writers Association's award of Footballer of the Year.

Spurs finished eighth in the league that season. Liverpool beat them in the UEFA Cup at the semi-final stage. They beat everybody, in fact – they won the League Championship. But on 6th December, in the League Cup fifth-round replay after that earlier draw at Anfield, Spurs won 3-1, with a goal from Pratt and a Chivers double. It was proof to everyone that, if they wanted to, they could match any side in the land.

Weeks later, at Molineux for the first leg of the League Cup semi-final, Pratt and Peters put them two up against Wolves after 15 minues in a tie that finished 2-1. Behind after a Terry Naylor own goal in the second leg, Peters scored a 70th-minute equaliser. After John Richards put Wolves ahead again two minutes from the end, Chivers got Spurs to Wembley with a goal in extra-time.

So Spurs were in a League Cup Final again, two years after their 1971 triumph. That day at Wembley, Coates didn't even start against Norwich. He was on the bench until Pratt went off injured in the 24th minute. Taking up a place in midfield, a role he much preferred to that of a forward, he was in his element. The only goal of a drab game came from one of Chivers's trademark long throw-ins, flicked on by Peters. Coates, unmarked, won the cup for Spurs with a 20-yarder.

Coates was well happy. He was on his way to getting a permanent place in midfield at last. And his fan mail shot up like nobody's business. Nicholson, too, was as pleased as Nicholson ever could be. It meant that Spurs were back in Europe again.

What it would lead to, nobody could have foreseen.

CHAPTER NINETEEN

GAME OVER

In 1991 Bernie Kingsley took the day off work to have his hair cut before the European Cup Winners' Cup game against Porto. 'It was in Mehmet's barber shop by White Hart Lane station,' says Bernie. 'There was this old bloke sitting in the chair. I didn't really notice him. He was just another old guy having his hair cut. But Mehmet knew I was part of the Tottenham Supporters Trust and he introduced me. It was Bill. Amazing. I was kind of in awe.'

Mehmet's was where Nicholson usually had his hair cut. Over half a century the style never varied – bristly and no-nonsense, the same cut that he was given in the army. 'Long hair is fine in the pop world, but not in football,' he told his biographer Brian Scovell.

Nicholson's last big signing for Tottenham was Alfie Conn from Rangers, who had enough hair to stuff a mattress. 'It was long and flowing, like a Cavalier's,' says Danny Keene, who liked Conn so much that later on he called one of his two fantasy football teams 'Alfie Conn's Sideburns' (the other one was 'Macnamara's Band'). 'That wasn't for Bill. Bill wanted them in a shirt and tie, clean shaven, short back and sides.'

But it wasn't really the hair. It was what Alfie Conn cost – £150,000, with a £7,000 signing-on fee and a weekly wage of £180 – that made Nicholson's eyes water. Plus, it was more of a desperation signing than anything. Conn wasn't Nicholson's type of player. He was a flamboyant ball-artist, a teaser, an individualist who would dribble the ball from one side of the pitch to the other just for the sheer joy of it. He had a powerful shot, too, and the crowd loved him in the same way they would later love David Ginola. He scored a hat-trick on his debut against Newcastle. He taunted Leeds, taking the ball to the side of the pitch and sitting on it. To everyone except Nicholson, he was the new 'King of White Hart Lane'. To Nicholson, he was a player who didn't find space, use the ball accurately or blend with the team. Plus, added Nicholson, 'He wore his hair extremely long in an unbecoming manner for a professional footballer.'

Then again, there weren't many footballers out there who were Nicholson's type by then. Later on, in his autobiography, he talked about watching a match with Eddie Baily in the mid-eighties: 'The ball was continually in the air, with defenders and goalkeepers belting it from one end of the pitch to the other. None of the players wanted to control the ball and make an accurate pass. Every kick was a long one, transferring responsibility as far away as possible. Players didn't seem too bothered if they failed to control the ball and it went into touch.'

'Bill was coming to the end of his time,' said Joe Kinnear. 'His touch was probably failing. He didn't seem in tune with all the new things happening, the new tactics, the new attitudes, the new ways of doing things, on and off the pitch. He'd begun to say to himself, lots of times, that he didn't like the way football was going, all the money coming in, all the greed and commercialism. In his day, as he was always telling us, people played for the love of the game, as he had done.'

So Nicholson's disillusionment was palpable. Something had gone wrong with the game he loved. It was the decade of terrace wars and organised violence. In 1973 there was the introduction of crowd segregation and fencing. Manchester United's Red Army racketed up and down the country, creating bedlam. A Bolton Wanderers fan stabbed a young Blackpool fan to death. The hooliganism sickened Nicholson.

As did the dizzy inflation of transfer fees. He resented paying bloated amounts of money for players he felt unworthy of wearing the Spurs shirt. He was thrown when players started to assert themselves financially.

Martin Peters and Mike England headed a players' delegation to argue about a new bonus structure that they felt was insultingly small. It was the first time he had been challenged en masse by the players. 'He got really nasty,' Martin Chivers recalled in his autobiography, *Big Chiv*. 'The worm had turned and he didn't like it; what's more, he didn't know how to cope with it. His attitude was that we should just be proud to be wearing the Spurs shirt without thinking of benefits in monetary terms.'

It was obvious that football didn't bring him pleasure any more. At home games, he and Baily would sit in the row behind the directors' box, just in front of the press seats. You'd listen to them, a crusty duo of carping disillusionment, having a go at the most expensive player – usually Ralph Coates. 'It was around this time that football plummeted to a level never before experienced in this country,' Nicholson recalled in his autobiography. 'There was a meanness about the way the game was played. I have to admit I didn't enjoy watching it. There were fewer goals and more arguments, more dissension, more professional fouls.'

Meanwhile, a new kind of manager, mouthy and dandified, was dominating football. It was impossible to imagine Nicholson on ITV's *The Panel*, swapping banter with Derek 'The Doog' Dougan and Brian Clough, someone he'd cuffed round the head for being cheeky as an Under-23 international. Nicholson would rather have sawn off his own head than worn the kind of ice-cream suits favoured by Ron Atkinson and John Bond.

Nor would he go along with the growing culture of backhanders, with players demanding covert payments to cover the cost of tax paid on profits from their transfer, and managers wanting their cut from the fee. 'Bill,' said Brian Scovell, 'was as honest as an archbishop.' Despite enquiries about new additions, the only fresh faces in 1973/74 had been the homegrown talents of Ray Evans and Chris McGrath. Spurs had a poor season, going out in the first stage of both domestic cups and finishing in mid-table. At the Lane towards the end of December, just 14,034 fans bothered to turn up for the Stoke game. Spurs won 2-1, so at least those who did turn up saw a victory. It wasn't often that happened around that time. By the end of the season Spurs' tally of 45 points in the league tied with 1912/13 as the worst in club's history. Arsenal accrued the same number of league points but beat them on goal difference.

As was often the case with Spurs, the European run (in the UEFA Cup) had been a season-saver. They played some good football and beat top-class sides – well, Nicholson said they were, according to Chivers: 'Bill kept seeing the "best teams ever" in Europe when he analysed our opponents.' The performance that stood out was the quarter-final against FC Cologne – 5-1 on aggregate against a side that had been unbeaten at home in Europe. After dispatching Lokomotive Leipzig 4-1 in the semis, Spurs faced a final against the Dutch team Feyenoord of Rotterdam.

Before the first leg, there were skirmishes outside White Hart Lane and some of the coaches carrying Feyenoord supporters were pelted with stones. Inside the Lane, the Dutch retaliated by lobbing urine-filled beer bottles and cans onto Spurs fans in the lower tiers. Then Spurs ended up drawing a game they should have won, but, after a Mike England goal six minutes from half-time, they were suckered four minutes later by one of Wim van Hanegem's famous curlers from a free kick, and a Feyenoord own goal by Joop van Daele in the second half was cancelled out by Theo de Jong's equaliser five minutes from time.

When it came to the second leg in Rotterdam, some fans were looking for retribution. Comprehensively well-fuelled by the end of the ferry trip, they arrived in a mood that was ugly even before kick-off. 'We got to the stadium, and right outside there were two or three hundred Feyenoord fans giving it large, goading us, so it went from there,' said one fan, Phil, quoted in Steve E. Hale's *Mr Tottenham Hotspur*. 'Their Old Bill split it up, and then we all started going into the stadium. Things quietened down for a while. The match started, and most of us – me included – just settled down to watch the game, even though we were still getting pelted and gobbed at by the Feyenoord mob who were right next to us. Then Feyenoord scored, and that was it. We sort of all knew that the game was up, because they had two away goals from the first leg, and to be fair they did look a useful side. So it went mad.'

It was a mistake by Pat Jennings that led to the first Feyenoord goal, the Spurs keeper dropping a cross from Peter Ressel for Wim Rijsbergen to head home. On the terraces, some of the Spurs fans ran at the Feyenoord fans and the police moved in. The terraces swarmed like a giant anthill as people ducked to avoid bits of burning stadium. 'Suddenly smoke and flames started to engulf one part of the ground,' recalled Chivers. 'I looked up and saw a person hanging off the stand and behind him seats being thrown into the air like missiles, some of them on fire. It was scary stuff.'

As the half-time whistle went, the players fled down the tunnel to regroup. Nicholson left Eddie Baily to give the team talk and went out again with a megaphone to plead with the supporters to calm down. No one was listening. The dry, crisp voice of Yorkshire was drowned out by sirens, firecrackers, shouting and the clang of flying crash barriers. When Nicholson came back into the dressing room, his eyes were red-rimmed and watery. He looked like an old man. 'I remember thinking, "That's probably the end for him",' says Perryman.

The mayhem carried on through most of the second half. Feyenoord scored again but the football was, in the main, an irrelevance. Sitting on the team coach as it sped away from the stadium towards the next day's headlines of 'Hooligans Shame Spurs' and 'Rioting Fans Shame Britain', Nicholson appeared inconsolable. 'He had absolutely no under-standing of such behaviour,' said Chivers, 'and I remember him looking sadly out of the window of the coach back to our hotel and saying, "What have they done to my game?"'

'While we were waiting for the police to let us out, some bloke said to me: "Did you hear Bill Nick at half-time, speaking on a loudspeaker?"' said Phil. 'I said, "Yeah, of course – didn't you?" He just shrugged and said: "He was saying something about calming down, that's how it sounded to me. Easy for him to say, he wasn't getting spat at." And the sad thing is, that's genuinely how some of us felt at the time; like Bill didn't have any idea what was going on up there – and in a way, he didn't. Of course, the reason Bill didn't know what was going on was because we were acting like a bunch of arseholes, and the whole world knows that he was a nice bloke. It was totally alien to him.'

The 1974/75 season got under way. Spurs did not make a promising start. They lost at home to Ipswich and three further defeats followed. One of them was to Carlisle, who had just been promoted. It was Tottenham Hotspur's worst start to a season for 62 years. Nicholson and Chivers, who was going through a divorce and needed the money, were embroiled in a contract dispute. Chivers rejected what was offered via the medium of the press and asked for a transfer. Nicholson dropped him, then changed his mind and yanked him out of Siberia for the crunch home game against Manchester City. Spurs lost 2-1.

Alan Mullery has a telling anecdote about that period of Nicholson's tenure. In the summer of 1974, Spurs played Fulham in a pre-season friendly. 'I met him outside the Cottage and he looked troubled,' said Mullery. 'I asked him what was wrong and he opened up to me. "I think I've lost the respect of the players," he said.'

'It was no secret that Bill was becoming increasingly disillusioned with a lot of aspects of the modern game,' said Martin Peters. 'He absolutely hated hooliganism, and the events in Rotterdam were the worst he had seen. This was his club being shamed, and after the first few games of the 1974/75 season it was clear that he didn't really have his heart in it.'

In the weeks leading up to his personal crisis, Nicholson was still on the lookout for players, and had spoken to Gordon Jago, the QPR manager, about swapping Chivers for Gerry Francis or Stan Bowles. Then Spurs lost 4-0 to Middlesbrough at White Hart Lane in the League Cup second round, and every last drop of resolve deserted him. That night he told Sidney Wale he was going. Wale tried to change his mind at a cocktail party the following Sunday morning. When that didn't work, he asked Nicholson to stay on for two weeks until they could find a replacement.

Acting on the assumption that he would be allowed to nominate his successor, Nicholson started interviewing. As far he was concerned, one candidate stood out. Danny Blanchflower knew the set-up and the tradition and had a powerful emotional attachment to the club and its ideals. The fans felt the same about him. Nicholson's plan was to stay on as general advisor. It was, really, a reworking of the relationship they'd had in the glory days. More than that, Nicholson had Blanchflower's successor in mind too. He interviewed Johnny Giles, the former Leeds captain, for the job of player-coach. Both men were up for working in the set-up Nicholson envisaged.

On the day of the board meeting scheduled to discuss the applications for a new manager, Blanchflower waited for the call from Tottenham offering him the job. He killed time by playing golf with his journalist mates. On the way round, he expanded enthusiastically about his plans for Spurs. He wanted a club that was an academy for the kids, where the fans could moan about things in the programme, where the players treated fans with respect, where the game would be about attack, not defence. He speculated about playing with four men up front. He deliberated over whether or not a Jaguar would be the appropriate car for a Spurs manager. That was Blanchflower. Doing things in style. With a flourish.

Back home, he went on waiting for the call from White Hart Lane. The phone never rang. Nicholson, much to his surprise, wasn't invited to the board meeting either. He had already told Wale that he had interviewed Blanchflower and Giles and had prepared a report recommending them both. The directors never got to read it. They held the meeting without him.

According to Nicholson, what caused his resignation wasn't the trouble with Chivers. It wasn't the night in Rotterdam, or the failure to buy new players, or the disastrous start to the season, although losing 4-0 to Middlesbrough was the tipping point. 'The simple truth was that I was burned out,' he said. 'I had no more to offer.'

If Nicholson hadn't been in such a frazzled state, it's possible that he would have paused to ask himself whether it was sensible to start interviewing candidates for a job he had just resigned from, without sounding out his former employer first. True, the directors had never interfered in his management of the club before, but now he wasn't really the manager. He might also have been more cautious about going for Blanchflower. Spurs were at the bottom of the table. They did not need a manager whose uncompromising commitment to flamboyant, attacking football was such that he would tackle a relegation fight with four forwards. A manager who had been out of the game for 10 years. A manager whose outspokenness, dominating personality and independent-mindedness went alongside huge support among the fans and a low opinion of the people who ran football. A man who once wrote: 'There have been times when I have caused the Tottenham directors some concern by standing up for the things which I have believed.' Blanchflower, the directors feared, would waltz in and take over the club.

Nevertheless, the directors' reaction shocked Nicholson. Wale was furious that he had talked to Blanchflower and Giles without telling him first. They didn't want him around the club in any capacity, either. They were afraid he'd turn into Tottenham's Matt Busby, fatally undermining the influence of his successor.

So Nicholson's leave-taking was an aggrieved, unpleasant one. Angrily he told Wale that what he had done had been for the benefit of the club. For 16 years he had virtually run Tottenham Hotspur. They, the directors, had had an easy time in those years, enjoying the matches and the glory and leaving him to take the strain. They had asked him to carry on for those two weeks, and never before had they queried any of his decisions.

'In those days, a manager who'd had great success, like Bill Shankly at Liverpool, did help to appoint the next manager, or help pick his successor,' said Joe Kinnear. 'Bill Nick was only doing what he thought was best for the club, a club he'd worked for all his life, for almost 40 years, since he'd joined them as a boy in 1936. He'd been totally loyal to them. And what did they say? What amounted to "Get lost".'

For his 16 years as manager of Tottenham Hotspur, during which he made the name of the club world-famous and built a team of players who still live on in people's minds, Nicholson was given a £10,000 payoff. The club refused him a testimonial, saying they already had three players due for one. After that, he severed all contact with them.

He was not the only one to receive cavalier treatment. There was no room now for Eddie Baily at White Hart Lane. A new man would be coming in and would want to bring his own team. So Baily was sacked. He received a £4,000 redundancy payment. The following Monday, the two of them went down to the Labour Exchange and signed on.

CHAPTER TWENTY

'I'M A SPURS MAN'

Practically the first words spoken by Terry Neill at the press conference to announce Bill Nicholson's replacement were: 'I am as surprised as you are to find myself at Tottenham.' There have been more inspiring rallying cries.

Still, there wasn't much else he could say. The astonishment that permeated the Spurs part of north London centred on where Neill had spent most of his playing career. It's claimed that on being informed of Neill's CV one member of Tottenham's board of directors said, 'Oh, did he play for Arsenal, then?'

Yep, just a bit. Neill was centre-back there from 1959 to 1970 and made 241 appearances, a considerable number of them as captain. You can't be much more indelibly stamped with the Arsenal trademark than that. After he quit, he spent four years as player-manager at Hull City, but for all his assurances that 'from now on I am a Spurs man', those intervening seasons at Boothferry Park weren't sufficient to disinfect him as far as the Tottenham fans were concerned.

Mind you, the Spurs board had what they thought was wisest – a complete break from the Nicholson-Baily duo. Here was a young manager who, at 32, was the wettest behind the ears in the whole of the First Division and who, in contrast to Eddie and Bill, had a talkative, upbeat personality, the kind that would puff out the players' chests a bit and apply Savlon to egos bruised by the old regime.

'He was good for me,' says Steve Perryman. 'Eddie had decided I'd gone – he said I never sprinted, I never jogged anywhere. So I'm thinking I'm on my way. It had become a drudge for me with Bill. He'd just become all-consumed. With the top players he couldn't sign, with the young players who waited to take his every instruction. I couldn't understand what Terry said at first because he had this thick Northern Irish accent, but he was calm. Didn't shout. And at the end of a session, when we were changing in the dressing room, he put his hand on my shoulder and said, "Just to let you know, you're going nowhere."

'He said I never got in front of the ball, and he was right. He gave us some new ways of playing and the game became more relaxed. I was running forward. I was opening up the game for myself. I think I scored something like six goals in 15 games.'

If Perryman was won over, others were not. 'It was only when Terry Neill came in that we realised that the great era was over and rebuilding was on its way,' said John Pratt. 'I remember one morning turning up for training and saying to Steve Perryman, "Heck, we're the only ones left." Until then, everyone had known Bill and had known they were wanted. I was only ever on a one-year contract in 16 years at White Hart Lane. Suddenly we didn't know what sort of players the new manager was looking for and if we were going to be in a job any longer. It was an unsettling time.'

'The idea of Tottenham without Bill was quite weird,' said Martin Peters. 'Nobody could quite believe it.'

Fresh faces like Nicholson's last signing, Alfie Conn, newcomers like John Duncan and Don McAllister, plus Chris Jones, the 16-year-old Neil McNab, Mike Dillon and Keith Osgood, all promoted from the apprentice ranks, were brought in rapidly. Too rapidly, maybe.

There was dissatisfaction from a dressing room group of Tottenham giants like Mike England, Martin Peters and Martin Chivers: strong-willed, powerful characters who had not only had their hands on more silverware than their manager had as a player, but were also close to Neill in age, and in England's case a couple of years his senior.

They didn't take to Neill's training methods, for a start. Nicholson and Baily had been imaginative and technical. They had concentrated on coaching with the ball. With Neill in charge, the focus was on fitness and stamina. That, anyway, is how things looked from where Chivers was sat. 'I hated it,' he recalls in *Big Chiv*. 'He used to give us these jackets with the pockets filled with sand to weigh you down. We had to run and sprint with them. It was just power running all the time. We hardly did any constructive things with the ball. It is the typical answer for any coach who has got a problem. The first thing coaches think when a team is not playing well is, "Ah, they are not fit enough."

'Most of the first-team players remaining at Spurs were not exactly spring chickens but had reached the top of their professions with enormous achievements under their belts and a lot of knowledge of the game. I think Neill found that daunting. He had played against them only recently and he knew that people like Martin Peters and Mike England knew more about the game than he did and that is no exaggeration. Also, he was coming in to manage a team that was a family.'

It was a family that was rapidly breaking up. In March, when Spurs were in the bottom six of the table and Peters offered his opinion that he could do a better coaching job than the manager, Neill briskly dispatched him to Norwich City. Before the end of the season England had left too, abruptly announcing his retirement from football because his ankles had gone. The young winger Chris McGrath was loaned to Millwall. Chivers was finding it difficult to blend with Duncan, his new striking partner, and Neill stuck him in the reserves. He only came back for the last game of the season.

Which had its comic absurdities. Spurs needed at least a draw against Leeds at White Hart Lane to avoid the drop into the Second Division. In order to maximise their chances Neill fell back on the services of a clairvoyant and hypnotist called Romark, who had once bragged that he could drive through London blindfolded. That said, when attempting to prove it he only managed to get 30 yards down the road before crashing into the back of a parked police car. Romark's other claim to celebrity was that he'd put a curse on Crystal Palace. That was after Malcolm Allison hired him to psych the team out of the Third Division and subsequently failed to pay him. Palace made it out of the Third eventually anyway.

The weird thing was that as far as Spurs were concerned, the hypnosis seemed to work. First Romark told Chivers that he could see headlines saying 'Chivers Back With A Goal'. Then he put Cyril Knowles into a trance and told him he was a rod of iron. The next day, the rod of iron fired Spurs into the lead. Conn put them two up and then cockily sat on the ball, and Chivers made it 3-1. Leeds were goaded into retaliating with a Peter Lorimer goal before Knowles scored a second. The game finished 4-2, not a bad result. And there was a headline in one of the next day's papers that read: 'Chivers Back With A Goal'. 'It was probably one of the worst Spurs sides I've ever seen,' says supporter Rick Mayston. 'But when Knowles scored it was one of the greatest moments.'

Who knows? Maybe it was less down to Romark than the fact that Leeds had nothing to play for that day. Neill's team of raw youngsters and creaking legends, on the other hand, had been facing the drop. They had been driven on by pride and desperation, and hadn't been found wanting. However it came about, they had kept Spurs in the First Division.

The sale of Peters to Norwich had netted £50,000, but that summer there were no new signings to reinforce a diminished, misfiring squad. In fact, Neill was still waving the pruning shears around. Phil Beal went to Brighton, where Alan Mullery had just kicked off his managerial career, and Joe Kinnear was about to follow him there. The first game of the 1975/76 season, against Middlesbrough, was his last in a Spurs shirt. He got a good send-off – Spurs won 1-0 with a Perryman goal.

Kinnear's place at right-back was filled by Terry Naylor, who had been on the edges of the first team since 1970, and whose defending was about as soft-hearted and accommodating as his nickname, 'Meathook', suggested. For the opening weeks of the season, there were few other changes in the side. John Pratt, Neil McNab, Steve Perryman and Jimmy Neighbour made up the midfield and Neill opted to partner Chris Jones with Chivers in attack. Cyril Knowles stayed at left-back and Keith Osgood and Don McAllister provided the heart of the defence who, in spite of Pat Jennings's presence behind them, had a bad September, shipping seven goals. Six of them were against Manchester United and Derby and it left Spurs nearer the bottom of the table than the top.

At last Neill got out the cheque book, bringing in Willie Young, Aberdeen's peppery ginger-haired centre-back, to replace McAllister. Re-jigging the defence seemed to work; Spurs went nine league matches unbeaten. That season, there was also a League Cup run, with Spurs crushing Third Division Doncaster Rovers 7-2 to reach the semi-final. Back in the attack, Duncan helped himself to a hat-trick and Chivers scored twice. For the big man, though, the old problems hadn't gone away. 'I hated this period of my career at Spurs,' Chivers recalls. 'I just did not fit in with Neill's team and his methods which included some strange bonding antics. I found it embarrassing when we were asked to put our arms round each other and do the "hokey-cokey" in the dressing room. I was too old and sedate for all that nonsense and I showed it.'

The last four in the League Cup was as near to Wembley as Spurs got. Newcastle saw to that first. Pratt's goal and Jennings's wonder-saves at White Hart Lane meant they took a small advantage to St James' Park for the second leg, but it wasn't enough. The 3-1 defeat by Newcastle was followed by an exit from the FA Cup, beaten 2-1 in a third-round replay away to Stoke.

Being shown the door in the cups didn't impact on Spurs in the league, however. There was a classy 2-1 victory over Ipswich at Portman Road, then a 2-1 revenge win over Stoke. Which was significant for another reason. Glenn Hoddle played his first full game for Tottenham Hotspur.

Hoddle had come on to Spurs' radar as an 11-year-old Harlow schoolboy after Martin Chivers and Ray Evans went along to present the prizes at a local junior cup final and realized that here was a special talent in the making. Back at White Hart Lane, Chivers passed on his name and Hoddle was invited to train with the club. Seven years later, the rest of football was about to find out about him. His debut first-team appearance had been brief but promising, coming on late in the game as a sub at Norwich six months earlier after Knowles's knee had given up the ghost. That day he nearly scored. This time, in his first full match, there was no 'nearly' about the beautifully angled, rising drive that made it into the net past the mighty Peter Shilton. 'The ball had run loose of a defender 25 yards out and I heard John Pratt yell, "Hit it!"' said Hoddle. 'And I did.' It was the match-winner.

Playing in five out of the next six games, Hoddle demonstrated his promise as the side strung together wins over Aston Villa, Wolves and Burnley before making way for Neighbour for the end-of-campaign run-in. In those final games, Spurs were true to type. There were stirring goal-fests at the Lane – a 5-0 rout of Sheffield United and a 4-1 stroll against Coventry. They went to Highbury and strikes from Pratt and Duncan had the game won by half-time. Now they were sixth in the table. It was heady stuff. And short-lived. In a final pair of fixtures, they lost away to Birmingham and at home to Newcastle.

Still, a good League Cup run, a strong finish to the season – a Spurs team under Terry Neill might actually be going places. But in the summer of 1976, Neill left. He blamed disagreements with the directors during the club's end-of-season tour to Canada, New Zealand and Australia. That said, he had also just learned that Bertie Mee, the long-serving Arsenal manager, was leaving Highbury. Neill took over from Mee in time for start of the next season. 'Okay, I admit it,' he said. 'I am and always will be an Arsenal man at heart.'

So, less than two years after taking on Terry Neill, Spurs had to find a new manager again. There was no extensive search, none of the media speculation that would later characterise the hunt for future incumbents. The rest of the football world may not have known it, but they had the right man on site already.

Back in the summer of 1975, Neill had made one addition to the coaching staff. A very important one. To work with the first team, he had recruited a little-known Yorkshire-born coach who had just been sacked as part of a cost-cutting exercise by Newcastle United. As a player, Keith Burkinshaw had not so much set the football world alight as caused it to smoulder slightly in a dark corner. He'd been on

Liverpool's books for seven years in the 1950s, during which time he played in one league game. After that he went to Workington Town in Division 3 (North), made 293 league appearances and scored nine goals as a hard-working, determined wing-half, then saw out his playing days at Scunthorpe. Let go by Newcastle, he arrived at White Hart Lane with a massive point to prove.

And though it was going to take him a while, this unassuming but stubborn and strong-willed man from Yorkshire would do just that.

CHAPTER TWENTY-ONE

'I'M GOING TO MAKE THIS A TEAM'

The new occupant of the manager's office at White Hart Lane was the polar opposite of the man he replaced. Neill had been affable and chatty. Burkinshaw was thoughtful and still, the sort of man who stands on the edge of the circle in the pub, saying nothing, just listening. But he gave the impression that as he listened he was absorbing and processing an awful lot.

Mind you, it seemed that Burkinshaw was the last person to hear about Neill's departure. After the club's end-of-season tour finished, he had taken his wife and kids on holiday to Croatia, and the first he heard of the latest drama at the Lane was when he picked up a newspaper. It was, he said without overstating the case, 'a complete shock'.

For Burkinshaw, the future suddenly seemed tormentingly uncertain. He had shifted his family down from Newcastle to London just a year earlier and now, as he wondered whether he was still wanted at White Hart Lane, it was looking like a pointless disruption to their lives. Then again, what did he have to lose? He applied for the manager's job.

The players helped to swing it for him. In the short time he'd worked with them, they'd been impressed. Mention Burkinshaw's name to them even now and you can hear the warmth and respect in their response. 'He was a very honest manager,' says Gary Mabbutt. 'Very down to earth, a lovely, lovely man, a gentleman.'

'He is very honest, he likes discipline, he likes order' – that's Ricky Villa's verdict.

And here's Steve Perryman on the subject: 'He cared about the team, about it improving, about Tottenham Hotspur; he cared about living up to the tradition. And he was absolutely committed. He said to me once, "Trust me, Steve, I am going to make this a team." And he did.'

Someone who shared the players' approval was the chairman of Tottenham Hotspur. Sidney Wale had already made up his own mind about the set-up under Neill's management. 'Burkinshaw did the work while Terry appeared on TV,' he commented drily. Plus Wale could see the parallels between Burkinshaw and another Yorkshireman, from whom absence had most definitely made the heart beat stronger. 'He was never a publicity-seeker. He was more the sort of manager we'd been used to, and we liked.'

'The two of them were astonishingly similar in almost every respect,' says Brian Scovell, Nicholson's biographer. 'Like Bill, he also believed in playing attacking football and didn't like cheats. He was totally honest and never minced his words: he gave it to them straight.'

'Keith told you how it was,' says Garry Brooke.

Key was Burkinshaw's belief in what Nicholson had believed in: 'I was determined we'd play with flair and style. To me, that was as important as the results.' Here was someone who believed in The Spurs Way. He loved the flair players. He loved the ones who could pass.

Not that there were many of those around at White Hart Lane in the summer of 1976. Burkinshaw already knew the problems with the squad he had inherited. Cyril Knowles had retired midway through the previous season, while Chivers had been sold to the Swiss club Servette of Geneva in Neill's final spate of clearing-out. Alfie Conn had long since tucked the ball under his arm and gone back to Scotland to join Celtic. Meanwhile, Ralph Coates was getting on a bit and Jimmy Neighbour was about to move on to Norwich City. The squad at Burkinshaw's disposal lacked depth and experience. More damningly, some just weren't good enough.

'I thought,' said Burkinshaw understatedly, 'we were looking at a difficult campaign.'

Even so, he hadn't imagined how difficult. The season began with a 3-1 defeat to Ipswich at Portman Road. Four days later, Newcastle did them 2-0 at White Hart Lane. The following Saturday they didn't concede any goals against Middlesbrough, but they didn't score any either. But at the time, one point from three games wasn't particularly alarming for the fans. Queens Park Rangers, who had missed out on the title by a single point three months back, were doing even worse, they rationalised. And the following weekend Spurs came back from 2-0 down at half-time against Manchester United. Moores, Coates and Pratt all found the net. It was an exhilarating victory, one that was followed by a 1-0 home win against Leeds. Only five games in and 13th place didn't seem too bad. The crisis was over.

Except it wasn't. Spurs only won one out of their next 10 matches. One of them a 3-2 defeat to Third Division Wrexham at White Hart Lane in the League Cup. If that was embarrassing, though, it was nothing compared to what happened in mid-October when they travelled to Derby.

Twice league champions over the previous six seasons, in the running for another title just a few months back, Derby County were having the sort of season when nothing went right. On the day Spurs arrived, they hadn't won all season and had mustered seven goals in eight matches. Now they beat that total in a single game, with their Scotland international Bruce Rioch scoring four in Derby's 8-2 win.

Knocked out of kilter, Spurs careered closer and closer to the drop zone. Mini-revivals were followed by long drawn-out slumps. Battling for survival against West Ham, Bristol City and Sunderland, Tottenham lost to all of them. When 1976 ended they were third from bottom.

And the new year brought no turnaround, no Spurs rollercoaster ride, no FA Cup run even – Cardiff dumped them out of the competition in the third round. By the end of February, Spurs were bottom of a densely packed five-club pile. When, in March, the defending champions and league leaders Liverpool came to White Hart Lane, and were sent away beaten thanks to a Ralph Coates goal, a result that brought yet another renewal of hope, it was almost cruel.

Because that, more or less, was as good as it got. A win over QPR moved Spurs above them into 17th place, but they'd played four games more than the boys from Loftus Road. With eight games left to maintain First Division status, they only managed two more wins. The goal stream turned into a drought. They lost the north London derby at Highbury, 1-0, then the next day they went to Ashton Gate and lost 1-0 to Bristol City. The Easter programme had seen them drop back into the bottom three, Bristol City were bottom on 25 points, then Tottenham were one of five clubs on 27 points, and they'd played more games than everyone else.

Draws at home to Sunderland and away to Stoke came either side of a defeat at Villa Park. By 23rd April, Spurs were in 19th place on 29 points. The two clubs immediately below them, Coventry and West Ham, were only one point behind, with several games in hand. So by the time they came to their next match, Spurs had dropped into the bottom three again.

They were at home against Aston Villa, who were chasing a UEFA Cup place. Goals from Hoddle, Jones and Taylor gave Spurs a 3-1 win. But in the meantime, Sunderland had gone to eighth-placed West Bromwich Albion and surprisingly come away with the points. The killer day, though, was 7th May at Manchester City, who were in second place and pushing for a title they hadn't won in almost 10 years. City won 5-0. 'It was my worst Spurs experience of all time,' says supporter Rick Mayston. 'I knew there was just no way back, but you stand there and watch them knowing you're relegated. I'd never known Spurs as anything but top flight.'

From then on, it was effectively over. Slumped in the away dressing room at Maine Road, the team took in the bad news on *Sports Report* on BBC Radio 2. Everyone around them had gained at least a point.

Now bottom of the table, two points adrift, with just one game left and a goal difference of at least minus five to make up, they needed to ram home a pile of goals against Leicester City. Even that by itself wouldn't be enough. West Ham had to pick up no more than a point from their final two matches. For the Spurs fans there was hope, though – those last fixtures were against Liverpool and Manchester United.

Against Leicester, Spurs nevertheless fought for their survival. John Pratt and Jimmy Holmes scored; they won 2-0. But meanwhile in a goalless draw at Anfield West Ham were nicking the point they needed to stay up and send Spurs down.

Bottom of the league. Spurs were relegated after 27 years in the top flight. At first the fans were defiant. That afternoon against Leicester, they'd invaded the pitch, banners already painted with the message 'We Shall Return'. But they'd never known Spurs as anything but a top club, the club of Blanchflower, Mackay and Greaves, the club that stood for everything that was bright and shining about football. As the reality began to sink in, it's almost impossible to describe the intensity of the humiliation and dejection around White Hart Lane.

To compound the pain, Pat Jennings left that August. He was 32, had made 472 league appearances, saved countless goals and scored one (the upfield punt in the 1967 Charity Shield that beat Manchester United's Alex Stepney). Two seasons back, he had made world-class saves to keep Spurs in the First Division. This time he had consistently been their greatest performer. The combination of dependability and brilliance hadn't gone unnoticed by his fellow pros – the PFA made him Players' Player of the Year, the first goalkeeper ever to get the award. It hadn't gone unnoticed by Arsenal either. After a contract dispute, Burkinshaw let Jennings go. Up the road to where the shirts were red and the football was boring.

Beyond White Hart Lane, there were questions: was Burkinshaw the right man for Tottenham? The chairman wasn't one of the people who were asking, though. 'I still think you're a good prospect,' Sidney Wale told Burkinshaw. 'And I want you to stay.'

So the fightback began. In this, Burkinshaw had one crucial asset – Steve Perryman, the boy who had stepped up to captain the side aged 20 when Peters failed a fitness test, the man who did exactly what it said on the tin. During Nicholson's time, Perryman had demonstrated the ability to perform roles not often combined in a single player. He was a workhorse, but a playmaker too. That and a scorer of rare but crucial goals, like the two half-volleys struck from the edge of the box to capsize AC Milan in the 1972 UEFA Cup semi-final. Then there was the Andy Lochhead shot he cleared off the line at the last gasp of the 1971 League Cup Final. The man was par excellence, a rescuer of lost causes. Small wonder that with Martin Peters gone Burkinshaw had handed him the captaincy on a permanent basis and stuck him in the centre of defence.

For Peter Shreeve, Burkinshaw's right-hand man and coach, Perryman was 'an excellent, excellent player. Nobody really appreciated how good he actually was. His technique was brilliant. He had a great jam tart and he loved the club – he would have slept there if he could'.'

John Syer, the psychologist brought in by Burkinshaw to work with the team, sums him up this way: 'Steve Perryman took care of us the same way he took care of everyone. When we got to the hotel on away games, he'd invite us up to his room, order tea and biscuits and make sure we understood what the team needed from each of the players. He was the greatest captain of any team in any sport that I've ever been involved with. The way he built up relationships was unique.'

For Graham Roberts, he was a fantastic influence, a superstar, the best he ever played with. 'His distribution was fantastic and nothing was ever too much trouble for him if it would help the team out, help his team-mates. He would bollock you – but only in the right way; it was only for your needs and benefit. That's what a captain is, a leader from the front, and that was Steve.'

Or as Paul Miller put it: 'He didn't stand no shit from anybody.'

As for the fans, they loved him. 'He was dependable,' says Rob White. 'He was the bloke who won't let you down. He was this force who was trying everything, putting all his power into trying to improve Tottenham. It was this admirable, unbelievable quality which not many players have.'

'We'd dropped down into the Second Division and there was Perryman saying, "It's my responsibility to lead us out again,"' says Martin Cloake. 'He was Lord Kitchener! It was "Your Captain Needs You!" Spurs were this great club that had fallen on hard times. They should be in Division One. Support your team! You *had* to go.'

Back in the Second Division for the first time since 1950, Spurs had to adjust to the cup-finals-every-week mentality that was life in the lower reaches. Which they did, staying in the top four alongside Bolton, Brighton and Southampton all season, followed all over the country by numbers of fans so vast that grateful second-tier clubs enjoyed record gates; 52,000 piled into White Hart Lane for the top-of-the-table clash with Bolton in the spring.

One game stood out from all the others, though – 26th October, 1977. Tottenham Hotspur 9 Bristol Rovers 0. Four of the goals came from Colin Lee, signed 48 hours earlier from Torquay. Ian Moores bagged a hat-trick. Peter Taylor got on the score-sheet, too. So did a youngster called Glenn Hoddle, claiming the final goal of the day. It was the club's record winning margin in a league match. No one knew how crucial those goals would turn out to be.

Because when it came to spring, Spurs developed the jitters. They dropped points. It was between them, Brighton and Southampton for the last two promotion places, and Spurs' sole advantage over Brighton was the superior goal average given to them by those nine goals at Bristol Rovers.

In one of those weird twists of fate, their last fixture was against Southampton. Both sides needed a draw for promotion; defeat for either would have meant staying down. The game was a no-risks 0-0 stalemate. No one cared, though. Spurs had got themselves promoted straight back.

Spurs weren't just back in the First Division again, they were going to be in there with that season's midfield sensation, Hoddle. A 20-year-old who had joined Spurs as a 16-year-old apprentice, who wore his shirt hanging loose outside his shorts, and who over the next decade would turn out to be one of the most brilliant and divisive characters of English football, the kind who you only see – and even then you have to be lucky – once in a lifetime. The enigma. 'The Perfect Ten'. Or 'God', as some preferred to call him.

Midway through the 2011/12 season when, in concurrent attempts to revive Premier League campaigns that threatened to self-destruct,

Fergie brought back Paul Scholes and Thierry Henry dusted off his shinpads for Arsène Wenger, the *Daily Mail*'s Saturday Debate posed the question: 'Who would you bring back?'

Jamie Redknapp chose Gazza – 'He was different class at his peak.'

Jamie's dad went for George Best: 'Simply the greatest player to have graced these shores.' For the journalist Michael Walker, the answer had to be Danny Blanchflower: 'Those who have backed Tottenham at big prices to win the league are now in a state of agitation. Blanchflower's return would ease that. He has the Spurs been-there-done-that T-shirt.' As for Nasser Hussain, the former England cricket captain, being an Arsenal supporter didn't stop him going for another Spurs great. 'I would love to see Glenn Hoddle playing again,' he said.

It's a yearning shared by a lot of people, not just Spurs fans and the odd rogue Arsenal supporter. You could argue forever about who's been the most gifted player to wear a Tottenham shirt, but he has to be a prime candidate. Hoddle is the player kids wanted to be. People remember those silky skills. The languid style. The balance and vision. They remember the saying at the time. If you wanted to stop Spurs, you stopped Hoddle.

Here was someone who, according to Steve Perryman, played as if he had a set of golf clubs where his feet should be and could hit a two iron, or a seven iron, or a nine iron. Who had, as Tony Galvin said, 'the ability to hit the perfect long ball.' For Graham Roberts, he was 'probably the best player that Spurs have ever had'. Or as the comedian Jasper Carrott put it: 'I hear that Hoddle's found God. That must have been one hell of a pass.'

For Hoddle, the season spent getting out of the Second Division was a learning curve. To deal with the rustic tackling, he made himself stronger on the ball. He established a crucial and necessary playing relationship with Perryman in which he was the creative force and Perryman the ball-winner and protector. Because of Burkinshaw's nagging, he put some effort into defending as well as attacking – not, it must be said, with limitless enthusiasm or consistency. 'At that time he shoved down my throat his feelings that I shirked my defensive responsibilities,' Hoddle said later. 'That's where he and I disagreed.

Of course, I'm fully aware of my deficiencies. But I do have the ability to open up opposition defences and be creative. That, in my opinion, is more important; it is positive play, not negative.'

'He wasn't there yet,' says Burkinshaw, 'but everyone at Tottenham and in football knew he would soon be the main man.'

That said, the team that Burkinshaw had promised to make was still a work in progress. That summer, as Spurs prepared to return to the place they belonged, he was about to add to it with one of the most original and audacious transfer deals in football history.

CHAPTER TWENTY-TWO

...AND STILL RICKY VILLA!

That summer's World Cup in Argentina provided a bleak reminder of the state of English football in the 1970s. In 1974, England had failed to qualify and Alf Ramsey, the only manager to deliver the Jules Rimet trophy to a grateful nation, had been sacked. His successor, Don Revie, had walked out in the summer of 1977, announcing 24 hours later that he was now manager of the United Arab Emirates. To qualify for the 1978 tournament, England were down to relying on Italy to lose to Luxembourg on 3rd December. Pigs failed to fly on the day, leaving Scotland and Ally McLeod's Tartan Army, a side of ludicrously-inflated self-belief, to shoulder the burden of British disappointment in South America.

Nowhere was the gulf between English and Argentinian football more underlined than in midfield, and it was embodied in the diminutive, perpetually busy form of Osvaldo Ardiles. Here was an artist, a skilful grafter, quick and brave, the link man between hard-bitten, uncompromising defence and fluid, fast-moving attack. And with the abject state of Argentina's economy, and the recent lifting of the players' union ban on foreigners playing for British clubs, the ambitious, highly intelligent Ardiles – he was a qualified lawyer – was looking for a move to England.

Which is where Bill Nicholson came in.

Nicholson was at Tottenham Hotspur again, brought back by Burkinshaw. It was one of the first things he did when he took over as Spurs manager. Until then, there had been a stand-off between ex-manager and club, the outcome of the bust-up over Blanchflower and Giles. Since he hadn't even been invited to attend matches at White Hart Lane, Nicholson had been keeping in touch with the game by helping out with the scouting at West Ham. 'I felt sorry for Bill,' said Joe Kinnear, 'the way he was just allowed to creep out of the club.'

But if the boardroom hadn't understood what Nicholson meant to the fans, if they hadn't seen that what he had achieved was built into the very soul of the place, Burkinshaw had. 'Here was this blue-and-white-blooded Spurs man,' he said, 'across town earning his corn at West Ham when he could be helping Tottenham.'

So the old man came back on a modest salary, with the job description of head scout. He was in his element again, watching as many as five games a week, travelling all over the country in his ancient Vauxhall Cavalier, often with Darkie at his side, armed with the Thermos flask and sandwiches.

Thirty-eight years in the game, years of obsessive watching of players and matches, had given him not just knowledge of who did and who didn't deserve to wear a Spurs shirt but an unequalled collection of contacts. One was Harry Haslam, another Yorkshireman.

In those days, Haslam was managing Sheffield United, and in the search for untapped talent he had set up a South American network that began at Bramall Lane, where the Uruguayan Oscar Arce was on the coaching staff. Earlier that year, he had brought a gifted Argentinian midfielder, Alex Sabella, to England for £160,000, though the rumour was that he had been offered a 17-year-old called Diego Maradona but couldn't afford the £200,000 asking price. Arce tipped him off that Ardiles was available. With the £400,000 asking price way above his budget, Haslam phoned Nicholson.

'I had seen Ardiles on television and had been impressed by him,' Nicholson wrote in his autobiography. 'He was obviously a player who would improve our side.' Spurs bought some plane tickets fast.

'I met Ossie in a hotel on a Sunday and there was an immediate connection between us,' said Burkinshaw later. 'I knew he was a man I could work with and he came back the next day with his wife and signed.'

Unable to believe how simple it had been, Burkinshaw then discovered Ardiles had a mate who was also looking for a move. Ricky Villa was a big, hippyish-looking midfielder with a Zapata moustache who had made a couple of brief showings as a sub at the World Cup. He was, in consequence, much more of an unknown quantity to Burkinshaw who thought, nevertheless, that it would be good for Ardiles to have a friend to help him settle in England. 'I phoned Sidney Wale and asked him how much we had in the bank. He called back 20 minutes later and gave me the green light. I think it took all of 10 minutes to get Ricky to sign. We got the two of them for £750,000.'

And it was ground-breaking. That kind of thing just didn't happen in football – two Argentinian World Cup players coming to England. Not just that. They were coming to Spurs. Not Arsenal. Not Liverpool. Not Manchester United. This was what the club stood for, what Tottenham Hotspur was about. These were players who embodied the style that had been hard-wired into its very being from the days of John Cameron at the start of the century. Paul Miller called it a defining moment, as pivotal as winning the Double. 'It changed our history. They changed our club. Forever.'

Glenn Hoddle's appraisal, as they got together on the training ground for the first time, was glowing. 'I loved playing with Ossie and Ricky. It was special. Ossie was certainly the most astute player I played with. He read the game better than anyone. Ricardo was probably the more technically gifted player. I remember we played a friendly in pre-season against Royal Antwerp. In the game, me and Ricky played a series of one-twos through the middle of the pitch and I thought, "This is wonderful. This is someone who is on the same wavelength as me." And we just gelled, all three of us.' Villa returned the compliment: 'When Ossie and I saw Glenn, we turned to each other and said, 'Why have they signed us?'

This wasn't, however, an overnight transformation. Spurs in the 1978/79 season were largely a young side getting to grips with life back in the First Division, while simultaneously the two Argentinians struggled to acclimatise. Gordon Taylor of the PFA complained that their presence could mean two English players out of a job. Hard man Tommy Smith, who'd been the First Division's stand-out frightener for Liverpool and was now rattling his chains at Third Division Swansea, promised that Ardiles and Villa could expect some rough treatment in the English game. When Villa scored in the first game of the season, the equaliser in a 1-1 draw away to Nottingham Forest, the papers figured that Spurs had championship potential. Within two weeks, after they lost 4-1 to Aston Villa at White Hart Lane and went on to get obliterated 7-0 at Liverpool, the same papers were tipping them for a swift return to Division Two.

The press were wrong. Over the course of the next three seasons, Burkinshaw's Spurs developed into the most exhilarating outfit in the league, a strong, committed group of players kept in line by Perryman, their linchpin and captain, buoyed by the passion and joie de vivre of Ardiles and focused around the mysterious genius of Hoddle.

'We were the team of the moment because we were different from everybody else in the league,' says Ardiles. 'We played stylish football. We had Ricky Villa and Glenn Hoddle and we played in a very South American way, which a lot of English clubs weren't used to. They played more direct football and they played the long ball into the box. We really played very differently from the rest of the country. I loved it. It was a wonderful type of football to play.'

And as in the case of the push-and-run side, there was intelligence there. As Perryman puts it, 'None of us were mugs.'

Most of the youngsters had been brought through by Peter Shreeve, then the youth coach, and his assistant, the Double side's Ron Henry. Mark Falco, the bubble-perm-owning Micky Hazard, Garry Brooke and the flying full-back Chris Hughton all came in that way, as did Paul 'Maxie' Miller, the tough, sharp-witted defender who thrived on the big stage. For Micky Hazard, in particular, playing alongside Ardiles was an experience he remembers fondly. 'Ossie was probably one of the nicest people I ever met in my life,' he says. 'I obviously got on very well with the youth set-up guys but when you talk about players within the first-team set-up, Ossie was always there to help me, from start to finish. Thereby killing the myth that you're there to compete with each other for your place. You've got to have a squad of very good players to be successful, and as long as we win, that's all that matters.'

Then there were Tony Galvin and Graham Roberts, both of whom Nicholson fished out of non-League obscurity. Galvin, a winger with the unusual (for football) distinction of possessing a BA in Russian Studies from Hull University, was doing a teacher-training course in Nottingham and playing for Goole Town in the Northern Premier League when Nicholson was tipped off about him. The old man drove through apocalyptic winter weather to a night match in the Peak District where, huddled at the back of the grandstand away from the driving sleet, he watched Galvin carving tramline after tramline on a pitch covered by an inch of snow. Potential, pace, strength, two good feet. In Nicholson's words, 'To be recommended'.

In fact, as Galvin admits in *The Boys from White Hart Lane*, he might not have joined Spurs at all. On the day he was due to sign, Ronnie Fenton, Brian Clough's assistant at Nottingham Forest, called him up at his college hall of residence. 'They wanted me not to go, they'd got wind of it somehow,' he said. 'So I had to make a decision on the day – was I going to put Spurs off and go and see what Forest had to say? But I just made the decision: "No I'm not, I'm going to go to Tottenham." . . . I suppose it was because I knew they'd been and seen me so I felt a bit of a commitment, but to be fair when I was younger Tottenham had a bit of glamour about them and I had always liked them. It didn't bother me where they were at the time – you knew they'd come back – it was just because it was Tottenham.'

Spurs picked him up for £30,000. It was £10,000 more than they paid Weymouth for Graham Roberts two years later in 1980. Roberts's signing was a spectacularly accidental stroke of luck. Nicholson had been on a disappointing scouting trip to Swindon ('The match was uninteresting and the player I was watching had not impressed,' he observed drily) and was waiting on the platform for the train back to London when he got into conversation with a man listening to *Sports Report* on a transistor radio. A bit of a non-League anorak, the man told Nicholson that Weymouth were the most watchable side, with some strong young players. Roberts, he said, was the best of them.

Less than a week later, Nicholson drove from Tottenham to Weymouth to see for himself. That day, Roberts was playing in midfield and scored twice. He had, in the past, been turned down by Southampton, Bournemouth and Reading. One of his goals was a header which, said Nicholson, 'reminded me of Cliff Jones in his prime'. He was, it followed, good enough for Tottenham Hotspur.

That said, once Roberts became Paul Miller's partner in defence, he wasn't so much Cliff Jones Mark II as the spiritual offspring of Dave Mackay. He was ruggedly physical, he hated losing and he was celebrated less for his finesse than his willingness to kick holes in the opponents' midfield. 'Maxie would set them up and I would welly them,' he told Martin Cloake and Adam Powley in *The Boys from White Hart Lane*. He was brave, too. There's a classic photo of him at Wembley in the 1981 FA Cup Final, spitting out the teeth dislodged by an accidental kick from his team-mate Chris Hughton. They tried to stop him going back out for the second half, there was blood pouring out of his mouth, but no way. 'They'd have had to break my legs to keep me off,' he said.

That 1980/81 season was the one when Burkinshaw's team really branded themselves as the new great Spurs side. Their swagger and skill wasn't geared to grinding out the league victories that would have won them a title, but as a cup side no one could touch them. By then Burkinshaw had placed the last pieces in the jigsaw. Recognising the side had been short of a goalscorer, he signed two.

As personalities, Steve Archibald and Garth Crooks were pretty much direct opposites. The only thing they had in common was goals. Crooks, bought from Stoke, was a showman, a wide-eyed Northerner, excitable and bright – you needed more than the fingers of one hand to count his O Levels. 'He said big words,' claimed Tony Parks. Archibald, in contrast, was scruffy and moody. The Scot's prickliness soon got under Burkinshaw's skin. But, like Crooks, he was a brilliant finisher, chasing everything and scoring against everyone. Rapidly becoming the darling of 'The Shelf', he was serenaded at home games to the tune of a British Airways ad showing on TV at the time: 'We'll take more care of you, Archibald, Archibald.'

'They were showbiz, they were Hollywood,' says supporter Danny Keene. 'You had Hoddle, Ardiles, you had Micky Hazard who in any other era would have been a star if he hadn't always had to compete with Hoddle. You had Crooks and Archibald, one from the Potteries, one from Scotland. I remember wearing a bright yellow T-shirt on a baking hot day in 1980, watching them at home to Forest, first day of the season. Watching Crooks and Archibald just hit it off. 2-0.'

It was their goals that took Spurs to Wembley, in a season that Spurs went Rockney. The pop-rock duo Chas and Dave wrote them a cup final song. The lyrics of *Ossie's Dream* – (sample lyrics: 'Ossie's going to Wembley, his knees have gone all trembly') – may not have been up there with *Jerusalem,* but the team got to sing it on *Top of the Pops*, with Ardiles piping the immortal line, 'In the cup for Tottingham'.

The cup took a lot of winning for Tottingham, mind. The semi-final was against Wolves at Hillsborough, and Spurs thought goals from Archibald and Hoddle had put them through until a late equalising penalty mistakenly awarded by Clive Thomas led to extra-time and then a replay at Highbury four days later. 'Virtually every kid in north London bunked off school because you could just turn up and get in on the day,' remembers Martin Cloake. '58,000 Spurs fans inside Highbury. A fantastic performance by Spurs. Crooks scored two and we were superb. Proper Spurs football – width and speed, deadly, just everything.'

It was Ricky Villa who clinched the win over Wolves with a marvellously accomplished third goal scored from 30 yards out. It was Villa, too, who was to dominate everything that followed. The lasting image of the 9th May final against Manchester City is of his lonely, disconsolate trudge down the side of the pitch to the tunnel after Burkinshaw had substituted him. That game ended in a draw after extra-time, with Tottenham's record of being undefeated in cup finals made safe by City's Tommy Hutchinson, who earned the distinction of scoring at both ends, first giving City the lead after half an hour, then with 10 minutes left deflecting Hoddle's shot past Joe Corrigan.

So it was a reprieve for Spurs, but despair for Villa. He had failed, he had hardly had a touch of the ball, he had been taken off. He was bitterly disappointed, in himself, in Keith Burkinshaw. But in the dressing room afterwards, Burkinshaw sat down with him. 'You'll play in the replay,' Burkinshaw said. And for that, Villa repaid him a thousand times over.

'We heard on the radio that tickets were going on sale on Sunday morning.' says Martin Cloake. 'So my mate came and knocked for me at 4am. There were no buses, so we started walking from Muswell Hill to Tottenham to get there before nine, and we weren't the only ones. There was this kind of movement of people. Older fellas who'd stayed up all night after being on the piss, it was like an exodus. We got to Wood Green and this policeman in a van said: "Where are you going?"

'"We're going to Spurs."

'"Jump in and we'll give you a lift."

'The copper dropped us at White Hart Lane. The queue already went all the way round the ground and then down Park Lane. We joined it around Northumberland Park station, and we got tickets for the replay, the best cup final ever.'

For some, it was the best goal ever, too. It was Tottenham Hotspur 3 Manchester City 2. It was John Motson, the BBC commentator, shouting: ' . . . And *still* Ricky Villa!'

'I'd driven down from Sheffield for the replay and the car broke down outside the Pantiles pub in Neasden,' says supporter Ivan Cohen. 'I walked the rest of the way. And it was one of the best matches I've ever seen. In my mind's eye I still see Ricky Villa dribbling in and out, it's almost in slow motion, you're going, "Shoot for f***'s sake, shoot!" and even now every time I see it on TV I get a little tingle in the back of the neck.'

Villa had scored once already by the time that happened, seven minutes after the start. Three minutes later, City had equalised, then they'd gone ahead from a penalty five minutes into the second half. With 19 minutes left Spurs equalised through Crooks. Then, seven minutes later, Villa ran almost half the length of the pitch, with City players swarming around him and the unmarked Archibald screaming at him for the final pass. Instead Villa found a sliver of space, and sent the ball through it.

The Saturday just gone, he'd been dismissed as a failure. Now he'd won the cup for Tottenham, with a goal that no one's ever forgotten. Like they'll always remember how, afterwards, he ran all the way across the pitch and launched himself into Burkinshaw's arms. This was redemption. This was gratitude.

'I watched the rest of the game through one lens of my glasses because someone sitting on a stanchion behind me literally jumped on my head,' says Rick Mayston. 'But it was one of the best moments of my life.'

'I'll never forget that 1981 final,' recalls Norman Jay, now an acclaimed DJ. 'I got the sack from my job for taking time off to go to the replay. Ricky's goal was at our end; it was packed. We were willing him "hit it, hit it!" And when it went in, there was just this deafening noise and whole wave of people. I've been to a World Cup Final, and that pales by comparison to a cup final spectacle – that kind of fervent, almost religious passion.'

'The match didn't finish till close on 10pm,' says Morris Keston. 'We were driving back to the Chanticleer club for the official celebration with the players and we couldn't get in to Tottenham High Road. It was around midnight and it was jam-packed, blocked solid. Cars, flags, horns blowing, 60–70,000 crowd, unbelievable. We parked not far from Bruce Grove library and had to walk the rest of the way.'

A quarter of a million showed up for the civic parade the following weekend. Spurs fever spread beyond British shores, too. Villa's goal inspired the forming of the Malta branch of the Spurs Supporters Club.

'It's your first trophy, for the players you've come through with, for your family,' Paul Miller said later. 'It is a magic moment that defines your life really. And the way we did it – the romance, the Argentinians, the record, the parade down the High Road afterwards – it was all wonderful. And knowing we were on the verge of something great. We knew it was just the start, it wasn't a one-off.'

In saying it was the start of something, Miller got it right. Spurs were on the brink of a new era. But just what it would bring was something no one could have predicted.

CHAPTER TWENTY-THREE

TWO CUPS AND A WALKOUT

On 2nd April, 1982, Argentinian forces invaded the Falkland Islands, entering the capital Port Stanley in the early hours of the morning. The garrison of the Royal Marines was outnumbered and outgunned, and after some brief skirmishes Governor Sir Rex Hunt ordered them to lay down their arms.

Eight thousand miles away, Burkinshaw went to bed on the Friday night anticipating nothing more testing than the next day's FA Cup semi-final against Leicester at Villa Park. He woke up on Saturday morning to learn that Britain was at war with Argentina.

The choice Burkinshaw had to make was starkly simple. Did he play Ardiles and Villa and get vilified for being unpatriotic or did he leave out two of his key players? In the end he fielded both of them. Spurs won 2-0, while the Leicester fans showed their diplomatic sympathy by unleashing a continuous barrage of stick.

That was the last game Ardiles played for Spurs that season. He left to join the Argentina squad's preparations for the 1982 World Cup. It wasn't a cop-out, said Burkinshaw, it had been agreed that he could go before the war even started. Still, it left Burkinshaw with the issue of what to do about Villa. Everyone, he said, had an opinion, including the person who sent him a death threat. In the end he decided not to play him in the final. Which meant going to Wembley without two of his main men.

The way the run-up to Wembley had begun was extremely satisfying – a 1-0 victory over Arsenal at the Lane. Emphasising the point that divine justice was no empty concept, Crooks's goal went in under the body of Pat Jennings. The omens were good. Spurs were going for three trophies and were in with a shout for all of them. But then Liverpool beat them in the Milk Cup Final, with Spurs caught by a sucker-punch of a late equaliser and losing 3-1 after extra-time. It was the first time Spurs had lost in a major Wembley final. Paul Miller took it badly. 'I walked off,' he said. 'I didn't do a lap of honour. I was disgusted with it.'

Steve Perryman believes that if they'd won this trophy this Tottenham team would have gone on to win the league and many other trophies. 'Liverpool, as great as they were, won many games in the last five minutes,' he says. "That was part of being great, they never gave up. Our legs went. We sat down for the extra-time team talk; they didn't. I saw a picture where I was stood up talking to the other players who were all sitting down on the turf. Maybe they were too tired, but Liverpool had this thing over us.

'I don't think it [the loss] affected us in terms of team spirit . . . but if we'd overcome Liverpool in a major game, that would have been a hell of a step forward. It didn't knock us, but we could have won so much more had it gone our way.'

Instead, in April, Spurs went out in the semi-final of the European Cup Winners' Cup to Barcelona. By the time they reached Wembley to face Queens Park Rangers, they'd finished fourth in the league. The FA Cup was their only hope of getting something from the season.

It wasn't a great game. They'd played a lot of matches, they were without Ardiles and Villa, QPR played with Second Division dogged-ness and 90 lacklustre minutes came and went, goalless. In extra-time, Hoddle scored and they thought they had it won. Then Terry Fenwick bundled in the equaliser. With the match ending all-square after extra-time, they had to go back to Wembley on the Thursday night and do it all over again.

The year before, the replay against Manchester City had been a classic, with Villa scoring what would later be chosen as the FA Cup Final 'Goal of the Century'. This one wasn't anything to tell the grandchildren about. Spurs' players were exhausted. Heavy snow that winter had meant the postponement of half a dozen league games. With the cup fixtures added, Spurs' 15-man squad had got through 10 games in 20 days at one point. By the day of the replay, Miller, Hoddle and Galvin were all playing through injuries. Spurs won through a sixth-minute penalty, taken by Hoddle after Tony Currie had brought down Roberts in the box. After that it was just a question of hanging on to notch up the seventh FA Cup Final without defeat.

'I think the FA Cup in 1982 passed me by, really,' remembers Micky Hazard. 'Maybe it was because it was my first experience of playing in a cup final, but it was weird, like an out-of-body experience. Steve Perryman said he had it in the semi-final against Wolves in 1981, the same sensation. I was watching the game and my body was running around doing these things at the same time. I was in the game but I wasn't actually there. I was in a dream.'

It was a while before Spurs got their mojo back. Most of the 1982/83 season was a let-down. The FA Cup and League Cup went elsewhere, and so did the European Cup Winners' Cup. Even the return of Ardiles, who had been on loan to Paris St Germain while the Falklands War ran its course, wasn't enough of a lift. Then, with the signing of Alan Brazil from Ipswich Town in March, a Glasgow Scot with a head of magnificent blond topiary, Spurs rallied. By the time the season ended, they were fourth. With Liverpool, Watford and Manchester United, who finished above them, already qualified, Spurs clinched a place in Europe for 1983/84. Which was to end with one of the most dramatic, triumphant and emotional finales in Spurs' history.

Maybe the first month of the season should have been taken as a warning of the tumultuous highs and lows that the end of that season would bring. Near the end of Spurs' first home game against Coventry, Steve Archibald had a Carlos Tevez moment. When he picked up an injury on top of a knee problem already in place, he walked off the pitch and refused to go back on. Spurs, who had already used their subs, finished the game with 10 men. Burkinshaw's relationship with Archibald had never been warm. After the Coventry game, it froze over completely. Burkinshaw dropped him for a month, then put him on the bench for the away game at Watford on 24th September. It's a game most fans remember for the game-turning goal scored by Hoddle when, with Spurs 1-0 down, he got the ball with his back to goal, moved round a defender and chipped the ball in over the keeper's head. Archibald came off the bench to score the second and there was another from Hughton to make it 3-2 to Spurs.

Back in the side, Archibald scored 21 times in the league that season – the tally included doubles against Wolves, Luton, Sunderland and Arsenal – without him and Burkinshaw exchanging a word. Apart from a conversation about the transfer list that Archibald had been placed on. But with Ardiles struggling through injury and Spurs getting knocked out of both cups early doors and slipping down the league to eighth, there wasn't much for them or anyone else to talk about.

Except for the UEFA Cup. This began with a first-round demolition – 14-0 on aggregate – of the Irish side Drogheda and reached an early peak near the end of October in the second-round first leg against Feyenoord. Back then, the Feyenoord midfield was controlled by the ageing genius Johan Cruyff, who misguidedly assigned himself to mark Hoddle at White Hart Lane. Hoddle gave him a masterclass in creativity and control, topping it with a 40-yard pass that put Galvin through for Spurs' second goal. They were four ahead by half-time (though some classic Spurs generosity in defence let Feyenoord pull two back after the restart). 'I was a shadow without any presence,' was Cruyff's lament afterwards.

Spurs won the away leg 2-0, beat Bayern 2-1 on aggregate in the third round and came through 4-2 against FK Austria in the quarter-finals, the tasty nature of the home leg best summed up by the midfielder Istram Magyar who said: 'As for Miller and Roberts, they are both wrong in the head.' The semis against Hadjuk Split were about two of Peter Shreeve's homegrowns. In the first leg, Spurs scored first through Mark Falco but then let the lead slip through 10 bad minutes in the second half. With the away-goal advantage, it only needed Hazard's first European goal of the season, a 25-yarder after six minutes at White Hart Lane, to put Spurs into their first European final for 10 years. The last one had featured the riots of Rotterdam, an experience most people preferred to consign to the Room 101 of Spurs' history. This time it was going to be different.

Since letting Pat Jennings go to Arsenal in 1977, Burkinshaw had never found a copper-bottomed replacement. None of the three he tried –– Barry Daines, Mark Kendall and Milija Aleksic – had completely managed to fill the gap.

Then in the summer of 1981 he signed Ray Clemence from Liverpool. Already a veteran – he had done 14 years at Anfield – Clemence was 33 years old, with a career behind him that featured league titles, a European Cup, plus regular competition with Peter Shilton over who was going to mind the England net. But Burkinshaw had let Jennings go to Arsenal in the mistaken belief that he was past his best, and he wasn't going to make that mistake again. Clemence was organised, he was assertive, he was mentally strong. He was surely worth placing faith in.

While Clemence got on with lending some much-needed stability at the back, the other keepers departed except for Tony Parks, a homegrown coached from the age of 12 by Peter Shreeve and Ron Henry. Always the back-up keeper (at 16 he'd come on as a sub in a European Winners' Cup game), he had kept working on his game away from the spotlight. He expected life to be no different when Clemence came along. In the 1983/84 season, though, Clemence not only hit a patch of poor form but got injured against Fulham in the FA Cup – Roberts had to go in goal. The game ended in a draw and after that Parks was in business.

That is until the quarter-final against FK Austria at White Hart Lane. In that game he received a whack on the knee that needed stitches and subsequently became infected. This meant that a recharged Clemence was back in goal. Then, after the second leg against FK

Austria, during shooting practice on Friday morning, the last shot of the session caught Clemence on the edge of his finger and broke it.

So Parks came back again, and was so nervous against Hadjuk Split at White Hart Lane that he nearly juggled a cross into his own goal. But as the final approached, when he counted up the appearances, he worked out he'd been in the first team since January and had played 28 games, so it wasn't as if he was fresh out of the small time. He'd earned the right to be there facing Anderlecht.

That May, away to Anderlecht for the first leg, Spurs led through a Paul Miller header until five minutes from the end, when Morten Olsen toe-poked home a rebound from Frank Arnesen. By that time Perryman had been booked, for the second time in the tournament, which ruled him out of the second leg and pleased Anderlecht immensely. Spurs, surely, would struggle without his commitment.

It wasn't only Perryman who was missing from the starting 11 for the second leg. Clemence was out, so was Hoddle. Ardiles was on the bench. They were missing top, top players. The side was full of Peter Shreeve's homegrowns – Alistair Dick, Ian Crook, Mark Falco, Micky Hazard. And Parks. Jacky Munaron, his counterpart in the Anderlecht side, was Belgium's international goalkeeper. It wasn't just Spurs v Anderlecht, it was understudy v world class.

In the electric atmosphere that only European nights at White Hart Lane can provide, with a crowded Shelf packed out under the floodlights and Munaron playing a blinder, a stubborn Anderlecht went ahead on the hour. As Roberts, captain for the night, drove Spurs forward for the equaliser, Burkinshaw sent on Ardiles. The Argentinian was carrying an injury, but the move was the game-changer that inspired a relentless bombardment of Munaron's goal. With seven minutes left, Munaron batted away a shot from Archibald. As the ball was played back into the box, Ardiles got a toe to it and hit the bar. The last of the ensuing ricochets fell perfectly for Roberts, who scattered the ranks of defenders to blast the ball over the line. It might not have been true Spurs, but it was definitely true Roberts.

Thirty exhausted minutes of extra-time, with both sides feeling the pace, achieved nothing. So it was down to penalties. Roberts, captain for the night, put the first one away. Then Olsen, 1983 Danish Player of the Year, captain of Denmark, stepped up to face Parks.

Parks caught him glancing to the right. That, he decided, was where it was going. Olsen fired his shot low and Parks threw himself at it and turned the ball round the post.

Mark Falco, Gary Stevens and Steve Archibald all did the job for Spurs. Brylle, Scifor and Vercauteren answered them for Anderlecht. So, at 4–3, Danny Thomas prepared to take the final kick. The one that would give Spurs the trophy.

And he missed.

Fate had betrayed him. The devastation was plain on his face. The team grouped round him and led him back to the centre circle. Now it was down to Anderlecht's last man, Arnor Gudjohnsen, to score and send the shoot-out into sudden death. And it was down to Tony Parks to stop him. And he saved it.

'I got my hands on it, did a couple of rolls and got up and I was off.' he said. 'I genuinely didn't know what to do so I just ran. If that gate in the corner had been open, I would've been down at Seven Sisters in seconds. I remember Ray Clemence just clothes-lining me across the throat and I was under a pile of blokes. I looked up and saw Danny Thomas's face – the biggest thing in the penalty shoot-out was the two faces of Danny Thomas. The despair when he missed and the absolute ecstasy just seconds later.' And Roberts, who had been rejected by three clubs, who had come to Spurs through a chance meeting on a station platform between Bill Nicholson and a non-league anorak, lifted the trophy.

The triumph was mitigated by sadness, though. Years later, it was Ossie Ardiles who summed up the events of that night. 'We won the UEFA Cup,' he said, 'but this team was finishing its life.'

Ricky Villa had returned to Tottenham for the 1982/83 season, but this was the final year of his contract. Off he went to Miami to play for Fort Lauderdale Strikers in the North American League. Alan Brazil went to Manchester United for considerably more than Spurs had paid Ipswich. In August 1984, after appearing 189 times for Spurs and scoring 78 goals, Steve Archibald was transferred to Barcelona for

£1,150,000. When I interviewed him there in the summer of 1985, in the Catalonian sunshine, with Terry Venables as his manager, he was chatty and happy, not morose at all. Maybe El Tel was taking more care of him.

Those three weren't the only ones who left. At the beginning of April, Burkinshaw had given the board notice that he was quitting at the end of the season. Like a great film with a rubbish ending, he walked off the pitch after that triumphant UEFA Cup win and out of White Hart Lane for good.

To explain why that happened, you have to go back two years, to the arrival of one man at Tottenham Hotspur.

CHAPTER TWENTY-FOUR

DON DRAPER TAKES OVER SPURS

Oscar Wilde put the tragic irony of humanity's finest emotion in a nutshell when he said: 'Each man kills the thing he loves.' This isn't, of course, going to be a literary thesis. The point that is being made here is simply that the worst of outcomes can spring from the best of intentions. Which is what happened when Irving Scholar gained control of Tottenham Hotspur.

It came about like this. In 1979, inspired by the crowd-pulling potential of Ossie and Ricky, and the convenient timing of the club's centenary in 1982, the Tottenham board of directors committed themselves to rebuilding the dowdy and dilapidated West Stand. What made the idea all the more attractive was that planning restrictions at Highbury precluded the instalment of executive boxes at the home of their arch-rivals. The old wounds inflicted by Henry Norris back near the start of the century still pained. So cornering the north London corporate entertainment market in the face of the old enemy was a prospect that gave the board profound satisfaction.

The estimated building cost was £3 million, £200,000 more than the club's annual turnover. No problem. Leased for three years each at £90,000 a pop, the executive boxes, all 72 of them, would be the money-spinners that would soon have the stand paying for itself. The shortfall would be made up by a discreet appeal involving a thousand wealthy supporters contributing £10,000 each.

To which end, Arthur Richardson, Sidney Wale's successor as chairman, set up a special sales meeting at White Hart Lane to court them. One who turned up was the 33-year-old Irving Scholar, a multi-millionaire property developer and lifelong Spurs fan. In his teens he had stood on The Shelf. When it came to knowledge of club history, he was a human *Spurs Miscellany*. Domiciled in Monaco for tax purposes, he still managed to get to every home and away game most seasons. 'He was handsome,' says the author and football consultant Alex Fynn. 'He was Don Draper of *Mad Men*. Black hair. Angular face. Creative. The most generous of men. And Spurs was the love of his life.'

Scholar's original intention was simply to lease one of the new boxes. As a successful businessman and property developer, though, he recognised straight away that the stand's projected cost of £3 million was way too low, and offered Richardson his services as an unpaid advisor. Dismissing him as just another flash intruder who wanted to insinuate himself onto the board, Richardson turned the offer down.

The new West Stand was officially opened on Saturday, 6th February, 1982 by Sir Stanley Rous, the ageing president of the FA. Behind the scenes, the buzz of victory – Spurs beat Wolves 6-1 that day – was blemished somewhat by the knowledge that, as Scholar had predicted, the project had come in at more than a million pounds over budget. At the going rate for property in the early 1980s, that made it the most expensive stand in the country. Coupled with heavy spending on the team since the 1977/78 promotion season, the rebuilding of Archibald Leitch's ageing superstar had plunged the club into financial crisis.

St Paul's epiphany was on the road to Damascus. According to *Sick as a Parrot*, Chris Horrie's highly entertaining account of life at Spurs in the 1980s, Irving Scholar's was on the M1 on his way to watch Spurs away at Leeds when he decided he would rescue Tottenham Hotspur.

When Hunter Davies wrote *The Glory Game* in 1972 he described the set-up of the Tottenham board of directors thus: 'The Spurs board is a very tight little circle, like the board of all successful clubs. Getting into something like the Athenaeum is easy compared to getting on the board of Spurs. To be a director, the qualification is 10 shares, but even if you found someone willing to sell you 10 shares, the board has to approve every transfer. If they don't want you, even as a shareholder, that's it.'

The board of directors was made up of local businessmen, whose shares had mostly been handed down, over the decades, from father to son – Sidney Wale owned the most. The septuagenarian Arthur Richardson and his son Geoffrey ran a north London family waste paper business. Charles Cox, an elderly car dealer (he supplied motors to the royal family), had been the prime mover behind the veto of Blanchflower and Giles back in 1975. He was gone, to be replaced by Douglas Alexiou. But even Alexiou was part of the circle, being Sidney Wale's son-in-law.

Nevertheless, in partnership with another successful property developer, Paul Bobroff, Scholar stealthily set about stockpiling shares. Many belonged to little old ladies who had been left them by their husbands and believed them to be worthless. Judicious waving of cheque books brought more and more into Scholar's and Bobroff's possession.

But the real catalyst for the undoing of Arthur Richardson was his rift with Sidney Wale. That had originated in the close season after the 1982 FA Cup win, when Keith Burkinshaw took the team on a tour of Japan, Hong Kong and Bahrain. When Burkinshaw suggested that the directors and their wives might want to come along, Wale agreed but only to the inclusion of himself and Mrs W. When the others found out later that they'd missed out on the jolly, a peeved board, led by Arthur Richardson, moved to oust him.

It was the chance Scholar and Bobroff needed. Wale, in his own fit of pique, sold his shares to them. By November 1982 they had enough to wrest control from Richardson. Then in June 1983, with the intention of wiping out the debts and raising enough to spend on the star acquisitions who would bring the glory days back, they sold a new tranche of shares to make Tottenham a publicly owned company.

Two Tottenhams emerged. There was Tottenham Hotspur Football and Athletic Club – Douglas Alexiou, the sole survivor of the previous board, became chairman of that one. Then there was Tottenham Hotspur plc, the holding company, through which Spurs became the first football club to have a listing on the Stock Exchange. The flotation, which raised £3.8 million, was over-subscribed by three-and-a-half times. Small blocks of shares were bought by a large number of supporters. They weren't thinking about making a profit; they just wanted to feel part of the club.

Scholar's plan was to set up a commercial operation alongside the football that would generate enough money to subsidise the team. Within two years he had yanked Tottenham Hotspur towards modernity as the club exploited business possibilities no one in the English game had ever thought of before. The rest of football quickly cottoned on, in Manchester United's case by luring away Scholar's fellow-innovator Edward Freedman, who within a year at Tottenham had successfully paved the way on replica kits, videos, books and premium rate phone lines.

With the Wale and Richardson families gone, everything changed. Suddenly this was no longer a cosy family club run by local businessmen. Traditionally, the Spurs board had avoided publicity in order to put off any bothersome invasion of vulgar interlopers. In the same spirit, it had regarded advertising as a blight on White Hart Lane. Tottenham had been one of the very few clubs left that banned it from the ground. 'We've got an image at Spurs which we must maintain,' said one of the directors in *The Glory Game*. 'You don't have to lower it to get money. I don't want disc jockeys on the pitch or other things which some clubs have.'

But Scholar was smart enough and young enough to understand the value of television. He brought in Saatchi & Saatchi as Tottenham's advertising agency and marketing consultants. 'They thought we would do an image campaign,' says Alex Fynn, who was in charge of the account. '"Nonsense," we said. "You need to sell more season tickets and improve attendances."' A series of ads went out before the first home game of the season, against Coventry. It was another Spurs first

– no club had run a television advertising campaign before. 'The obligatory touch of televisual surprise,' wrote Chris Horrie, 'was provided by Mrs Ridlington, a bespectacled, white-haired granny who was pictured following the team on to the pitch, bedecked in her supporters' scarf.'

'Make sure you're one of the team' was the selling idea of the campaign. Unfortunately, it was a hostage to fortune. Then the team started struggling and the cry from the terraces was, 'Bring on Mrs Ridlington!'

'Ads only work when they're representing success,' says Alex Fynn. 'They were great pre-season. Then the team started doing badly. We were selling a poor product. So it stopped.'

But for a while that was the only dip in an otherwise upward trajectory. The share issue wiped out the debts and the club was moving into profit. Blue-chip companies were leasing the executive boxes and the banqueting suites were stuffed with punters – £1,500 would buy you the Bill Nicholson Suite for a day. From there you could take in the new-style pre-match entertainment. Gone were the police dogs jumping through hoops. In came Gerry and the Pacemakers, along came parades of camels and elephants – the latter in spite of severe misgivings by the groundsman: 'If one of those elephants s***s on the pitch . . .' One of the back office staff was therefore deployed to follow behind with a shovel. Then there was the grand plan to have the players parachute onto the pitch. Sadly, the insurance company decided it was a bad idea, so the back office had to do it instead. They all landed on the pitch apart from one who touched down outside the stadium. Unfortunately, he was the one who was carrying the match ball. Along with all this new pizazz, ticket prices went up.

Then Keith Burkinshaw walked out.

Not only were there two Tottenham Hotspurs, there were also two Irving Scholars. One was the innovative businessman, who put into place a series of projects designed to give the club a sound financial base. The other Irving Scholar was the fan who owned the club. Knowing what mattered to the fans, he organised the first testimonial for Bill Nicholson. He loved Spurs, he loved the players and was determined to do the best he could for them. When Ardiles, towards the end of his career, tentatively asked for a one-year contract at £75,000, Scholar sent him away with a two-year one at £80,000 a year. 'When it appeared that Danny Thomas would never recover from his horrendous knee injury,' wrote Alex Fynn and H. Davidson in *Dream On*, 'Scholar, rather than immediately claiming insurance, gave the player a new contract for a year with a 16 per cent salary increase.' He also, unfortunately, gave undisclosed loans to players without putting into place any structure for repayment, an indulgence that would later result in swingeing penalties being visited on the club by the Football Association.

Whereas the old board had kept a distance from the players, Scholar was on first-name terms with them all. In the past, the chairman never went down into the dressing room, except maybe to say a stilted 'Well done, lads' after a cup triumph. Scholar suffered no such awkwardness. Tony Parks recalls him after the 1984 UEFA Cup penalty shoot-out, sitting by the door with the trophy in his lap (he was in a wheelchair at the time, with his leg in a plaster cast having torn an Achilles tendon while taking part in a first-team practice match at Cheshunt). To him, owning Spurs was like having a giant book of living Panini stickers. He was hands-on. Too hands-on for Burkinshaw.

'He wanted to buy the players and arrange their contracts,' Burkinshaw said later. 'I wouldn't budge, and he made it clear that he wouldn't budge either, so that was the end of our relationship.'

So after three cups and the boldest bit of transfer dealing in history, Burkinshaw left. There was one more thing to add to his legacy, a comment attributed to him in the press that, even though he denies saying it, pretty much sums up what he felt about Spurs at the time: 'There used to be a football club over there.'

There still was. For the time being, at least.

The summer after Burkinshaw walked out, Scholar started the hunt for a new manager. The press conjectured that it was going to be Argentina coach and one-man ash cloud Luis Cesar Menotti, whose chain-smoking presence in the technical area was one of the leitmotifs of the 1978 World Cup. Scholar himself claimed later on that he arranged to take up-and-coming young Scottish manager Alex Ferguson off Aberdeen's hands, only for Fergie to back off 10 days before Spurs were due to parade him in front of the media. The result was that Scholar promoted Peter Shreeve, the one-time Reading player who, as part of the White Hart Lane fixtures and fittings since 1974, had been operating as Burkinshaw's assistant.

'Everybody who has been in that situation will say that becoming manager after being coach is a difficult step to take,' Shreeve recalled in *The Boys from White Hart Lane*. 'Everyone will also say, "Be yourself." I was determined not to change. We all worked hard together when I was coach so why should I do anything different as manager? But there's an inevitable difference when you change roles. When I was the youth-team coach, I was "Uncle Peter"; when I became first-team coach, I was "that so-and-so Shreevesie". The level of demand was that much higher – we needed to produce victories, not defeats. Some people might say I was a better Uncle Peter than I was the other, which might be fair comment.'

That season anyway, 'that so-and-so-Shreevsie' got most of it right, partly thanks to some neat work in the transfer market where, to polyfilla the holes in the front line left by the sale of Archibald and Brazil, Spurs invested in Les Allen's boy Clive from QPR, with John Chiedozie brought in from Notts County to act as his supplier. The buys looked sound. On the opening day of the season, away to Everton, with Hazard as playmaker in place of the injured Hoddle, Allen scored two and Chiedozie one in a 4-1 win.

After taking three points from the first two matches at the Lane, there followed a mini-slump away to Sheffield Wednesday and Sunderland (where Roberts and Allen both collected red cards). But then came six wins on the spin, with Garth Crooks regaining his place from Allen and bagging not just four in the 9-1 aggregate win over Halifax Town in the League Cup competition, but also three against Portuguese outfit Sporting Braga as Tottenham began their defence of the UEFA Cup. It meant an impressive 9-0 victory over two legs. At that stage, Spurs were unstoppable. Home to Liverpool – it was

Perryman's 600th league game for Spurs – another Crooks goal won it for them 1-0. They were second, three points behind Arsenal, until they lost to Manchester United at Old Trafford and Everton overtook them.

In the middle of all this, the defence of the UEFA Cup was going on. After seven months out with an Achilles injury, Hoddle came on as a sub for Hazard in the second-round tie against Brugge in Belgium. With Brugge 2-0 up, Hoddle lasted 23 minutes, picking up yellow then red for successive niggling offences. Allen came on for Crooks and scored three minutes from time to give Spurs the crucial away goal. Back home, he scored the match-winner as Spurs beat Liverpool twice in 19 days in the third round of the League Cup.

With a three-goal win over Brugge in the second leg of the UEFA Cup, Spurs were up against Bohemians Prague in the next round. They were lucky boys to have Clemence in the home leg. Outclassed, they won the game 2-0 thanks to an own goal and an 89th-minute drive from their best player on the night, Gary Stevens. Seven minutes into the return leg, Falco headed his 15th goal of the season to put Spurs 3-0 up on aggregate and take the pressure off. The Czech side vented their frustration on Hoddle who was carried off on a stretcher at half-time, suffering from a dead leg, concussion, and a deep cut over his eye that required 12 stitches.

Hoddle was not the only one on the sick list. Shreeve was hoping to bring back Ardiles, who had only managed 13 games in two-and-a-half years after a stress fracture to his shin and surgery on a long-term knee problem. In the event he was three months away from a comeback. Against Sunderland, Clive Allen suffered an excruciating groin injury, self-inflicted when he crossed the ball with his left foot, as Spurs left the League Cup at the fifth-round stage. Allen only managed three more minutes on a football pitch during the rest of the season.

Even so, that winter Spurs started to look convincing for the title, with seven wins and six draws including a 2-1 beating of Arsenal at Highbury. Then the bandwagon started to rattle slightly. Liverpool booted them out of the FA Cup. Gary Mabbutt broke his leg against

West Brom. At White Hart Lane, Steve Perryman scored the only goal of the game in the first leg of the UEFA Cup quarter-final against Real Madrid, deflecting a cross from the byline. Unfortunately, it was into his own net. In Spurs' next home match, a 2-1 defeat by Manchester United, Gary Stevens damaged knee ligaments during a goalmouth skirmish and joined Allen and Mabbutt as long-term invalids. The UEFA Cup slipped out of Spurs' hands in the Santiago Bernabeu with a 0-0 draw that featured Perryman getting sent off in the 79th minute.

So if Spurs wanted silverware, it would have to be the league. With nine of the remaining 14 games at home, they had to be favourites. Ardiles came back and scored in a 5-1 defeat of Southampton, but within days Hughton, playing for the Republic of Ireland in a friendly at Wembley, injured his knee. He was challenging for a ball with Hoddle at the time.

With the squad thinning out like a piece of pulled chewing gum, Spurs lost their next three home games against Aston Villa, Arsenal and Ipswich. The crucial game was the one against Everton, and they lost that too. Everton went on to win the title and Liverpool beat Spurs for second place on goal difference.

There were the usual what-might-have-beens. If Allen hadn't missed 27 games through injury. If Ardiles had been able to come back earlier. If Chiedozie's crosses from the byline had matched the standard of his runs up the flank. In fact, Chiedozie had only one more season left at White Hart Lane. Plagued by injury and supplanted in the line-up, he only played once more for Spurs. The name of the player who took his place is indelibly associated, through no fault of his own, with triggering off the most critical period in Spurs' history.

CHAPTER TWENTY-FIVE

WHERE'S ALL THE PLAYERS GONE?

On 1st July, 1985, Shreeve signed Christopher Roland Waddle from Newcastle, the club that had rescued him from non-League Tow Law Town as a 19-year-old to play in a side that included Kevin Keegan and Peter Beardsley. It cost Newcastle £1,000 to sign the winger then known as 'Widdly', who had been making ends meet by working in a meat pie factory (he made the seasonings for sausages, allowing the press to describe any goal scored by him as 'sizzling'.) Spurs paid £590,000 for him, buying Newcastle time to stave off relegation to the Second Division for four more years. It was not going to be the last time that Waddle had his uses as an appreciating asset.

It's impossible to say what prompted him to do it, but Waddle sported two hairdos at once. The one at the front was a bouffant. At the back, slightly lighter in tone, was a Jennifer Aniston, shoulder length with demure flick-ups. He once had a penalty shoot-out with the German striker Rudi Völler to decide who had the best mullet. He won and was awarded Mullet of the Year. His really awesome talent, though, was with the ball at his feet. He learned what he needed to know while playing 40-a-side games in his native Sunderland between teams featuring a wild mismatch of ages (as an eight-year-old, he often found himself nutmegging people 20 years older and several feet taller) and strips. In those conditions, the only way to ensure someone passed to him was to stand out in some way. So he became a master dribbler.

He wasn't necessarily a footballer's natural shape. Slim but unwieldy off the ball, he wasn't blessed with outstanding pace either but, bounding rather than running down the wing, the ball apparently connected by some invisible magnetic influence, he was a profoundly confusing force that defeated a succession of defenders. Against them he would stamp one leg then the other as though treading out a fire, drop one shoulder, wiggle a knee in one direction then head in the other. They never seemed to learn.

Waddle scored twice on his league debut, a 4–0 home win over Watford on the opening day of the 1985/86 season, but he was joining a team that was in transition. Even though he clicked with Clive Allen up front, even with Paul Allen − Clive's cousin − joining Hoddle and Ardiles in midfield, Shreeve's rejigged line-up was less successful than anticipated. There was an end–of–days feeling about everything. Like Hoddle and Ardiles, Galvin, Roberts, Miller and Hughton were all veterans of the Burkinshaw glory days. Perryman had played in the era of Chivers and Gilzean, Mullery and Jennings. The result was a mid–table finish, not high enough for Irving Scholar. Shreeve was sacked.

Asked later about the end of a job that had started so promisingly, he was good-naturedly fatalistic. 'The posse catches up with you,' he told the writers Martin Cloake and Adam Powley. 'In a John Wayne film the cowboys get together and go off and hunt the villain as a posse. It doesn't matter who you are, how good you are, the posse catches up with you. Circumstances come together and they get you. That's when they say, "All the best, Pete; fantastic, but see you later."' (And they did, but that's another story.)

To replace Shreeve, Scholar took on a youngish David Pleat, who had followed a career as a winger curtailed by injury by taking Luton Town from the Second Division to the First. There he prevented them from going down again and established a reputation along the way for putting together sides that played attractive attacking football. Mind you, his main claim to celebrity at the time was being televised skipping joyfully, all Hush Puppies and flapping tie, onto the pitch after a last-minute goal by the Serbian defender Raddy Antic against Manchester City prevented Luton from plummeting back into Division Two in 1983.

At White Hart Lane, Scholar's new manager cut a grimmer figure as he went for a clear-out of old stock. Roberts knew where he stood almost immediately. 'I got a phone call from Pleat. The first words he ever said to me were, "You're not my sort of player, you're on the list and as soon as I get the right offer you'll be sold."'

Perryman had made his last appearance at White Hart Lane on 2nd March, 1986, when Spurs lost 2-1 to Liverpool. The defeat meant they had only won once in eight league games, a 2-1 victory at Sheffield Wednesday in their previous match. After an FA Cup defeat to Everton two days later, Shreeve had dropped him. There was no attempt to use his emotional intelligence and motivational skills or reward his dogged loyalty to Spurs by putting him on the coaching staff. After a record 655 appearances in a one-club career that began in 1969, he was shunted off to Oxford United.

In place of Roberts, Pleat signed Richard Gough from Dundee for £750,000 and installed him as captain in defence alongside Mabbutt. Steve Hodge came in from Aston Villa to join Ardiles, Paul Allen, Hoddle and Waddle (now inevitably rechristened 'Wad' to go with 'Hod') in a five-man midfield that for the time was revolutionary. In front, Clive Allen played as a lone forward. Fully fit, in a reshaped line-up, he was Roy of the Rovers, jumping off the pages of the comic. He shot, he scored. Forty-nine goals – 33 in the league, 16 more in the cups – resulted.

Outside the penalty box, Allen was on the average side of remarkable. Inside, where mysteriously he seemed to appear just in the right place for the ball to land at his feet when he saw it lift off someone else's boot, he was as deadly as Greaves, whose record he broke. Even in that era it was almost unfeasible for one man to notch up so many. His goalscoring enabled Spurs to chase a treble of title, league and FA Cup. Against Arsenal in the Littlewoods Cup semi-final, Spurs' class and performance were summed up in a quote from *The Independent*:

'No attacking side can be more difficult to deal with than Spurs at the moment.'

'At the moment' was the operative phrase.

Spurs won the first leg at Highbury 1-0, courtesy of an Allen goal (who else?). He scored again to make it 2-0 on aggregate in the return at White Hart Lane. An announcement over the tannoy at half-time informed fans that tickets for the final would be on sale at the Park Lane ticket office at the end of the game. Legend has it that George Graham used the announcement to fire his team up (David Pleat reckons it's more likely 'someone in the tunnel mentioned it as they came out'), but, whatever, Arsenal fought back vigorously and goals from Viv Anderson and Niall Quinn forced a replay.

A third Allen goal of the tie gave Spurs the lead in the third match, but again Arsenal stormed back to win 2-1, the late David Rocastle grabbing the winner. 'Arguably, this tie was when the fortunes of each club turned,' says Martin Cloake, 'with Arsenal on the up, and Spurs on the way down.'

In a rerun of the 1984/85 season, the title slipped away too, with Everton and Liverpool finishing above them. Which left the FA Cup.

Having overpowered Watford in the semi-final, Spurs faced a side that, surely, they could not lose to. No one fancied Coventry. They were a team without pedigree. That was how it looked to the fans, anyway, when Clive Allen scored after two minutes. Sure, Coventry equalised soon afterwards, but Mabbutt put Spurs back in the lead again. And then Coventry, the side no one thought had a prayer, drew level to take the game into extra-time. In the extra period, a cross hit Mabbutt and looped over Ray Clemence's head into the goal. Coventry City 3 Spurs 2. The unthinkable had happened. Spurs had lost an FA Cup Final. The season that had promised everything, the season that was going to see them win another Double, had left them with nothing.

'The fact is,' David Lacey wrote in *The Guardian*, 'that failing to finish opponents off is one of the prime reasons why Tottenham, after playing some of the most attractive football, have ended the season without a prize.'

It's easy to conclude that the 1987 cup final is something Mabbutt would prefer to forget, but he sees it differently. 'It was a great cup final,' he says. 'To be honest, you go and block a cross and 99 out of a 100 times it works. But it just hit my knee and I could see it going over Ray's head into the corner. I'm still a legend in Coventry. Free food and drink for life.' Coventry fans so appreciated what he did for them that they named a fanzine after the iconic moment: *Gary Mabbutt's Knee*.

Any regrets he has are centred on the loss of Gough, whose partnership with Mabbutt in defence had begun to chip away at Tottenham's reputation for flawed defending but who, early in the 1987/88 season, was allowed to return to Scotland. Said to be 'homesick', he joined Rangers, becoming the first Scottish player to be signed for over £1 million. The Spurs board made little effort to keep him, though no one wondered why. 'We had out best chance of a league title under David Pleat,' says Mabbutt. 'I had my best partnership in defence with Richard Gough. We had one season together, great understanding, comfortable at the back. It was,' he concludes wistfully, 'one of the best squads ever assembled.'

That day at Wembley was Hoddle's last appearance in a Spurs shirt too. He left for Arsène Wenger's Monaco, announcing that he was going where his style of play would be more appreciated. There are a number of ways you can sum up Hoddle in his time at Spurs. You can paint him as the press and a succession of England managers saw him, a frustrating enigma who entranced with his vision and creative play, didn't do his share of hard graft and faded as the game went on. Or you can just run the goals through your mind: the one after the amazing run against Oxford United, the volley against Manchester United, the one against Nottingham Forest, when the ball didn't touch down once from the goalie's clearance upfield to Gerry Armstrong's head-on to the volley he put past Peter Shilton.

'I wasn't a great goalscorer, but I scored great goals,' is how he sums himself up. His response to accusations of being a luxury player had echoes of Danny Blanchflower's riposte: 'It's the bad players who are a luxury.'

'I used to laugh my head off when people said it,' Hoddle told a

Times journalist in 2008. 'I'd think, "What about the run-of-the-mill players – there are hundreds of them in this country. Are they not luxury players?"'

By the time he went to Monaco, Hoddle was coming to the end of an England career that never took off in the way it should have done. Fifty-three caps might be judged good going by most standards, but to be unwilling to build a side round a phenomenon like Hoddle, a player as unique and marvellous and game-changing as a Maradona or a Ronaldo or a Messi, just exposes the timidity and lack of imagination of the England management in his era.

England weren't good enough for him. Tottenham Hotspur in the years between 1977 and 1986, the years of Ardiles and Villa, Crooks and Archibald, Perryman and Mabbutt, were. And here's Hoddle now, beating practically the whole Oxford side on his own to score his farewell goal, blowing kisses to the crowd as the applause rains down . . .

Some fans carried on wearing his name across their shirts. And in our hearts some of us still do.

Looking back on that losing cup final against Coventry, two things stand out. The first was the shambles over the kit that day. Half the team (including Glenn Hoddle) took to the pitch wearing shirts missing sponsor Holsten's logo due to a pre-match mix-up. The other shambles was the own goal in extra-time. Together they were a metaphor for the chaos that was about to engulf the Scholar regime.

First off, they needed a new manager again. When, in the summer of 1986, Irving Scholar had prised David Pleat away from Luton Town to take over from Peter Shreeve, it was a smart appointment. In his first season, Pleat had brought them close to another Double. Then it went pear-shaped. Eighteen months into the job, Pleat found himself the subject of a sequence of mortifying allegations about his private life in the tabloids. Resignation duly followed. But the dice seemed to have rolled Scholar's way. His first choice for Shreeve's replacement had always been the charismatic, multi-talented Englishman coaching Barcelona, but Terry Venables had opted to stay in Catalonia. Pleat got the job instead. Now, conveniently, Scholar's primary target was available.

A month earlier, after the fans had turned on him after a bad start to the season, Venables had jacked in the Barcelona job and headed off on holiday to Florida. Not that he anticipated an extended spell on gardening leave. There was already a tasty project being lined up for him in the form of an offer to manage Juventus. That was before Irving Scholar got on his case. Forty-eight hours after Pleat's sacking, the Tottenham chairman had tracked Venables down to a hotel in West Palm Beach and talked him into passing up Juventus in favour of Spurs.

Venables arrived at White Hart Lane that November, sweeping through the gates in a black BMW whose tyres must have sagged under the weight of the hopes it was carrying. True, when he'd briefly played for Spurs, the fans had been decidedly underwhelmed, but everyone had forgotten about that. On the terraces banners saying 'Welcome Home El Tel' proclaimed the faith. Here was the coaching genius who had delivered the Spanish title to Barcelona for the first time in 11 years, the Dagenham boy whose versatile and restless mind had, back in the 1970s, co-produced four novels with the writer Gordon Williams and co-created a TV detective series, *Hazell*, while simultaneously pursuing a managerial career with Crystal Palace and then Queens Park Rangers. Here was Scholar's Messiah. Here was the man who was going to bring back the glory days to Tottenham Hotspur.

Right from the start Venables had few illusions about the mission in front of him. His first game ended with a 2-0 defeat by Liverpool. True, Liverpool were the best team in the land, but a week later Spurs lost 1-0 at home to tail-enders Charlton Athletic. The great team built by Burkinshaw and thrillingly reshaped by Pleat had lost Hoddle and Gough, two of its main men. With Ray Clemence nearing pensioning-off time, Spurs were shipping goals again. Gary Stevens, the holding midfielder who had been there since the last days of Burkinshaw and who might have dealt with the most glaring examples of defensive casualness, was injured. Steve Hodge, one fifth of the midfield, wanted out. And up front, Clive Allen had lost the thread of last season's form, while his new partnership with the Belgian striker Nico Claesen had so far failed to come good. In the words of Paul Miller: 'When Terry

Venables took over the club he said, "Where's all the players gone?"'

Not that Venables's earliest foray into the transfer market set the heart racing. The first item ticked off on his shopping list was Terry Fenwick, the leggy full-back brought on by him at QPR. Which was the cause of the first spat with his chairman, for whom Fenwick wasn't sprinkled with enough stardust. 'Scholar,' said Venables, 'was uninterested in signing defenders, preferring the "great box office", as he described it, of signing star attackers.'

In response, Venables pointed out that it was actually Arsenal, the great proponents of a solid defence, who were winning things. 'It can't always be showbiz-style and there are going to be days when you have to earn the right to play attractive football,' he said later.

So in February, he brought in Bobby Mimms from Everton as Clemence's successor, and Paul Stewart from Manchester City to boost the impact of Allen and Claesen up front. The quick fix didn't work. After New Year's Day, Spurs won just three more games in the league. That season they finished 13th, three places lower than they'd been when Venables arrived, having scored 26 goals in 25 games, and 38 in total in the league. It was the lowest tally since the club joined the Football League in 1908. Plus Port Vale of the Third Division knocked them out of the FA Cup. Only six months after being welcomed back as 'El Tel', *The Spur* fanzine, happily followed by *The Sun*, had rechristened him 'El Veg'.

But with the recruitment of one player, Venables was hoping that would all change.

In 2007, while I was writing about Bill Nicholson for the *Tottenham Hotspur Opus*, I asked the *Daily Mirror* journalist Ken Jones to explain how someone so apparently down-to-earth and pragmatic could have put together the most sparkling and inspiring side in the history of football. 'It's a mystery, really,' Jones told me. 'Bill Nick himself was a dour wing half-back as player but a romantic when it came to coaching. He put his imprint on that Double team.'

Then again, you might have guessed there was another side to Nicholson if you glimpsed his handwriting. 'In 1959, when I had just started out as a reporter, one of my first games was at Tottenham,' says Nicholson's biographer Brian Scovell. 'I was sitting behind Bill, and I watched him making notes in *copperplate* [extravagant calligraphic writing].' Terry Dyson puts it more succinctly. 'It was flowery!'

If you want confirmation, it's there in a screwed-up piece of paper found in Bill's waste basket by a cleaner just before Christmas 1987 and passed on to Gerry Lambert, Tottenham's head of security. Written after a scouting mission to Newcastle, Nicholson's assessment of Paul Gascoigne reads in places more like a beautifully-penned love poem than a set of scouting notes.

19.12.87
West Ham 2 Newcastle 1
Has two good feet. 5ft 10. 20.
   He has explosive pace off the mark. He seldom stands and watches, in fact he always wants the ball, but he is a bit undisciplined and often goes where he pleases. He has great control and confidence on the ball, and good vision. He virtually invites the tackle but always seems to be that little bit faster than his opponent. He screens the ball well and he turns so tightly with the ball with a full knowledge of what and who is around him. Some of his passing was exceptional too so that I can't think of anyone else in the F/C with similar ability . . . He was very reckless in the tackle that got him his caution . . . But he is still very young and just has to be recommended.

It was a more considered assessment than the one Jack Charlton had given Gascoigne when he joined Newcastle. That one was, 'There's a lot of fat there, but I'm told underneath you've got a bit of skill.'

That understatement was true. Gascoigne wasn't just England's most naturally talented prospect, he was also its most captivating and compelling to watch. 'He was a swashbuckling footballer who could go past opponents as if they weren't there,' said his contemporary, Jamie Redknapp. 'He wasn't the quickest but would use his elbow to muscle past someone, or he'd shift the ball quickly from one foot to the other and be away.'

A month later at Newcastle, Venables saw for himself what this chunky, pugnacious 20-year-old could do. 'I had selected Terry Fenwick to mark him, and early in the game as Gascoigne took possession, Terry tightened himself right up and really hit him as hard as he could but Gazza just leaned in to him and Terry bounced off,' recalled Venables later. 'We knew about Gazza's skills, but now we discovered that you could not kick him out of the game either.'

Gascoigne was impish and child-like, he seemed devoid of fear and he was the sort of player who as long as he was on the pitch made you think you were in with a chance. Cole Moreton in *The Independent* likened him to 'a manic kid rushing around the playground, nicking the ball off the big boys and beating them for skill every time'. Wild-eyed, pink-faced, sometimes he just ran around where the fancy took him. After he came on as sub and scored in England's 5-0 defeat of Albania, Bobby Robson said, 'If the ball had been kicked out of the ground, he would have chased it.'

This wayward enthusiasm often morphed into a kind of deranged recklessness. When he was a trainee at Newcastle, he got into a strop because he felt picked on, so he commandeered a groundsman's tractor and rammed it into the dressing room wall. But like no other player, Gascoigne inspired extraordinary affection in fans (and, later, celebrity mates like Chris Evans and Danny Baker), an affection which in due course he happily utilised by getting them involved in mad exploits – one fan found himself being driven off on the roof of a van after Gascoigne persuaded him to climb up there to retrieve a traffic cone placed on it.

That, of course, would happen way into the future. Back then, at St James' Park in January 1988, with Gascoigne scoring both goals in Newcastle's 2-0 win, Venables was convinced. Here was the player to lead his revival of Spurs.

Which was a problem because Liverpool and Manchester United were after him too. In fact, by that summer Gascoigne had already told Fergie he was up for a move to Old Trafford. That was before Gascoigne's fellow north-easterner Chris Waddle was put on the case. Sweet-talked down to London to have a look at the White Hart Lane set-up, Gascoigne and an entourage of mates were put up at the club's expense at the West Lodge Park Hotel in Hadley Wood. They wrought havoc. After finalising the deal with Scholar, Gascoigne expressed his gratitude: 'We'd like to thank you for the best three days of our lives.' Gascoigne's £2 million transfer fee was a new British record. Probably the hotel bill was, too.

Early in 2012, Ferguson was still harbouring regrets at missing out. 'Gascoigne was unbelievable,' Ferguson told his interviewer, DJ Spoony, on Radio 5 Live. 'We should have got him . . . If you look at English football since they won the World Cup in 1966, you would have to say Gascoigne is the one real world star they have produced. He could have played for Brazil.'

And instead he was playing for Spurs. Though not on the opening day of the 1988/89 season. While the rest of the football world was thronging through the late summer sunshine to their ground of choice, and while the Spurs fans were keyed up with near manic anticipation at the prospect of a Gascoigne-Waddle-Stewart attack knocking in a shedload of goals against mediocre Coventry, the players were being rerouted to Mill Hill for an afternoon of training.

To explain just why that came about needs a bit of a back-flip in time. Intent on pressing ahead with the commercial development of White Hart Lane, the Tottenham directors had given the go-ahead for the rebuilding of Archibald Leitch's East Stand. The plan was for it to match the standard – and the money-stream – of the West Stand, which meant increasing the number of executive boxes from 72 to 108. That, in turn, involved getting rid of its famous middle section of terracing, The Shelf.

In so doing, they would be destroying a revered totem of Spurs' history. At other grounds, the club's hardcore fans traditionally massed behind the goal. Spurs fans were unusual. They gathered along the side, on The Shelf, where they had the finest view in the ground. Then in February 1987, they discovered it was to be ripped apart.

'It was a magnificent standing area,' says Rick Mayston. 'It was very important to me; it was where I'd stood for years.' Mayston proceeded to start a campaign group, Left On The Shelf, which, at the final game of the 1987/88 season, staged the largest sit-in ever seen at an English ground to mark the end of the best terrace in the country. More than that, they got the stand listed, and won a concession to retain part of the standing area underneath the executive boxes. The protests and subsequent amendments to the plans, though, delayed the building work. By 17th August, 1988, the opening day of the season, with the main works completed but rubble still left over the place, the ground was declared unsafe and the game against Coventry had to be called off.

As a punishment, the Football League deducted two points from Tottenham's Division One total, though that was later rescinded and replaced with a £15,000 fine. Meanwhile, Gascoigne's Spurs debut came the following week against Newcastle.

Gascoigne was to get less than a hero's welcome at his old club. Outside St James' Park, someone set up a stall selling Mars bars in a garage forecourt in response to Gazza's revelation in a recent interview that he was partial to them. Every time he went near the crowd, fans pelted him with them. He was the turncoat, the traitor, the fat bastard who'd left them to get rich. Venables took him off before the end and he was booed all the way to the tunnel.

Otherwise it wasn't a bad afternoon for Spurs. Two down by half-time, they came back with a goal. Waddle scored straight from the kick-off, and a follow-up by Terry Fenwick made it 2-2. It had been a show of talent and spirit. Close to £5 million had been spent on the squad in just six months. There was real confidence around the place that the title was there for the taking.

Instead, a week into November 1988, Spurs were bottom of the First Division after losing 3-1 at home to Derby County. 'What's the difference between Spurs and the Star of David?' went the joke doing the rounds (and it wouldn't be for the last time, either). Answer: 'The Star of David's got six points.' Winning just once in their first 10 league games, they had made their worst start to a season since the last days of Nicholson. In the papers, Gascoigne was being labelled a £2 million turkey. Stewart, who had crowned his debut by missing a penalty, was failing to pose any kind of goal threat, scoring just once in those first 10 games. Some of the fans took against him – Venables knew all about how that felt, having suffered the same sort of treatment playing for Tottenham back in the '60s.

But the fury directed at Mimms, now widely known as 'Booby Mimms', was even more vigorous. The demoralised, luckless goalkeeper was also the butt of his team-mates' frustration as he conceded 22 goals in the first quarter of the season.

The dismal run continued into the new year. Spurs lost 2-0 to Arsenal before being knocked out of the FA Cup by Second Division Bradford City at Valley Parade. That performance sealed Mimms's fate. Venables replaced him with the Norwegian goalkeeper Erik Thorsvedt, who promptly marked his debut by dropping the ball into his own net against Nottingham Forest.

That said, as Thorsvedt eased himself into the role (and won himself the nickname of 'Erik The Viking' to signify the fans' approval), Gascoigne's form improved, and with Fenwick moving back to partner Mabbutt, the season revived. Waddle went on to have his best season ever, scoring 14 league goals, two more than Stewart. In their final 15 games, Spurs only lost twice and finished in sixth place. Arsenal were champions, mind.

'Which was a truly terrible moment,' says Martin Cloake, 'because at that time Arsenal didn't win things.'

That summer Venables tried to find a solution to the goal shortage by homing in on Matt Le Tissier. The Southampton striker was enthusiastic, leaving Venables with a 'signed' contract which Venables stashed away in the safe ready to produce at the end of the season when Le Tissier's contract with Southampton had expired, so he could register it with the FA and the Football League. Then, abruptly, Le Tissier pulled out of the move, later explaining that his fiancée hadn't fancied moving to London.

So Le Tissier stayed with Southampton and Venables lobbed £1.5 million Barcelona's way to capture Gary Lineker. Included in the price was Nayim, already on loan to Spurs. 'On this occasion,' said Venables later, 'the Tottenham board readily agreed to make the money available to buy players rather than clothing companies, even though it later transpired that the club barely had two coppers left to rub together.'

Lineker had charm, intelligence, ambition, good manners and a cool head – he'd never received a single yellow card, let alone a red. He was also the finest deliverer of goals in Europe. He'd been the inexhaustible supplier of them at Leicester and Everton and the winner of the Golden Boot at the 1986 World Cup in Mexico. That was the year he went to Barcelona, brought there for £2.8 million by Venables. He did the business there, too, in a side that won the Copa del Rey and the Cup Winners' Cup. But then Johann Cruyff took over, started playing him out of position and then left him out of the first team. Lineker, not surprisingly, grabbed the opportunity to get back together with his former manager.

For the fans, it seemed as if they were about to enter Elysium. They had their own holy trinity, they had the Law, Best and Charlton of the era: Gascoigne, Lineker and Waddle. Flair, vision and skill. In their thousands they convinced themselves that Spurs were capable of clinching their first title in nearly three decades. Then, on the morning of the press conference scheduled to unveil Tottenham's new signing to the world, Scholar bounced into Venables's office with jaw-dropping news. 'You're never going to believe this,' he jabbered excitedly, 'but we've just had an offer of £2 million for Waddle.'

'Yeah, so what?'

'It's from Bernard Tapie.'

The owner of Olympique de Marseille was a high-rolling Eurocrat, and the fact that he was behind the bid altered Venables's thinking. If Tapie's heart was set on Waddle, he might be prepared to up the bid considerably. 'If we did have to lose Waddle,' Venables said later, 'we could at least use the money to add some common sense to the "great box office" by buying two or three defenders to sort out the defence.'

'Tell him we want £6 million,' he told Scholar.

They didn't get it, not quite. But over several weeks Scholar managed to push it up to an incredible £4.25 million, then the third-highest transfer fee in the history of the game. Neither Scholar nor Venables had wanted to lose him, but for that money Spurs were always going to allow Waddle to leave for the South of France.

And even then, as things turned out, it wasn't enough. Not nearly enough.

CHAPTER TWENTY-SIX

GAZZAMANIA

In the dressing room everyone was gobsmacked by Waddle's departure. 'We had just bought Gary Lineker,' says Mabbutt, 'so Waddle would have been the perfect player to give him quality crosses into the box. With Gazza coming through the middle as well, it would have been a mouth-watering prospect.' Selling him, he concluded, made no sense. The fans felt the same way. A cover, now iconic, of *The Spur* fanzine had Lineker shaking hands with Venables and saying, 'I'm really looking forward to playing with Chris Waddle,' while Venables responds with, 'Er, there's something I've been meaning to tell you.' Tongue in cheek, the fanzine also launched a 'Buy Back Chris Waddle' campaign – donations of £10,000 or more required.

The sale had made perfect sense to Venables when he had agreed to it. He'd thought the massive profits would be ploughed back into the squad. Instead, just a third of the money came his way, restricting his purchases to the modest rather than the spectacular. Steve Sedgeley, smart on the ball if deficient in pace, arrived from Coventry for £750,000. Pat van den Hauwe, whose nickname 'Psycho' was no barrier to a rather interesting celebrity life (his fame peaked when he married Bill Wyman's ex, Mandy Smith), signed from Everton for £575,000.

Even that was pushing the boat out a bit far. The simple truth was that Spurs could barely afford even those players. Scholar's business plan had been to develop the commercial side of Tottenham Hotspur plc in order to bankroll the star acquisitions. As part of that, the club had signed a deal with the Danish sportswear company Hummel to market replica Spurs shirts in the UK. The hoped-for success in shouldering adidas and Umbro out of the market didn't happen, though the business trundled along. Then, fatally, the brand was expanded to produce a range of sporty fashionwear (fans of a certain age will recall Hoddle in Hummel). Along with other acquisitions came more clothing companies. Martex made women's fashionwear and Stumps produced cricket and tennis gear.

Which was when the law of unintended consequences intervened. All the commercial ventures into which Spurs had diversified to generate income for the club were now achieving precisely the opposite; they were bleeding money.

'The rest of the Waddle cash disappeared down the plughole of Tottenham's debts, and within six months, instead of buying more players, I was being told to sell more of the ones we already had,' Venables said later.

Meanwhile, the price of refurbishing the East Stand, originally costed out at £4.5 million, had doubled. In the boardroom, the heat was on. The financially giddying heights of the 1980s were all but over. It transpired that when the club had moved for Lineker earlier in the summer they hadn't been able to buy him outright because of the debts of the plc. They had made a £600,000 down payment, one half of the £1.2 million transfer fee, and Scholar had had to guarantee the rest of the deal with his own money. Now the plc didn't have enough in the coffers to come up with the final payments. Nor did Scholar himself. The prospect loomed of Lineker being repossessed by Barcelona.

But there was no way Spurs would be able to justify letting their star striker go. In Waddle's case it had been simple. As soon as the player realised he'd be able to set himself up for life with the move to Marseille, he was all for it. In Lineker's case, that excuse was a non-starter. If Lineker went, the whole world would know about Tottenham's increasingly desperate financial plight.

So Scholar organised a secret loan of £1.1 million from the newspaper publisher Robert Maxwell to cover the transfer of Lineker and prevent his being recalled to Barcelona. He just had to hope that his boardroom colleagues would not find out that he was short of money and borrowing on the quiet. Otherwise, all hell would be let loose.

After the usual stuttering start – one win out of six games launched the 1989/90 season – Spurs produced a streak of form that had them winning eight of their final 10 games to claim third place in the table behind Liverpool and Arsenal, playing the kind of attractive football that was Venables's trademark. Lineker bagged 24 league goals and Gascoigne came good to the extent that his place in the England squad for the 1990 World Cup in Italy now seemed certain.

A few months earlier, that hadn't been the case. Bobby Robson, the England manager, had been unimpressed by Gascoigne's inability to perform to a team plan or be anything but a brilliant, reckless, crowd-seducing individualist. After the friendly against Albania, he had pronounced him 'daft as a brush.' A fat lot Gascoigne cared. He just appeared at the next England training get-together with a toilet brush stuffed down one of his socks.

Robson, by now a derided figure in the tabloids, caved in to public pressure and included him in the 1990 World Cup squad. He had been helped in his decision by Gascoigne's thrilling performance in a warm-up friendly against Czechslovakia. At Wembley, the whole country could see what he was capable of as he scored one goal and set up the other three in England's 4-2 win.

But the incredible displays came at a price. To play like that, Gascoigne had to be pumped up on adrenaline. In his case, the supply was not just plentiful but complicated by the lack of a stop valve. In Italy, as part of the World Cup television coverage, the teams were lined up for the cameras and each player was asked to mouth his name. Gascoigne settled for 'f***ing w*****'. The BBC had to use the footage all through the tournament. He grabbed the controls of the plane flying the England squad to Naples, setting it three miles off course. At the team hotel, he played marathon games of tennis in the midday sun and his 24/7 manic energy kept the others awake. The only way to shut him up was to give him sedative injections.

But it was also in Italy that Gascoigne became a celebrity far beyond football as his verve and energy carried England through to a semi-final against West Germany. The defining moment happened there, in the 1-1 draw in Turin when, five minutes into extra-time, Gascoigne fouled the German player Thomas Berthold, more through over-enthusiasm than evil intent. Inevitably, Berthold took the opportunity to make a drama out of it. As the referee reached for the yellow card, the cameras zoomed in on the moment it registered on Gascoigne's face that this was his second booking of the tournament, and that if England got through to the final he wouldn't be playing in it.

He was in anguish, utterly disbelieving, his shoulders slumped in pain. Knowing how his team-mate ticked, Lineker looked over to the bench. Tapping his finger against the side of his forehead, he mouthed to Robson: 'Just keep an eye on him.'

The match was still poised at 1-1 as the whistle blew to mark the end of extra-time. As Robson went to console him, Gascoigne's tears flowed. And after the match, Gazza's tears were bigger news than the fact that England subsequently lost on penalties. Because a player never cried like that, like a vulnerable child, wiping away the tears with the hem of his white England shirt. A blubbing Gazza replaced house prices and schools as the hot topic at swanky London dinner parties. The normally staid *Times* feature pages commissioned an article on the phenomenon (I know – I wrote it). Gianni Agnelli, the president of Juventus, called him 'a dog of war with the face of a child.' The novelist and Spurs fan Salman Rushdie asked rhetorically: 'Before Paul Gascoigne, did anyone become a national hero and dead-cert million-aire by crying?' More than 200,000 people turned up at Luton airport for the England team's homecoming. Gascoigne rose to the occasion by wearing a pair of fake plastic breasts and stomach with 'Gazza' written around the belly button.

Back in England, he carried on taking everyone by storm. He appeared in two TV ads, one for Woolworths in which he cried after unwrapping a present only to find out it was a rugby ball and another, with Lineker, in which he cried when Lineker stopped him eating his Walker's Crisps. He cracked jokes on *Saint and Greavsie*, and enjoyed wild drinking sessions and japes with his mates. His beaming mug and chubby body appeared on front pages, got up variously as a Roman centurion, a clown, Oliver Hardy and Braveheart.

On the first day of the new season, still the focus of near-demented media attention, he opened the scoring in the 3-1 home win against Manchester City. Lineker got the other two. Against Derby County two weeks later, his hat-trick moved Arthur Cox, the Derby manager, to comment: 'If he were a Brazilian or Argentinean, you would kiss his shoes.' Under the headline 'Gascoigne Tops A Bill That Is Full Of Talent,' the following Monday's *The Times* commented: 'The advance publicity was right, the rave reviews fully justified. The Greatest Show on Earth, presented by Tottenham Hotspur and starring Paul Gascoigne, duly brought the house down at White Hart Lane on Saturday.'

By the end of October, Spurs were unbeaten in their first 10 games and sitting third in the First Division. The defence had conceded only four goals. It was the best run since the Double season.

Then everything did a back-flip. The first half of the season rapidly started looking like a golden era as Spurs won just three out of the remaining 24 league games. Without the money to strengthen the squad the previous summer, Venables had had to confine himself to buying the left-back Justin Edinburgh from Southend United. 'The shortage of cash and the uncertainty about Spurs' future was beginning to have an impact on the field as well as off,' he complained. 'By early in the new year, the team was knackered, cut apart by injuries, and with no money for signings, there were no quality players to replace the injured.'

As Venables indicated, Spurs' only chance of qualifying for Europe 'would be to enter the Eurovision Song Contest or win the FA Cup'. With the club's two recognised troubadours, Hoddle and Waddle of *Diamond Lights* fame, now playing in France, the cup was the only option. In stormy weather, a goal by Paul Stewart at his former club, Blackpool, saw Spurs progress through the FA Cup third round. From then on, Gascoigne inspired them towards Wembley. Towards the end of January, he scored two and made two – for Lineker and Mabbutt

– in the fourth-round defeat of Oxford United. The night before the fifth round, away to Portsmouth, he played squash for an hour but retained enough energy the following day to score two more in Spurs' 2-1 win. In the quarter-finals, Spurs were dragging 1-0 behind Notts County at half-time, but an equaliser from Nayim and the winner from Gascoigne put them in the last four of the tournament, with Arsenal to beat if they wanted to reach the final.

But by then the big question was not whether they had a chance of beating the champions elect, the one everyone was asking was how much longer Gascoigne would be around.

Even before the cup run started, the fact that the club were in big trouble had become common knowledge. Back in September 1990, *The Sunday Times* had exposed Scholar's secret £1.1 million loan from Robert Maxwell. The covert nature of the deal had turned out to be a divisive error, with board members angry at being left out of the loop. That autumn, Tottenham Hotspur's share price was suspended on the Stock Exchange. Its debts were ballooning. They were £10 million short with current net liabilities of £17.7 million. The weekly interest bill was £40,000. Back then, that wasn't loose change, and the Midland Bank had placed Spurs in their 'Intensive Care Unit'. In other words, the club was hanging from the cliff edge and the bank was threatening to stamp on its fingers.

At the club's AGM in January 1991, held at the Chanticleer club in the back of White Hart Lane, several hundred fan shareholders turned up. They were led by the Tottenham Independent Supporters Association, newly formed by several activist fans with the object of getting together a bloc of small shareholders to vote. Along with beefs such as the recent 40 per cent hike in the cost of season tickets, the loss of The Shelf and the sale of Waddle, the priority as far as they were concerned was to find out what was happening at the club and who was responsible. They were treated to the devastating news that the club were under pressure to sell their main asset, Gascoigne, and were prepared to listen to offers. Close to the end of a stormy, emotional meeting, one fan took over the mike with the words: 'I've been sitting next to Bill Nicholson all through this meeting. If anyone should be on the board, it's Bill.' He was asked to stand up, at which everyone rose to applaud him.

By February, the directors were hawking Gascoigne around the big European clubs. Enter the newspaper publisher Robert Maxwell, already a highly unpopular figure in the game, long before the business empire on which his dealings were based turned out to be built on a foundation as firm as cobwebs. As owner of Oxford United, he had attempted to take over Reading, with the intention of merging the two clubs into a new one called Thames Valley Royals, based at that hotbed of footballing passion, Didcot. Thwarted in that venture and a subsequent attempt to take control of Manchester United, he handed Oxford over to his son Kevin and took possession of Derby County. Now the corpulent caliban began to circle above Spurs, with the guarantee that if he took over Gascoigne would stay at the club. So desperate was Scholar to hang on to the player that he joined forces with him.

The prospect horrified Venables. There was, he decided, only one solution. He would take control of Spurs himself. He had personal wealth, but not enough and during Spurs' journey to the cup final he was simultaneously trying to keep the side's morale from crumbling in the face of what was happening to their club while putting together a consortium to take it over. In March, a bid put together with the Scottish property developer Larry Gillick failed. His situation at the time was complicated by a double hernia injury to Gascoigne, which required an operation. There were two options, both of which entailed a gamble. He could defer it until after the semi-final against Arsenal, leaving the player at risk of breaking down. Or the operation could be done, with the resultant uncertainty about whether Gascoigne would be fit enough to play.

In the end, Gascoigne went under the knife and was rushed back into action against Arsenal. Wembley had been earmarked for the occasion – the first time a semi-final was being held there – because the whole of north London wanted tickets. Managed by George Graham, Arsenal were about to clinch their second title in three years. The compelling need Spurs always felt to beat them was given added urgency by the desire not to let them become the first club to win the Double twice.

So for the fans this felt like the real final. Maybe Gascoigne felt that way too. In the dressing room, the lunatic gibbering which for him always preceded a game of any magnitude was so intense on this occasion that it drowned out Venables's pre-match team talk. Barely fit after the operation, he eased himself into the game with all the diffidence of a torpedo, scoring after five minutes with a 35-yard free kick of such ferocity, power and swerving accuracy that David Seaman was left with an armful of nothing. It was, said the keeper later, 'one of the best free kicks I've never seen'.

Arsenal 0 Gascoigne 1. No other footballer could have done it. And in a way you just wish you could have left it right there, at Wembley in mid-afternoon on 14th April 1991, with the Arsenal players standing slack-jawed and Gascoigne running round the pitch in celebration, stopping off at the bench where, pink-faced and slippery with sweat, he flung his arms round Venables and guffawed in his ear: 'The silly bastard only tried to save it, didn't he?'

Because that afternoon we saw a supreme footballer at the height of his powers. Five minutes after the first goal, his was the assist that allowed Lineker to increase Spurs' lead. Arsenal were two down after 10 minutes. Alan Smith got one back for them before half-time, but with 20 minutes left Lineker scored again to take Spurs to the final. Gascoigne, having faded after half an hour, had been substituted by then. As he left the pitch, everyone in the world who wasn't Arsenal rose to applaud a man whose magical combination of sublime ability and colossal force of personality had almost on his own felled an outstanding side that had lost just one league game that season. '*That*,' said the commentator Barry Davies on the TV, 'was *Schoolboys' Own* stuff.' In *The Guardian*, David Lacey described it as an 'inspired display of individual, highly idiosyncratic football'. 'I don't think he ever played better,' says Mabbutt. 'What Diego Maradona did for Argentina at the 1986 World Cup, Gazza did for us in every round to reach the FA Cup Final. He was majestic.'

You sort of knew you'd never see anything like it again. So when, with three weeks to go until the cup final, Spurs agreed to sell him to the Italian club Lazio for £7.9 million, you just felt grateful you'd seen it at all.

Venables wasn't going to give up on taking Spurs off Scholar's hands. Which is where Morris Keston, 'Superfan', the man who has devoted most of his life and a large part of his fortune to following Tottenham, enters the story. 'The night before the final,' says Keston, 'I had a phone call from Philip Green, who was a friend of mine and a long-standing Spurs supporter. "Morris," he said, "Stop whatever you're doing and come to my office. No time to tell you what it's about, but I want you here at a meeting which will be of great interest to you. I'll fill you in when you get here."

'At that time, Philip wasn't as big as he is now, but he was the chairman and chief executive of a publicly listed fashion group and his office was in Baker Street. I got there and clocked Terry Venables at one side of the table, and I thought if Terry was away from the squad on the night before the final, something important was going on.

'Tony Berry, one of the Tottenham directors, was sitting next to him, and there were a couple of other club officials who I knew by sight, and someone else I didn't know, whom Philip introduced as Peter Robinson, Irving Scholar's solicitor.

'Philip held a piece of paper in the air and said, "Morris, this is a cheque for a million pounds which I'm about to make payable to Irving Scholar for his Tottenham shares, which will enable Terry to buy him out and save the club. If Scholar accepts the deal, you'll be chairman." I was thrilled, wasn't I?

'So then Peter Robinson got on the phone to Irving and put the deal to him, and Irving said, "All right, but I want the deal closed tonight." Then Philip took over the phone and said to Irving, "No, I've got to clear it with the Midland Bank first."

'But Irving wanted the deal closed that night, he wouldn't budge. He maybe thought there was another way out. The phone calls went backwards and forwards until 7.45 when Terry said, "I can't stay any longer, I've got to go to the team at the Royal Lancaster Hotel." After he left, the meeting went on until 10pm and Irving was still saying the deal had to be closed that night, so Philip said, "Then the deal is dead," and tore up the cheque. That was the end of my chance to be chairman of Spurs.'

Earlier in the day Venables had been to see Gascoigne's representatives, Mel Stein, his lawyer, and Len Lazarus, his accountant, in an attempt to persuade them that if Gascoigne stayed with Spurs he would build a team round him to win the league. That, Venables argued, would boost his value even higher. Plus if Venables's takeover of the club went ahead, he would make Gascoigne better paid than anyone in the British game. Stein and Lazarus remained unmoved. Later, while Venables and Scholar were failing to come to any agreement, Gascoigne signed a contract with Lazio that would bring him an immediate £2 million and an annual salary of £1 million a year, and would provide Tottenham Hotspur with a financial lifeline of £7.9 million pounds.

Maybe the fact that his future had been decided at last left Gascoigne less hyperactive than usual the night before his last game for Spurs. Whatever the reason, for once he didn't need to be zapped by the team doctor to help him sleep. The next day, though, he was as wired as he had ever been. 'If Paul Gascoigne was hoping to make a big impact in his last game in a Tottenham shirt, he was not to be disappointed, but not in the way he would have wanted,' Venables wrote later. 'If he had set fire to the stadium, he could not have earned more column inches.'

The danger signs were obvious within 90 seconds of the kick-off. In a rush of demented-looking instability, Gascoigne launched himself studs-first into Garry Parker's chest. The tackle didn't even earn him a booking. Ten minutes later, he crash-landed on Gary Charles on the edge of the Spurs penalty area.

Charles was unscathed. It looked like Gascoigne was too. Checked over by the Spurs physio, he got to his feet and took up position in a wall for the free kick he had just conceded. Then, just after Stuart Pearce struck the ball into the top corner of the net to put Forest into the lead, he crumpled like a shot animal.

Spurs were now a goal down with nearly 80 minutes' playing time left. Their talisman, their greatest player, had been stretchered off. Far from falling apart, though, they seemed stronger. 'Gascoigne's injury did have one side-benefit to the team,' Venables said later. 'Until Gazza went off, I had actually not got the balance of the side quite right.' Nayim came on as substitute to be deployed on the left, Samways moved into the middle, and alongside him David Howells, solid, unfussy, a bit of a Scott Parker, provided the vision, awareness and hard work. Even then, nothing came easy. With 25 minutes gone, a decent-looking Lineker goal was given offside. Five minutes later, running onto a Paul Stewart pass, he was awarded a penalty after the Forest goalkeeper, Mark Crossley, brought him down. Then Crossley, lucky not to have been sent off, turned Lineker's penalty kick aside.

But the equaliser had to come. Seven minutes into the second half, Stewart ran on to a pass from an Allen-Nayim move and shot across Crossley to make it 1-1. It was still that way at the end of the 90 minutes.

Before extra-time, Venables galvanised his players on the pitch. Brian Clough, by then in the grip of the alcoholism that was gradually destroying his health, ignored his players and sat on the bench talking to a policeman. Whether or not the eccentricity of the gesture unnerved his team, Forest looked vulnerable once play restarted. In the first half of extra-time, Stewart headed on Nayim's cross to the far post. Under pressure from Mabbutt, the England defender Des Walker headed into his own net. It was enough to win Spurs' eighth FA Cup.

Even as Mabbutt was lifting the cup, Tottenham were coming to terms with the news that Gascoigne had snapped a cruciate ligament in his right knee. It was almost the worst injury he could have suffered. He would be out for a year. He might never play again. His move to Lazio was in jeopardy and so, it followed, was the future of Tottenham Hotspur Football Club.

CHAPTER TWENTY-SEVEN

WHEN ALAN MET TERRY

Alan Sugar and Terry Venables met for the first time over a hi-fi unit cunningly disguised as separates encased in a plastic wood cabinet. It had real chipboard speakers, a tuner with a quality knob that stuck and a tape deck that performed the usual function of tape decks of the time, which was to chew up tapes. The Amstrad Tower System was part of the range of electronic goods that had made Sugar his fortune. Venables was advertising it for him under the strapline 'Great players'. Sugar's impression of him at the time was of 'a chirpy chappy, a shrewd lad.'

Baron Sugar of Clapton – who was, of course, just plain Alan back then – maintains that he didn't know what possessed him. But on the Monday following the 1991 FA Cup Final triumph, he decided to renew the acquaintance, one that had lain dormant for more than a decade, by calling Venables to arrange a meeting at the Hilton in Park Lane later that week. All he knew, he said later, was what his friends and his kids had told him – that Spurs was in danger of being shut down.

'It was one of those things you tended to hear in the background but not pay too much attention to.' Then he watched the drama of the cup final unfold on TV and his attention was grabbed. 'From what I could gather from the newspapers, Venables was at loggerheads with

Scholar who, as chairman, had been cast as the bad guy, responsible for the demise of the club. Reading the papers, you got the impression that everything wrong with Spurs, both on the pitch and in financial terms, was down to Scholar. Scholar was the devil and Venables was the white knight – only without any money.'

As the founder of Amstrad – Alan Michael Sugar Trading – money was something he did have. An East End boy, 46 years old, worth £157 million pounds, he was figuring in *The Sunday Times* Rich List as the 46th most loaded person in Britain. The fortune came out of a decision he took at 21 that there was a bigger future in manufacturing his own TVs and radios than selling someone else's.

For the men in his family, Tottenham was their club, though by the time Sugar was rich enough to start thinking about buying it, affordable electronic goods had consumed all his time and he had to admit to not seeing them play for about five years. In fact, his disengagement with Tottenham was such that when someone mentioned the Double, he allegedly asked: 'What Double?'

Not that it looked like a problem. The last bloke was noted for his encyclopaedic knowledge of everything Tottenham Hotspur and look where it had got everyone. So a month after Sugar's phone call, pausing only to bat off an attempt by Robert Maxwell to wrestle the club away at the last minute, Sugar and Venables won control. The pair each invested £3.25 million to equally own just over 35 per cent of the club's shares between them. For Sugar the money was easy to find. Venables struggled, borrowing around £2 million to get his stake and fulfil his dream of owning a football club. Sugar installed himself as chairman and booted Scholar out.

It was an undignified departure for a man whose primary objective had been to bring the glory days back to White Hart Lane, whose initiatives were all conceived out of passion for Spurs and a burning desire to make it a great club again. But if you go through them now, the details of some of Scholar's regime at Tottenham read like comedy. The man put in charge of selling the clothing ranges was someone whose previous job had been flogging corsets. While Scholar was making an impassioned speech to a parliamentary committee, denouncing Margaret Thatcher's National Identity Scheme for football, Tottenham Hotspur's Synchro Systems was simultaneously bidding for the right to administer the scheme.

'Irving Scholar was a fan who owned the club,' says Alex Fynn. 'Every minute, he was thinking of something he could do to improve Spurs. Where he came unstuck was that he confused the obligations of a chairman with the commitment of someone who loved the club more than any other fan.'

There was a symmetry about that downfall. He took over Spurs as the result of a financial crisis — the West Stand — and left as the result of a financial crisis — the East Stand and a diversification into non-football industries. 'How,' asks Alex Fynn rhetorically, 'could property developers have cocked up the East Stand? How could entrepreneurs have diversified in such a way that it became a drain? How could a smart businessman put his faith in Robert Maxwell?'

'He was a great motivational force,' says Brian Scovell, 'but serving the interests of the club in the wrong way.

'It was a sad time for me,' says Gary Mabbutt. 'I was at Tottenham during the change from what things were. We were trailblazers. Irving Scholar was ahead of his time and saw the way things were going. He truly loved the club. But if it hadn't been for Alan Sugar we would have gone under.'

'I don't think he was a bad man — just misguided,' says Steve Perryman.

Scholar himself summed it all up in his biography, *Behind Closed Doors*. 'Somebody,' he wrote, 'has to pay the price of failure.' It was Bill Nicholson he meant, but he might just as well have been talking about himself.

On the face of it, Sugar and Venables looked the ideal pairing — the businessman and the football man. From the very start, though, the relationship between Sugar and the chirpy chappy who was his chief executive was an uneasy one. According to Venables, he took 'an instinctive dislike' to Sugar but recognised that working with him was his only chance of becoming the first former footballer to gain control of his own club. Sugar, for his part, claims he had been warned. 'You ain't gonna last 10 minutes with that Terry Venables bloke,' one Amstrad employee told him. 'I couldn't understand why he would form that opinion – it was quite uncharacteristic of him,' Sugar said later. 'I think what he was referring to was a clash of egos. Little did he know how spot on he was.'

The line spun at the time was that Sugar would look after the £11 million bank debt, while Venables looked after the 11 on the pitch. It was a misapprehension. Now ensconced in the boardroom, Venables relinquished the role of hands-on manager, bringing back Peter Shreeve from his interlude as assistant manager at QPR and Watford to act as team coach, with Ray Clemence as his assistant.

'To be fair to Venables,' said Sugar, 'he did say to me at the beginning he would be having a manager, but what he did say also was that he would spend all his time directing and helping the manager. Peter Shreeve was supposed to do the donkey work and he would be doing all the tactics and strategy. But that is not how it worked out. In that first year, he hardly got involved and left everything, near enough 100 per cent, to Shreeve.'

'I don't begrudge Terry his ambition, it was what he had always wanted, but most of the players thought he would remain as manager when he became the owner as well, and were shocked when he stepped down,' says Mabbutt. 'Terry had discussed appointing Peter Shreeve with me. Having worked for a number of years with Peter, I thought that it was a good appointment, but I thought it would be as his number two, not his replacement. Peter is an extremely good coach, but it was a real disappointment to lose Terry and never see him on the training field that season. After winning the FA Cup, we needed Terry to stick around to build on that, but we had to start all over again.'

That said, the arrangement seemed to work all right at first. Spurs won five of their first seven league games to occupy third place in the First Division by the end of September. Then, with a Venables-free dugout, they slid down the table. Gordon Durie, signed from Chelsea to shift some of the burden from Lineker, managed just seven league goals. It was only Lineker's ability consistently to come up with the goods – 29 goals in 35 games – that stopped Spurs being relegated. Which would have been a catastrophe just as the Premier League was to be launched in the summer of 1992.

Lineker himself was never going to play in the Premiership. For a humongously large and life-enhancing fee, he had signed for the Japanese club Grampus Eight. He was followed out of the door by Paul Walsh, off to Portsmouth. Paul Stewart headed for Liverpool. As for Gascoigne, in the last week of the season he made his final appearance in a Spurs shirt, playing for the reserves in a friendly against the Tottenham youth team. His injury hadn't turned out to be the complete disaster that it had threatened to be. Lazio still wanted him, though the fee was reduced from £7.9 million to a rumoured £5 million, four of which was stumped up at once and the rest would be due once it was certain that Gascoigne could play again. His farewell drew more cameras than the average league fixture. It featured a goal of suitable brilliance, following which he dived into a puddle on the pitch shouting 'Splish splosh, lotsa dosh.'

As it turned out, England hadn't quite seen the last of him. His recovery was set back by an injury received in a nightclub brawl and it was a few more months before he set foot in Italy. On his first night there he gave his minders the slip, put his shoes by an open window and hid in a wardrobe. They thought he'd jumped out and committed suicide.

While all this was going on, at boardroom level Sugar was becoming increasingly pained at the situation. The way he saw it, he was being treated rather too casually as the 'rich nutter' who, having parted with his money, would be content to stay in the background. In December 1991, he underwrote more shares in a rights issue, making his total investment £8 million. That gave him a bigger slice of the cake than Venables, who lacked the funds to underwrite his portion of the rights issue. Sugar was now firmly in control, leaving Venables to lament, 'I was reduced from an equal partner to a pawn . . . My days at Tottenham were numbered.'

'At the start, Sugar and Venables believed they could work together but that rose-tinted view was based on misconceptions,' says Alex Fynn. 'Venables thought Sugar would have his hands full looking after Amstrad and would be happy to act as a silent backer, leaving him to get on with what he always wanted to do, be in charge of the whole shooting match.'

Thus it was that the most surprising development of Spurs' season followed in May 1992. Venables sacked Peter Shreeve and announced he was taking more control of the footballing side. To which end, he installed a continental management structure with Doug Livermore as chief coach and Ray Clemence as his assistant, while he took overall control of first-team affairs.

That summer, he shopped tirelessly: Jason Cundy, Dean Austin, Neil Ruddock, Andy Gray and a talented 20-year-old from Portsmouth called Darren Anderton, later to labour under the alias of 'Sicknote'. The most significant arrival, though, was in August 1992. One week after scoring the first-ever Premier League goal shown live on Sky Sports for Nottingham Forest against Liverpool, Teddy Sheringham signed for Spurs. Sheringham, a bright boy from the East London suburbs, was comfortable as both a number 10 behind a partner or as a prolific goal-getter, as evidenced by the 21 he scored that season. In order to encourage his signature on the contract, Venables had expounded to Sheringham his grand plans for winning the title. It didn't happen. A slow start and a failure to improve left Spurs 15th in the Premier League at the end of January, only five points above the relegation zone again.

Things looked up. Near the end of February, Sheringham scored a hat-trick in a 4-0 home defeat of Leeds (Neil Ruddock scored the other) to register Spurs' best league win of the season. With Nick Barmby, a homegrown 18-year-old in his debut season, on his way to finishing as second top scorer behind Sheringham, with Anderton starting to fill the gap left by Waddle, Spurs were playing fluent, entertaining football again. The feeling was that the good times were on their way back, that Venables might deliver on his promise of a title challenge in the near future. In the last three-and-a-half months of the season, the mini-revival took them to a finish of eighth, two places above Arsenal. In the FA Cup, they reached the semi-finals, facing Arsenal at Wembley again. 'Sicknote was brought down in the box,' remembers Bernie Kingsley. 'The ref was Mr [Philip] Don and he refused to give a penalty. That changed the course of history in my view. If we'd won, we would have won the cup, Sugar wouldn't have sacked Venables and we would have carried on with a great team.'

Well, maybe. Back in real life, Sugar was fuming. Venables's reluctance to consult him was frustrating. He found Venables's popularity with the fans annoying and personally insulting. Venables did not spend enough time with the first team. He was the one, he said, who so far had got nothing out of it but without him Tottenham probably would not still exist. The arrangement with Venables, it followed, was never going to work. A Spurs board meeting on 6th May, 1993, culminated in Sugar handing his chief executive a letter asking him to resign, sell his shares and leave the club.

'We did not like each other,' claimed Venables. 'That was it. No one could believe that was all there was to it, but that was the top and bottom of it.' Voted out as chief executive, Venables obtained a High Court injunction to put the sacking on hold.

'On arrival at the High Court in The Strand for the first day of the hearing, there were huge crowds standing outside, screaming my name, snarling abuse at me and calling me "Judas",' Sugar said later. 'As we walked up the staircase inside the court building, crowds of fans were standing above, spitting on me and Ann, who'd decided to be there to support me, as the whole world had ganged up on me.'

On 15th June, after three days of hearings, the High Court lifted the injunction and ruled that there was nothing to suggest the Spurs board could not fire their chief executive.

A week later, the Spurs board met at White Hart Lane to discuss the resolution to remove Venables as chief executive, and by two votes to one he was chucked overboard. As far as the fans were concerned, it was a massively unpopular move. The way they saw it, Venables, the best coach in the country, had been shafted by the heartless money men. In the forecourt of the club, Tel's blue-and-white army gathered to scream for Sugar's head along with press and cameramen. Venables was seen as the victim, the football man ousted by the money men. Sugar escaped through a side entrance. 'Never mind Bambi's mum,' said Sugar. 'I was the man who shot Bambi.'

'Spurs fans enjoyed Terry's time. I know I did,' says Mabbutt. 'He won his only trophy in the English game, brought in great players like Gazza and Gary Lineker and his sides always tried to play attractive football. There were missed opportunities, and maybe we could have enjoyed even greater success if Terry hadn't gone up to the boardroom, but overall the players were very disappointed to see him leave.'

Which wasn't quite how Sugar viewed the departure.

When a wounded Venables asked Alan Sugar how he would be able to replace him, he was told: 'I'll just get some other geezer in.'

He soon did. And if the fans were looking for calm and order to be restored at Tottenham, they hadn't seen anything yet.

CHAPTER TWENTY-EIGHT

SOME OTHER GEEZER

Five days after his court victory, Sugar unveiled his new geezer. In a cute move that mollified and distracted fans gutted by the loss of Venables, he brought in Ossie Ardiles, one of the most passionately loved characters in the Tottenham story. Ardiles's managerial career had just featured a couple of mixed years — he lasted a season at Newcastle before being sacked, but then took West Bromwich Albion into the First Division. It was time for a bigger challenge, and Sugar hadn't exactly had to jemmy him away from the Midlands club. 'I always thought it was my destiny to be Spurs manager one day,' Ardiles said.

Bringing in two more Spurs legends, Steve Perryman and Pat Jennings, as his coaching team, Ardiles then went into the transfer market. Given his largest ever transfer budget — £4 million — Tottenham's new manager rather surprisingly went for quantity over quality. Fans looking for a return to the days when Spurs was the greatest show on earth, to the sort of head-rush that came with the signing of a Lineker or a Gascoigne, had to content themselves with Colin Calderwood, Jason Dozzell, David Kerslake and Kevin Scott.

That said, Ardiles's early weeks in charge went promisingly — a 1-0 away win at Newcastle on the opening day of the season, 11 goals from Sheringham in the first 12 games, fifth in the table by the start of October. 'The fans loved it,' says Mabbutt. 'We were just total football. Everything was just great – training, passing, playing, it was the beautiful game.'

Sugar was loving it too. 'My ego is saying to me, "Okay Sugar, you're there now, mate, you're in charge, and the eyes of the football world are on you,"' he said that October. 'Knowing my character, I've got to make sure this is a success . . . I'm not going to shoot my mouth off about what we're going to do this season, but our ultimate goal is a place in Europe. I can only be pleased with the way things have gone so far.'

Not for much longer. First, Sheringham picked up an injury at Old Trafford. Eight games followed without a win. Plus in November, against Wimbledon, Mabbutt suffered the worst injury of his career.

'It was John Fashanu, bless him,' says Mabbutt. 'It broke my eye socket and cheekbone. I had maxio-facial surgery that night. Many places had to be rearranged – at the time they were worried about my sight and I've still got no feeling in the right side of my face.'

Without their captain, with a defence that was as solid and unyielding as sponge, Spurs were out of both cup competitions and one point off the relegation zone by the end of February. By the time Mabbutt came back, wearing a protective face mask, with an eye that still needed a further visit to hospital to be properly put back in place, there were 14 games left to stave off relegation. In the stands, to the tune of 'Spurs are on their way to Wembley', as they lost 4-1 at home to West Ham, the away fans chanted 'Spurs are on their way to Endsleigh' – the insurance company that sponsored the lower divisions at the time.

What had made the winter months more demoralising and disheartening was the death of Danny Blanchflower in December 1993. Alzheimer's disease, the illness that afflicted him in his last years, was cruel for a man who had once articulated so profoundly and authentically what the game, and Tottenham Hotspur, was about: 'It's about glory. It's about doing things in style, with a flourish. It's about going out and beating the other lot, not waiting for them to die of boredom.' To the fans he would always represent the soul of Spurs, forever the white-shirted captain leading out the team, with the ball in his hand, to the sound of *Macnamara's Band*. He was Danny Blanchflower, the best Spur ever, the leader of the band. And at that point, coming to the end of another season of crushed hopes, struggling to stay on the top step after what seemed like an eternity of troubles, the transitional seasons, the sale of loved players, the threat of extinction, the board-room melodramas, it was impossible not to dwell on how far the club had strayed from the spirit of Blanchflower's rallying cry. And equally difficult not to wonder when Spurs would live up to it again.

That season Spurs survived, just, by beating Southampton at home and Oldham away. It was only a 15th-place finish, three points above the drop zone, but they were still in the Premier League. Though how much longer they would be there was suddenly open to question.

Five days after the season ended, they faced an FA charge of misconduct over irregular payments to players between 1983 and 1989. Made in the Irving Scholar era, these undeclared 'loans' had been uncovered by Sugar when he took over and divulged by him voluntarily to the FA in the belief that openness would moderate any punishment doled out. Now, it seemed, the FA were not inclined to temper justice with leniency. There was a frighteningly strong possibility that if Spurs were found guilty, they would be demoted to the First Division. All that struggle, all those weeks of effort to stay up, all that ecstatic relief when they'd saved themselves from the drop – the possibility that it was going to count for nothing looked threateningly, bleakly real.

Though it didn't come to that, the way it turned out was almost as bad. On 14th June, 1994, Spurs were deducted 12 points for the 1994/95 Premier League season, banned from the FA Cup for a year and fined £600,000. They hadn't been punished with compulsory relegation after all. So what? Having 12 points clipped off the tally before they started virtually amounted to the same thing. It amounted to the most severe sentence meted out by the English game's ruling body to one of its members. Steve Davis of the Tottenham Independent Supporters Association termed it 'a disaster . . . The FA Cup is the trophy associated with Tottenham and it's probably the only thing we have a chance of winning next season.'

For Sugar, it was a bitter pill to swallow. After all, Spurs themselves had told the FA of the offences. Everyone knew that at the end of the following season four clubs were due to be relegated as the Premiership was pared down to 20. Spurs would be competing at a huge disadvantage. They'd only just avoided relegation by four points. 'It's slow torture,' said David Howells. 'They might just as well have gone ahead and relegated us. I'm absolutely staggered.'

Sugar set about getting the penalties overturned and, determined to lift morale after the crushing malevolence of the punishment, gave Ardiles the financial backing to buy big. Just who Ardiles was going to get was another matter. Effectively, he would be asking players to sign up for a nine-month relegation scrap. Even when the deducted points were reduced to six on appeal, the FA upped the fine to £1.5 million and kept the cup ban.

Then, in tune with the surreal tone of Tottenham Hotspur's existence at the time, one of the most jaw-dropping transfer coups in the history of football came to pass.

This was no furtive tapping up in a motorway service area, this was multi-millionaire to multi-millionaire-in-waiting, these were gods calling to each other from Olympian height to Olympian height. Well, from yacht to apartment in the world's most exclusive tax haven, anyway. Alan Sugar takes up the story:

'I was minding my own business in Monaco, actually on my boat at the time,' he recounts in his autobiography, 'and I got a most surprising phone call from a Swiss gentleman, who claimed to be the agent of Jürgen Klinsmann telling me he was back in Monaco where he lived and considering moving to the Premier League. And I said, "Yeah, so what? What's that got to do with us? Why are you phoning me?" You would have thought he would have been on the phone to Manchester United or Liverpool. He said, "Well, basically he wants a London club." Jürgen was much cleverer than anybody realised. He recognised that the Premier League was going to be the most powerful league in the world and I think he wanted to be part of it. I also think quite selfishly he wanted to live in London and there was a choice, Arsenal, us, Chelsea or West Ham.

'Once I realised they were serious the guy said to me, "Where are you?" and I said, "Well actually, I'm in Monaco harbour," and the fellow said, "I can't believe it, I'm phoning from Jürgen's apartment in Monaco, looking down on the harbour, where are you?" I said, "We're in the blue boat, fourth along from the left, and he replied, "I can't see you." I walked out with the mobile handset, waving, and he said, "I can see you waving, we'll be down in 10 minutes." And that's exactly what happened. Jürgen met all my family on board – most of them couldn't believe their eyes – we met the next day and I went round to Monaco, his club at the time, and signed the deal there and then.'

At the time, Klinsmann was probably the nation's most reviled footballer. Part of the West German side that had beaten Bobby Robson's team in the semis in Italia '90, his repertoire of over-the-top writhings and thespian dives so inflamed watching Brits that they even felt indignant for Argentina when he got Pedro Monzon sent off in the final. Well, for all of a few seconds, anyway.

So it says everything about Klinsmann's charm and guile that when he turned up at his first press conference at Spurs he had a snorkel and goggles in his backpack. 'The idea came from a German friend of mine who had lived in England and who at that time lived in Monaco,' said Klinsmann. 'He suggested bringing them to the press conference – but instead I simply asked the journalists if they know a diving school in London because I want to take some classes! But obviously it was the advice that my friend gave me, to make a joke out of it, that pretty much helped the situation.'

That was the media won over. Now for the rest of the country. Together with another new signing, Ilie Dumitrescu, the winger who had just become Romania's 1994 World Cup hero by scoring two of the goals that beat Argentina, Klinsmann made his Spurs debut on the opening day of the 1994/95 season as part of the most extravagantly gifted forward line the fans had ever seen.

Klinsmann, Dumitrescu, Sheringham, Barmby, Anderton. No way was Ardiles going to leave any of them out. This was the man who once said, 'If you left it to me, I would play with a goalkeeper and 10 front players.' This was his football dreamland. Away to Sheffield

Wednesday, he was true to his word. That day at Hillsborough, the world saw the birth of the 'Famous Five'.

It was also the debut of the 'Famous Dive'. 20th August 1994. Sheffield Wednesday 3 Tottenham Hotspur 4. The fourth Spurs goal was Klinsmann's, and he plunged like Tom Daley in celebration, joined by his his team-mates. Totally irresistible. Totally Spurs, too.

'It was Teddy Sheringham's idea,' said Klinsmann. 'Before the game he said, "When you score your first goal, we're all going to dive." That turned around a lot of people because they realised, "Hey, this German guy can make fun of himself!" I felt so comfortable with that group of players that I probably ended up playing the best season in my entire career.'

'Teddy had a little bit of everything,' said Darren Anderton. 'Some strikers are just target men, but Teddy was a complete team player. He was completely different to Jürgen Klinsmann. Jürgen was an out-and-out goalscorer, but Teddy was a level above because he could make the play – that's why I think Jürgen did so well when he was here, because he was playing with Teddy.'

Days later, Klinsmann scored both Spurs goals on his White Hart Lane debut in the 2-1 defeat of Everton. There were two more from him a week after that, in the 3-1 away win over Ipswich Town. In September, he scored a hat-trick as Spurs beat Watford 6-3 at Vicarage Road in the first-round first leg of the Coca Cola Cup.

But while Klinsmann was scoring hat-tricks, while Sheringham and Dumitrescu and Barmby and Anderton were knocking in goals at will, while all-out attack cancelled out a flimsy defence against lesser opposition, it was most definitely not the way to be playing in the Premier League. After winning three of their first four games, Spurs lost three in a row to Southampton, Leicester and, humiliatingly, 4-1 at home to Nottingham Forest.

'As a defence, we were constantly exposed and vulnerable,' said Justin Edinburgh. 'While everyone talked about the Famous Five, no one mentioned us. The defenders joked maybe we should be called the "S*** Four".'

Plus the Famous Five weren't getting along that famously. Dumitrescu, said Teddy Sheringham, was 'a showboater' and his prediction was that 'it was all going to end in tears'. So it did. Near the end of October, in spite of the arrival of another big signing, the Romanian playmaker Gica Popescu, Spurs lost 5–2 at Manchester City and were knocked out in the third round of the Coca Cola Cup 3–0 at Notts County, bottom of the First Division, winless at home for half a year.

Still banned from the FA Cup, adrift in mid-table, Spurs' hopes of a trophy were over after just two-and-a-half months. The fans turned against Ardiles, hammering on the coach and shouting, 'We want Ossie out' as it pulled away from Meadow Lane. His chairman noted their dismay. The hero of the Burkinshaw years lasted just one more game, a 3–1 win at home to West Ham, before Sugar opened the trap door and let him fall through it. Next day in *The Guardian*, the headline read: 'Ardiless. Football Latest: Sugar 2 Managers 0'

Symmetry was at work again. Two years earlier, Ardiles had been sacked by Newcastle, for the very same reasons that Spurs were now through with him: while his players scored goals for fun, he had problems at the back, and Newcastle struggled. Obviously, as Alex Fynn and H. Davidson pointed out in *Dream On*, 'somebody hadn't been paying attention.'

Jeered by the fans who 10 years back had worshipped and adored him, implacably booted out by Sugar, Ardiles made a heartbreaking exit from White Hart Lane. After one game in charge as caretaker manager, Perryman followed him. It was the second time that Tottenham's treatment of Perryman seemed unworthy of the man. 'I felt very sour about the whole thing,' Perryman said later. 'It was not the club I had known and loved as a young player.'

When he left Tottenham, Ardiles left English football. Managing successfully in Japan restored his morale. But Ardiles is not a man to bear a grudge. 'I would like, one day, to manage in England again,' he says now. 'Be positive. That is my motto.'

CHAPTER TWENTY-NINE

THE ONE WHO TURNED DOWN DENNIS BERGKAMP

Usefully for Spurs, an ideal-sounding replacement for Ardiles was ready and waiting. Gerry Francis had just walked away from Queen Park Rangers after falling out with their chairman. On 15th November, 1994, nine years after Bill Nicholson attempted to swap him for Martin Chivers, he walked into Spurs as their manager.

Captain of England at 23, pigeon-fancier, antique shop proprietor and owner of one of the most famous mullets in England, this was the man who had turned Queens Park Rangers into an established Premier League outfit which for the last two seasons had finished above Spurs in the league. He was also someone whose financial acumen had made him rich independently of the game. Someone who liked to leave the impression he wasn't too bothered about football any more.

'I wasn't looking for a new job,' recalled Francis. 'Also, if I'm honest I wasn't sure if me and Alan Sugar were going to get on with each other, so I only agreed a contract until the end of the season.'

But Spurs, he said, was a challenge he couldn't resist. With the club nestling near the bottom of the league and out of the FA Cup before it started, all-out-attack Ardiles-style was scrapped from the programme in favour of a strategy that was pretty much the direct opposite. Every day, Francis was out there working with the neglected back four in training. It was going to be good football, but starting from the back. The players were going to be playing as a disciplined unit – fit, honed, fast and ready to chase down anything. Tuesday training featured something new. Something called 'running', said Francis. 'It's bloody hard work, There aren't too many who want a ball afterwards. Mainly they want a basin.' Justin Edinburgh recorded that seeing knackered players throwing up by the side of the pitch became as mundane a sight as people doing sit-ups. Gica Popescu was said to drive home, crawl into bed and sleep for 18 hours.

After the initial blip of a 4–3 home defeat by Aston Villa in the first game of his reign, Francis focusing on the back looked to be paying off. David Howells, who had been highly-rated by Venables but spurned by Ardiles, came in to play a shielding role in front of the defence. Within a month, an arbitration panel reinstated Spurs to the FA Cup and overturned the six-point deduction (although they still had to pay the fine) and the team's fortunes seemed to have turned around with it.

By January, Spurs were hovering on the edge of the top six in the Premiership. By the time March was under way, they were starting on a promising FA Cup run. At Southampton, with the team two down at half-time and the fans steeling themselves for defeat, Ronny Rosenthal, just back from injury, came on as a substitute and scored twice in two minutes to take the game into extra-time. During which he made it a hat-trick, and goals from Sheringham, Barmby and Anderton made it Southampton 2 Spurs 6. Later that month, thousands of Spurs fans travelled to Anfield for the quarter-final. The result: Liverpool 1 Spurs 2, with Klinsmann scoring the winner two minutes from the end. Spurs were magical that day, in a game so evenly and superbly contested that even Liverpool fans stood and applauded them off the pitch.

That Klinsmann goal seemed to symbolise the revival. 'That was such a great win,' gushed the German striker. 'It was very emotional, like a fairytale about to come true.' Spurs' opponents in the semi-final were Everton, a club that had been batting its eyelids at relegation. Among the fans, the conviction grew. Klinsmann was going to take them to Wembley. Against Manchester United. In the press, we were calling it the dream final. It was looking as though Spurs had turned the corner, just when everything was going wrong in the red sector of north London, where the drama of Paul Merson's confessions of cocaine use, gambling and alcohol addiction and the sacking of their manager George Graham after an FA enquiry into alleged kickbacks on player transfers was giving Arsenal the most scandalous and turbulent season in its history.

But enjoying the other north London club's discomfiture was one thing. Capitalising on it was another. With the defeat of Liverpool, the season had peaked. Later on that month, in the FA Cup semi-final against Everton at Elland Road, Joe Royle's Dogs of War proceeded to outplay Spurs and beat them 4-1. Afterwards Royle marched into the press room and declared: 'Sorry about your dream final, lads. But bollocks to it. And that's with a double "l".'

So Spurs' adventure in the cup from which they had originally been banned was over. So was Sugar's love-in with Klinsmann when the German announced he was leaving for Bayern Munich at the end of the season.

'In the last months before I decided to leave, I would often ask Sugar what the plans were for next season – do they intend to get new players? I wanted to see if the club really wanted to go for the title,' said Klinsmann at the time. 'Sugar said we could invest money from the FA Cup run, something like £1.5 million. But if you want to be on the level of Blackburn, Manchester United and Newcastle, that is not going to work. So I thought, "Forget it".'

Klinsmann let slip the news to his best mate at Spurs first. 'I told him it wouldn't go down very well,' says Gary Mabbutt understatedly. Mabbutt was not wrong. In one of the most famous clothing deployment gestures since Sir Walter Raleigh chucked his cloak over a puddle for Elizabeth I to walk over, Sugar used the stage set of a BBC interview to screw up a signed Klinsmann shirt and throw it at the reporter with the accompanying sentiment, 'I wouldn't use it to wash my windscreen.'

An outraged, cruelly disappointed Sugar pursued the issue. As far as he was concerned, Klinsmann was reneging on a two-season deal. Trouble was, so cock-a-hoop had the chairman been to have bagged the German in the first place that he had failed to pursue the detail of a get-out clause in the contract stating that Klinsmann could leave after a season. Sugar had understood that it would be used only if Spurs were relegated. That hadn't been put in writing, though. 'He got upset,' said Klinsmann casually later, 'but no big problem.'

What was a problem was the faltering Premiership campaign. The season fizzled out, with the final 12 games featuring six draws, three wins and three defeats. For the fans, the feeling of dejection and disappointment was overwhelming. Spurs had finished seventh. They had blown their chance of Europe. Klinsmann had gone. So, it seemed, had everyone else. Following the German out of White Hart Lane were Gica Popescu, who joined Barcelona, Dumitrescu (shipped off on loan to Sevilla after being monstered by the tabloids) and the great young hope Nicky Barmby, who had come down from Hull at 16 to be developed through the Tottenham youth system, but was now giving homesickness for his native north east as his reason for accepting a record £6 million move to Bryan Robson's Middlesbrough.

But in May that year, a long way from White Hart Lane and its disappointments, there was a match taking place that ended up in Tottenham mythology. In the final of the European Cup Winners' Cup, Arsenal, the holders, were playing Real Zaragoza. With the score 1-1 and the match in the final minute of extra-time, it looked as if it was going down to penalties. Then Nayim, the midfielder signed by Zaragoza from Spurs two years back, looked up from the touch-line, noticed that David Seaman had meandered off his line, and sent a 50-yarder ballooning in off the bar.

Nayim from the halfway line. At the end of a season that had started with a flourish of which Blanchflower would have been proud and ended in a deflating sequence when nothing looked to be going right, it was something. Not much, but something.

The close season exodus was a depressing draining away of talent for Francis, though if he were to be asked what his biggest mistake at Tottenham was, he might admit that in the summer of 1995 he made a crucial misjudgement.

'The signing of Bergkamp in the wrong sector of north London has defined the recent history of our clubs,' opined Harry Harris in *Down Memory Lane*. Harris had taken a phone call from a Dutch journalist friend who told him that Bergkamp was unhappy at Inter Milan and wanted to try his luck in England. As Bergkamp had always been a Spurs fan because of his boyhood hero worship of Glenn Hoddle, he wanted to know if Spurs would be interested. Informed of Bergkamp's availability, Alan Sugar passed on the enquiry to Francis. Seeing Bergkamp as more of a midfield playmaker than the out-and-out striker he was looking for, Francis turned him down.

So Arsenal got Dennis Bergkamp. Spurs signed Chris Armstrong, Ruel Fox and Andy Sinton, who had been struggling to keep his place at Sheffield Wednesday. 'All worthy players, good Premiership material,' was Sheringham's opinion, 'but not the big names clubs like Arsenal and Chelsea had been signing. Not one of them was an improvement on what we'd had before.'

But telling Sugar that he was 'prepared to give it another year', Francis was confident that the 1995/96 season would feature a title challenge. That was before the third game of the season when Spurs lost 3-1 at home to a Liverpool side that were playing the kind of football that Spurs had given the game all those years ago – pass and move, each player working for each other, creating space and options. That day, Francis tipped Liverpool to be champions. The speed with which he stopped making noises about a title challenge of his own was partly caused by Armstrong's lacklustre start. Then there were the injuries to Sol Campbell and to Anderton, who by now was inhabiting the treatment room like an unexorcised ghost. It was Francis who was getting the blame from the fans, for recalling Anderton to the team without giving him enough time to recover.

Things improved and took the pressure off the manager for that season. Sheringham and Armstrong began to hit it off. Campbell returned to produce stand-out performances in defence. On New Year's Day, Spurs beat the league leaders Manchester United at White Hart Lane and reached third in the Premiership by the middle of January. More talk bubbled up about Spurs pushing on and going for the title. In the end, they finished eighth. But Francis had stopped them losing – after 50 matches in charge recording the fewest defeats of any previous manager in Spurs' history.

Over the following months, he spent moderately: Allan Nielsen from Brondby; the 20-year-old Norwegian striker Steffen Iversen from Rosenberg; and, from Cagliari, the Swiss centre-half Ramon Vega. Envisioning him as the ideal partner for Campbell in defence, Francis called him 'a real Tony Adams type'. Fans soon had another phrase for the gaffe-prone defender – 'dangerous at both ends' – and started calling him 'Suzanne', after the pop star of the same surname. Later, after Vega departed for Watford, one poster on the Bad, Stupid and Desperate fans website recalled him as 'like a skier on an uphill climb, all hunched shoulders, pumping arms and slowly sliding feet. He couldn't do *anything* – not even the most straightforward things – consistently'.

1996/97 turned out to be a gloom-filled, injury-wrecked season that started horribly when Mabbutt broke his leg in the 2-0 away win over Blackburn. Out of the first five games of the season, Spurs won one. When they lost to newly-promoted Leicester, they were booed off the pitch. At the end of November, they were knocked out in the fourth round of the Coca Cola Cup by Bolton Wanderers, losing 6-1. A month later, Newcastle United hammered them 7-1, one of the worst defeats in their history.

This time, there was no mid-season turnaround to take the pressure off Francis. For Justin Edinburgh, 'there was no brightness or buzz. There was an undercurrent of unhappiness amongst the lads. The big names had drifted away, and the players coming in were good, but certainly weren't players who could take us to the next level.' Sheringham's goal tally was seven, his worst ever at Tottenham. Armstrong broke his ankle, and at one point, when there were 15 first-team squad players undergoing treatment, Francis had to call in players from the youth squad. 'It got to the stage where I was handing out jelly babies at half-time to the kids I was having to play in the team,' he said.

Then there were the continuing absences of Anderton, who managed only 14 appearances, bringing forth a howl of resentment from Sugar. 'It was amazing how Anderton always seemed to manage to turn up and play for England,' he expostulated later, 'but when he returned to Tottenham he claimed his injury had come back again. I could not understand how Gerry was able to stand by and let this go on, but it seems you can't argue with someone who says they have pain.' Instead, Sugar argued with Sheringham about the length of his new contract, with the result that in the summer of 1997 Sheringham went for an astonishingly knockdown price of £3.5 million to Manchester United, saying he needed to play for a club that could win trophies.

Before the 1997/98 season got under way, however, the dismal exodus of talent was countered by a highly uncharacteristic signing. Scorned as mere decoration by Kenny Dalglish, who had just arrived at Newcastle to take over after Kevin Keegan's abrupt leave-taking, David Ginola found himself on the transfer list. In an attempt to appease the fans glaze-eyed from three seasons of pragmatic, increasingly unrewarding football, Francis took on the Frenchman known as 'Le Magnifique'.

Ginola could be exasperating, he could disappear when things weren't going well, but when he did what he did it was stunning.

'Ginola was one of my heroes,' says Paul Coyte, Tottenham's match-day announcer. 'I used to sit on the west wing, low down, and look at his feet. He was worth it! To watch that guy play, that's what we like as Spurs fans – that moment of genius that can turn a game around.'

Not often enough for Francis. Six weeks after the new season started, he told Sugar he felt he'd lost the support of the dressing room. It wasn't happening on the pitch and there wasn't much more he could do for the team. Plus the fans were calling for him to be sacked. He wanted to resign, but Sugar persuaded him to stay. He slogged on for another month, then quit for real.

'The thing about Tottenham,' he said later, 'is it's not just about winning. In most clubs winning is what it's all about, and people are happy with that, but at Tottenham you have to win with style as well, which puts even more pressure on. It's an impossible job.'

Which leaves you speculating how much less impossible it would have been if he hadn't turned his back on Bergkamp.

'Dennis Bergkamp was more fundamental in changing Arsenal than Thierry Henry,' says Patrick Barclay. 'Henry was a finisher but Bergkamp was a Danny Blanchflower, a designer who produced that speed and economy that were characteristic of Arsenal in the Highbury period. His father was a Tottenham fan and he learned much of his style from Glenn Hoddle, watching him on TV, and like us he would have noticed when Hoddle, at 18, didn't wait for the ball to touch the ground. Because he had no pace, he volleyed. That was behind Bergkamp's great volleying – stop the ball, volley, shoot with the other foot. There's no question that economy of movement was instilled in adolescence watching Glenn Hoddle in Amsterdam.'

'When we first started watching English football in Holland they showed one match a week on television,' concurs Bergkamp. 'Hoddle was the stand-out player. The way he moved the ball backwards and forwards with such ease was amazing. My favourite thing he used to do was the way he pulled the ball down out of the air as if it was the easiest thing in the world. Unlike so many players who had to try so hard to do that, he just let the ball sink softly on to his boot and therefore never lost control of it. I used to practise trying to do the same for hours.'

It's only a 'what if', of course. Bergkamp took a season or so to settle at Arsenal. It took a change of manager from Bruce Rioch to Wenger for him to show what he was capable of. But once he did, he was relentless. 'He never had a bad game,' says Barclay. 'He was galvanic.'

As for Francis, Alex Fynn sums up his three seasons at White Hart Lane with brisk severity: 'Criticised by the fans. Derided in the media for lobbing out £30 million on a bunch of underachievers.' Sugar was more inclined to be generous. 'He would have had a much fairer public hearing if he'd changed his name to Geraldo Francisco.'

Though signing Bergkamp might have done the trick.

CHAPTER THIRTY

THE ONE WHO TOOK THE TUBE

There are managerial entrances you remember, grand gestures that epitomise the person making them: the pomp and bravado of Jose Mourinho's 'I am a Special One' inaugural address at Chelsea in 2004; Kevin Keegan being received as the Messiah at Newcastle in 1982; even a Scholar-era Terry Venables sweeping through the gates of White Hart Lane in his black BMW, bringing with him, we thought, a touch of continental sophistication and glamour.

On 20th November, 1997, Christian Gross arrived at his media unveiling by tube, waving his ticket at the press with the announcement: 'I want this to become the ticket to my dreams.' It was intended to demonstrate his empathy with the travelling fan. Unluckily for him, it allowed the press to portray him as a podium-finish ass. 'From that moment on,' said Alan Sugar, 'he was dead meat. The media slaughtered him.'

To ridicule him was easy. For a start, Gross was virtually unknown in England to anyone who wasn't up to scratch on the more obscure details of the European football scene. When the press rang Alan Mullery for a reaction to the appointment, Mullery's knee-jerk response was: 'Christian who?' He was introduced by Gary Lineker as a 'relatively unknown species', while Gary Richardson asked him if he was scared. Another problem was the pronounced Swiss-German accent. He sounded, said Norman Giller in *Tottenham: The Managing Game*, like 'the Gestapo officer in *Allo Allo*'.

Then there was the team he inherited from Gerry Francis. Gross – who had, incidentally, also been pursued by both Borussia Mönchengladbach and Hamburg – had come to Tottenham on the back of taking Grasshoppers of Zurich to two titles in three years. Something similar never looked likely to happen with a Spurs side in what Sol Campbell admitted were 'dire straits', one that routinely caved in late on in games they should have won, one that was 16th in the table after 14 games and only a single point above the drop zone. Even then, Everton and Bolton, the two clubs keeping them away from it, both had a game in hand. They were solid enough in Gross's first match in charge, winning at Everton. But then the familiar routine reasserted itself in two home defeats. A 6-1 collapse at home to Chelsea was followed by a 4-0 loss at Coventry.

Two catalysts combined to make Gross's position worse. One was the rigorous training and dietary regime he imposed in order to instil a bit of backbone into a side he judged fragile and unfit. More ridicule was heaped on him when Fritz Schmidt, the fitness coach he'd always worked with, was denied a work permit – 'much to Anderton's relief' was the comment on Topspurs. The new discipline didn't go down well with other players, either. Les Ferdinand aggravated a leg injury, and pointed the finger at Gross for forcing him to train when he should have been resting. 'He was a really hard guy – training hard, playing hard,' said David Ginola, 'but he couldn't afford to play without me. You can play as hard as you want, but at the end of the day you need a lot of creativity and some skills. The game is not just playing hard, you need a bit of everything.'

The other catalyst was the return of Jürgen Klinsmann in December 1997, the rift with Sugar having been smoothed over. With Sheringham, the previous season's top scorer, now at Manchester United, and Ferdinand, Armstrong and Iversen all semi-permanent residents of a treatment room often more overcrowded than A & E on a Friday night, Gross was all in favour of the move. The outcome was bitterly ironic.

Though Klinsmann, already a Tottenham legend, was to contribute nine of the goals that would ultimately save Spurs from relegation, his return would further chip away at the shaky foundations of the regime Gross was trying to impose.

At 33, Klinsmann still fancied his chances of inclusion in Germany's squad for the rapidly approaching World Cup. But he'd fallen out with his manager at Sampdoria and had been dropped. Rejoining Tottenham, he figured, would give him enough time on the grass to clinch a place in Germany's 1998 World Cup squad. To which end, Klinsmann's new Spurs contract reputedly contained a clause stipulating that he would not be left out of the team. It was also rumoured that Sugar had guaranteed him a significant say over tactics and selection. The trouble was, no one had told Gross. First he'd been deprived of Schmidt. Then Sugar drafted in a rehabilitated David Pleat as director of football. Gross wasn't about to accept any further limitations on his authority and, unsurprisingly, he took against Klinsmann's muscling in.

'I had at the end my personal battles with Christian Gross, but that was also because the environment was very tense,' Klinsmann explained later. 'Spurs were struggling against relegation, and I thought it had to go this way and he thought it had to go that way.'

Mabbutt says that the disagreement stemmed from Gross's refusal to play David Ginola as the supplier of crosses to Klinsmann. Whatever the reason, Klinsmann was struggling to make an impact this time around. He also had the ear of the press to which he relayed the various gripes of dissatisfied players. There were whisperings that all was not well in the dressing room, and that the only player Gross talked to was his fellow countryman Ramon Vega. Then, in February, Klinsmann broke his nose in the FA Cup tie against Barnsley. Spurs lost 3-1, they were out of the cup and Klinsmann was out of the team.

Back in the side in March, Klinsmann openly fell out with Gross, threatening to walk out if his tactical input was ignored: 'I have totally different views about the way we should play and be led. There is a lot of tension between the team and Gross.' From the look of things during Klinsmann's comeback game against Bolton, he and Ginola were engaged in a stand-off too. Ginola's refusal to pass to him was so obvious it might just as well have been announced in a full-page ad in the programme. Instead, Le Magnifique combined with Clive Wilson to set up Allan Nielsen for the goal that hitched Spurs five points clear of the drop zone.

But from then on, the two of them did enough between them to warrant Spurs' survival in the Premier League. At White Hart Lane, Klinsmann opened the scoring against a title-chasing Liverpool and came up with his best performance since his return. Ginola, too, was a forceful, fluid presence in a 3-3 thriller that could have been a victory if Nielsen's overhead kick had hit the back of the net rather than the crossbar with a minute to go.

Without the suspended Ginola, Spurs went on to beat Crystal Palace 3-1. Klinsmann then proceeded to be the star of the match that finally completed Gross's rescue operation, wiping out any lingering suggestion that he had failed to make any significant impact with four goals – three of them in five minutes of striking brilliance so dazzling it was almost impossible to absorb – in Spurs' 6-2 win away to Wimbledon.

He signed off against Southampton at White Hart Lane on the last day of the 1997/98 season, after 15 appearances and nine goals. The ninth came six minutes after Spurs went one-down when Matt Le Tissier scored after 20 minutes. When Les Ferdinand chested the ball down into his path, Tottenham's most famous number 33 volleyed high into the top corner from outside the penalty area. Then, for the final time in Tottenham white, he took to the earth with glee.

There was a lot to be celebrated. Klinsmann had produced the goods. Spurs had won. Most importantly, they were still in the Premier League. But it was a sad occasion, even so. After 16 years, 11 of them as captain, and 619 appearances – he still holds the record of Tottenham's longest-serving player, a record unlikely now ever to be beaten – Gary Mabbutt had made his final appearance.

When Mabbutt came onto Tottenham Hotspur's radar, it was 1982 and Keith Burkinshaw was in charge. Bill Nicholson had already scouted the 21-year-old, not just in England Under-21 games but playing for Bristol Rovers, where on different occasions Mabbutt had shown himself as at ease and constructive at full-back, in central defence and as a midfielder. Given the existing sick list at Spurs, Mabbutt's versatility made him an ideal signing. What held Nicholson back was the perception that a prize such as Mabbutt would not come cheap. It was a misapprehension corrected in a tip-off by Peter Anderson, then manager of Third Division Millwall. Bristol Rovers, said Anderson, would be willing to let him go for less than half Nicholson's estimate of £300,000.

Mabbutt was so keen he cut his holiday short to sign. 'Where I was lucky,' he said, 'was that some players come to Tottenham and find it difficult to be accepted. When I signed, no one had heard of this boy from the West Country and Keith Burkinshaw said I might have to wait. Then because of pre-season injuries I was in the team in the first week, and I scored with a diving header against Luton. That gave me a special relationship with the Spurs crowd.'

His long and successful career as a footballer was all the more remarkable given that at 17 he had been diagnosed with Type 1 diabetes, entailing four self-inflicted injections and eight blood tests every day, and a life of dietary restriction. Hence he became something of an icon for many children with the condition. Soon after he came to London, the BBC got him to appear on Blue Peter, where he demonstrated how the injections were carried out using a syringe on an orange. His first experience of appearing on television also gave him first-hand experience of the BBC's still ingrained snobbishness. Having grown up in Eastville, near the old Bristol Rovers ground, he spoke with a pronounced Bristolian burr that the BBC suggested he might like to lose. 'They told me to say *door* and I said "Dorr", so they kept making me say "Open the *daw*," but I wasn't going to stop rolling my Rrrs. I love my Bristolian accent.'

He loved Spurs, too. After the 1987 FA Cup Final, George Graham tried to tempt him to Arsenal, Alex Ferguson waved the Manchester United cheque book at him and Kenny Dalglish had him on a wish list. 'Kenny called me after the cup final saying, "I want to sign you, Beardsley and Barnes." I was the only player he wanted but couldn't get. At that time, that's where the money was being made, being transferred, but it was a good time. Nice to be speaking to them and knowing they wanted your services, and it's a great honour to have three clubs come in for you, but I saw us gaining momentum. If, let's say, we had been fighting relegation every year and I'd fallen out with the manager, it might have been different, but I'd been at Tottenham for five years and was loving my football there.'

By the time he turned out for that final game against Southampton in May 1998, he had the kind of injury history normally only found in jump jockeys. 'Thing was, I'd had 16 operations in 16 years. A lot of them were the running repairs you have at the end of a season — knee, shoulder, hernia, double hernia.' Four more were on his face after the injury inflicted by John Fashanu.

'Every player who has ever played the game longs to be playing. You always wish you could go out there and perform. But though the mind may still be willing, the body's not. I'd had so many operations. Playing until 37, that's quite an achievement. I'd been diabetic 20 years, four injections and eight blood tests every day. Another club offered me a contract for one more year, but I'd had a wonderful innings, I was still pretty fit, and I didn't see the point in labouring on.'

When he packed up, he had nine offers of management. 'But I was talking to Bill Nicholson and he said the one thing he regretted was that he'd never seen his daughter grow up. He only realised it when he was walking her up the aisle. My first daughter had been born and if it was that hectic in Bill's era, it would be even more now.'

So he ran a sports management company and did some development work in South Africa, who made him their European ambassador when they were hosting the World Cup. He worked for the FA, too, on their disciplinary committee. Above all, he has stayed close to Tottenham Hotspur, for whom he works as a club ambassador. 'It's a cliché,' he says, 'but good news doesn't sell. All people want to hear about are the things that happen that aren't so good. No one would know Tottenham players have funded a house in South Africa for orphans. Each one of the players sponsors those children, and the club supplies the furniture and everything else for the running of the house.'

His best moment as a Spurs player remains the 1984 UEFA Cup

victory, the one when Tony Parks saved the penalty and nearly sprinted out of White Hart Lane from sheer joy. And his worst? That had to be his last game, the one against Southampton. 'When the final whistle blew, I'd been there for 16 years and I knew that was the last time. There were tears coursing down my face, tears coursing down the fans' faces. Saying goodbye to them, saying goodbye to the players and knowing I'd never be on that pitch again. That was my worst moment.'

With most players you usually measure their career in goals, or appearances, or the incremental rise and fall of transfer fees as they move from club to club. In Mabbutt's case, it's different. You measure his career in managers. When he signed for Spurs in 1982, Keith Burkinshaw was in charge. Peter Shreeve took over and went. So did David Pleat and Terry Venables, along with Peter Shreeve (again) and the Ray Clemence/Doug Livermore combo. He was still there through the years of Ossie Ardiles, Gerry Francis and Christian Gross. Gary Mabbutt is a living history of Tottenham Hotspur. The refusal to limit his life because of diabetes, the determination to go on playing in spite of injuries, shows the measure of the man. 'Legend' is a word that's applied rather too freely when it comes to describing footballers. When it comes to Gary Mabbutt, it's the only one you can use.

Saving Spurs from relegation that May had just been the starter position for Christian Gross. Arsenal, after all, had just pulled off another Double. So as the 1998/99 season got under way, the expectation of fans and club was of something a whole lot bigger than just survival. Gross seemed to agree. Determined to demonstrate how his stringent regime would be the key to glory, he brought the players in for pre-season training before the end of the World Cup. After which they crashed 3-1 at Wimbledon in the opening game of the season. Gross explained the defeat thus: 'The grass was too long.'

They followed that up with a 3-0 defeat at home to Sheffield Wednesday, played with all the passion of a patient leafing through old magazines in a dentist's waiting room. As he was driven away, Sugar had to run the gauntlet of protesting fans.

'Sugar usually rang to shout at me but this time he sounded depressed,' says Bernie Kingsley of the Tottenham Supporters Trust. 'We had a conversation for about half an hour and he didn't actually say he was going to sack the manager but he actually *asked* who we should get in. I talked about Hoddle, who was England manager at the time, and Klinsmann, because there'd been a strong rumour that after Klinsmann came back he went to Sugar and said, "Gross is useless, let me take over."'

Like a depressive who having made the decision to end it all is deceptively cheerful in the final hours, Gross appeared perversely upbeat. 'Believe it or not, in the week leading up to the Everton game, it was the calmest I have seen him since he came over,' said Les Ferdinand. 'Maybe he knew the writing was on the wall and decided to enjoy it for the last couple of days. There was certainly a change in his mood and his attitude.' Too late. Gross's Tottenham career ended as it had begun, with a victory over Everton at Goodison Park. After that, lampooned by the press, largely ignored by the players, let down by results, unable to persuade club and fans to give him longer than three matches to get it right, he was booted out.

'It was a bit of a knee-jerk, bringing in Christian Gross in the first place,' says Mabbutt. 'Not enough research had been done. He wasn't used to the British media and he didn't have enough experience of the English game. It was a bridge too far for him to come into a club where expectations were high. Technically, he had some very good ideas, but he didn't realise the man-management needed.'

The press couldn't resist wishing him good luck on his tube trip out of Tottenham. In actual fact, he made a dignified exit by taxi. 'I am more disappointed than angry,' he said. 'After only three games, I think it is too short a time to judge me and decide my fate. There were so many ideas that I had for the weeks and months ahead. I might have understood if I had been asked to go after three months, but after three matches? That cannot be right.'

Maybe so. Gross went on to win three Swiss titles with Basel, masterminding European defeats of Liverpool, Celtic, Deportivo and Juventus. And with hindsight, bearing in mind what was to follow, his record at White Hart Lane shouldn't be judged too severely. Gross took over a side of underperforming talents and crocks and tried to instil a necessary discipline and fitness to go with the mandatory flair. He was in charge for 30 matches, and won 18 of them. Okay, so he hadn't been the new Arsène Wenger. But then neither was the man who followed him. Far from it. Very far from it.

CHAPTER THIRTY-ONE

THE ONE IN
THE RAINCOAT

The journalist Norman Giller tells a story about the day George Graham came to Tottenham. 'George phoned me from Leeds at the end of summer 1998 and said: "I'm on the move again. Guess where to?"' says Giller. 'I came up with the daftest answer I could think of: "Spurs."

'"Bloody hell," said George, "How did you know? I've only just agreed to take the job."'

After Christian Gross, Spurs had been looking for a man who knew how a traditional English club ticked. But only a Spurs fan with a taste for comic absurdity could have relished the new appointment. George Graham and Tottenham Hotspur was a combination that went together like liver and crème de menthe.

For the fans, Graham was Arsenal. Soul-destroying Arsenal. You could never imagine him saying, as Bill Nicholson once did, 'It is better to fail aiming high than to succeed aiming low.' This was the man who once declared to former Tottenham director Douglas Alexiou, 'I love winning 1-0.' The man who still had Arsenal shares. The man whose teams featured impenetrable defence and spoiling tactics that drew yawns and often howls of protest from anyone who wasn't Arsenal. Not that he seemed to care. 'Yes, winning is boring, isn't it?'

Not just boring. Horrible, sometimes. Some fans could remember how when, as a laid-back midfielder, he was in the Arsenal side that clinched the League Championship part of the 1970/71 Double at White Hart Lane. Those were the days, of course, when Graham was known as 'Stroller', though by the time he returned to Highbury as manager in 1986 the persona of affable charmer had been smartly jettisoned. When Graham arrived at Highbury he was allegedly greeted by the manager's secretary, who had faithfully served for many years.

'Hello, George, it's nice to have you back,' she said.

'It's Mr Graham now,' he snapped.

But Graham's new severity had paid off. Arsenal then were a club whose reputation dwarfed their existing position. They'd won nothing since the 1979 FA Cup and were well adrift of the top clubs. Graham had proceeded to throw out most of the old guard, installing new signings and opening the dressing-room door to players from the youth team. Suddenly discipline was everything. So was winning. By Christmas 1986, they were top of the league. That hadn't happened for a decade. Over the next nine years, Arsenal went on to win six trophies, including two league titles and the 1994 European Cup Winners' Cup, underlining his reputation as one of the supreme tacticians of his era. True, he had been the main casualty of the bung scandals of 1995 and the FA's investigation into football's labyrinthine economy – Graham received a year's ban and lost his job. But, back in the game after serving his punishment, he went to Leeds and within two years had them qualifying for Europe.

No wonder, then, that Sugar fancied him to bring about a renaissance at White Hart Lane. It had been, he claimed, a tough but necessary decision: tasking the game's arch-pragmatist with the job of getting the club back in shape and performing in the way it should do. In Graham, he was giving Spurs the chance of glory by appointing a respected, successful manager who knew what it took.

And so, jacking in the Leeds job, Sugar's latest appointment arrived to the kind of reception that people give to a dawn raid by VAT inspectors. To quote Arsène Wenger: 'Once you have been an Arsenal man, it is difficult to go to Tottenham.'

Undeterred, Graham outlined his mission statement. 'I am totally focused on getting it right here,' he said. 'There is a lot of hard work to be done, and I anticipate a lot of changes. The aim is to be in the top six within two years.'

'I felt unclean about it,' said supporter Danny Keene, 'a degree of unease. But I also remember how poor and porous in defence we were, and I felt, "We've got somebody now who'll stop us losing."'

Not immediately. Four games into the job, George Graham's Spurs had chalked up one win, one draw and two defeats. Just over a month after he took over he was back at Highbury with a side featuring three central defenders. Arsenal 0 Spurs 0. This was most definitely not the Tottenham Hotspur of Nicholson and Blanchflower.

At least Graham backed away from offloading David Ginola, even if 'flamboyant entertainer' had never been a pair of words attached to a player deployed by Graham in his Highbury years. Realising there was no way he would win over the fans if he dispensed with the Frenchman, Graham took the less provoking option of retaining him while continually chivvying him about his work rate and substituting him. Ginola's response was to produce some of his best work for Spurs in that 1998/99 season – it was to earn him the PFA and FWA awards. The match-winner he scored at Oakwell, after a 40-yard zig-zag past five Barnsley defenders, in the FA Cup quarter-final is a prime example. 'It was like a skier performing a slalom,' says Danny Keene. 'He was a shining light for Spurs in a really fallow period.'

Uncreative, maybe, but not completely barren. In the knockout competitions Graham gave the club its best season since the start of the decade. The 1-0 win away to Barnsley clinched a first FA Cup semi-final in four years. That cup run ended there, in the semi at Old Trafford, with a two-goal defeat by Newcastle, but in the Worthington Cup – that year's moniker for the League Cup – Spurs went all the way. In November, there was a 3-1 fourth-round win over Liverpool at Anfield, the goals coming from Steffen Iversen, John Scales and Allan Nielsen. In December, they beat Manchester United 3-1 at the Lane, with two goals from Armstrong and one from Ginola. It earned them a semi-final against Wimbledon, by which time Graham had gone shopping in Europe. The man he brought back with him wore terrible clothes, couldn't score and, in the opinion of some, couldn't play. He was about to become a Spurs legend.

From the day in 1998 that Graham brought Steffen Freund to Tottenham from Borussia Dortmund, the would-be defensive enforcer in midfield bellowed and shoved and dived his way into the fans' affections with an excitable Latino manner wholly at odds with his take-no-prisoners playing style. He cemented his cult-hero status when, while suspended during the 1999/2000 season, he sat in the Lower East stand for the game against Arsenal (which Spurs won 2-1) and joined in the chants. 'He was Dave Mackay without the skill,' says journalist and fan Mat Snow. 'He really, really wanted to win. Against Arsenal once, Vieira was involved in some sort of trouble and Freund ran the entire length of the pitch to join in. His attitude was, if we can't outplay them, then at least we can get in their faces.'

What made Freund really special, though, was that he never managed to score. He was so cherished for his failure to rattle the rigging that whenever he got the ball everyone would chorus, 'Shoooooooot!'

'He couldn't hit a cow's arse with a banjo,' says Rob White, 'and we loved him for it. Spurs fans will all forgive lack of talent if there's lots of passion. He was definitely one of us.'

Freund isn't about to argue the point. 'I wasn't the best player, the fans are 100 per cent right. But if you talk about work-rate and attitude, that's me. I was always strong when I won the ball. I go on the pitch, I think, "We will win every game! I will try everything!"

'It was in November 1998, when Tottenham were looking for a holding midfielder, that David Pleat came over to watch me playing for Borussia Dortmund against Hamburg. I met David afterwards with my agent, Rune Hauge, in an Italian restaurant in Dortmund. Then George Graham watched me for 20 minutes against Kaiserslautern, said, "Fine", and flew home.

'My contract with Borussia Dortmund was finishing in the summer, but Spurs wanted me to sign in the January window. I had the feeling straight away that it would be the right move. Okay, they were in the middle of the table, but the club was one of the big five and that will never change. One of the biggest clubs in England, one of the biggest in the world, with some of the best supporters. I spoke to Jürgen [Klinsmann] before I signed. He said, "If everything's fine about your contract, sign for the club because it's special."

'I had to drive from Tottenham to my hotel in Waltham Abbey, so the club's press officer, John Fennelly, said he would give me a lead because I'd never driven on the left-hand side of the road before. There was only one car left in the car park, an old Suzuki, so I took that and it ran out of petrol halfway. Then we got to the hotel and it broke down. But I came over from the poor side of Germany; I had nothing. They said my clothes were terrible, I thought they were sexy! I would have been happy just to have good food!

'Ginola was really helpful and friendly when I came, because I didn't speak great English – growing up in East Germany, my second language was Russian. I didn't understand George Graham or Chris Hughton on the pitch, I didn't understand Chris's jokes or instructions. I was always running the wrong way because I didn't understand. In Germany, everyone concentrated in the dressing room. They would just sit there, very quiet. So when I got into the Spurs dressing room, I thought, 'What the f***'s going on?' The TV was on, people were listening to music, they were playing with the ball. I was the only one who concentrated.

'It was crazy for me at the beginning. In my first eight weeks, we played six times against Wimbledon. I always seemed to be up against Robbie Earle. I said, "Do we only play Wimbledon here?" It was not nice to watch! They didn't play pretty; long balls to John Hartson. The ball was only in the air and I was running around in the middle. It was really hard work. All the games finished 1-1 or 0-0.'

Except for one, the second leg of the Worthington Cup semi-final against Wimbledon. That featured a chipped first-half goal by Steffen Iversen, plus terrier-like defending combined with sustained and heroic singing by the fans. It got them to Wembley, and a final against Leicester.

Which, it had to be said, was an undistinguished one, memorable chiefly for Justin Edinburgh's sending off in the second half when, after being fouled by Robbie Savage he got up and gave his assailant a light slap. Savage clutched his face to his hands as if he had been head-butted by Mike Tyson and Edinburgh took the long walk back to the dressing-room. Down to 10 men, Spurs responded to the threat of extra-time by piling everyone forward, but the peak of excitement seemed to have been reached when Iversen's shot flapped the side netting. They were already in stoppage time when Nielsen plunged to score with a header.

Spurs lifted their first trophy in eight years. They were back in Europe. For Graham, it was job done. Even then, though, some of the fans found it hard to take. Many couldn't even bring themselves to utter his name. The victory chant that day was 'Man in a raincoat's blue-and-white army'. And for the subject of their serenade, the music was about to die.

In the league, the rest of the season petered out – Spurs took just one point from the last five games and finished mid-table. Then Nielsen fell out with Graham and went out on loan to Wolves before shifting permanently to Watford.

In the 1999/2000 season, Spurs' defensive frailty returned to haunt them. There were 15 league defeats, and after an FA Cup replay in December, Graham had to issue a public apology to the fans who had schlepped all the way up to Newcastle only to witness Spurs on the wrong end of a 6-1 thrashing.

But it was Europe that was to prove the tipping point. Back in cross-channel competition for the first time in seven years, Spurs' UEFA Cup second-round first leg against Kaiserslautern at White Hart Lane was an adequate night rather than a glory one – 1-0 to the Spurs, an Iversen penalty following a foul on Ginola.

When it came to the second leg in the first week of November, all that mattered for Graham was protecting the single-goal advantage. His decision to keep Ginola on the bench backfired. Discovering that Tottenham's one indisputably gifted forward was reduced that night to the role of bum on seat, Kaiserslautern changed their line-up. They won with two late goals. Nothing underlined more clearly Graham's stubborn refusal to acknowledge the shift from the defence-first mentality that had taken hold in the game since his years at Highbury.

To make matters worse, Arsenal were now enjoying a renaissance through playing the kind of football that by tradition belonged to Spurs. 'Without question, without a shadow of doubt, whether on principle or by happy coincidence, Arsenal stole Spurs' clothes,' says the journalist Patrick Barclay, 'because under Arsène Wenger, Arsenal became the cavaliers of football. It was Danny Blanchflower and Bill Nicholson. The pace of the transition from defence to attack, the elegance of the players – it was the glory game. I wrote at the time that Nicholson and Blanchflower would have been purring.'

Which Spurs fans were not. That 1999/2000 season ended with a 10th-place finish, just one higher than the season before. Picking up Neil Sullivan, the goalkeeper, and Ben Thatcher from newly-relegated Wimbledon to join two more ex-Dons, Chris Perry and Oyvind Leonhardsen, at White Hart Lane meant that since January 1998 Spurs had invested £23 million on new players. Yet Alan Sugar, however much money he threw at it, was still without a successful team, still having to field accusations of stinginess.

That, maybe, was what needled him into agreeing a club record fee of £11 million – getting on for top dollar in 2000 – for the Dynamo Kiev and Ukraine striker Sergei Rebrov. At the time, bagging the 26-year-old Rebrov appeared something of a coup – at Dynamo he had looked lethal and several clubs had been after him.

Intended to take Spurs to the next level, Rebrov struggled. Unfortunately, Ginola, who might have set him up to hit the back of the net, wasn't around any more. Graham had offloaded him to Aston Villa – a decision that was to prove a shrewd one when Ginola failed to fell any trees at the Midlands club.

Maybe Rebrov was intended to be a replacement for Sheringham rather than an out-and-out striker and never really got the chance to show what he could do. Ineffective without Andriy Shevchenko, his striking partner at Dynamo, too small to operate as a traditional target man, Rebrov went off like a damp rocket.

So did the 2000/01 season. With only one point to show from the previous four games, a 3-1 home win over Derby County, winless at the bottom of the table, was never going to soften fans' hearts. At the start of Graham's tenure, some had been prepared to give him a chance. Now everyone was angry, disappointed, resentful. These were people who had known the era of Lineker, Gascoigne and Waddle. They had gloried in Sheringham, Klinsmann and Barmby. They remembered the Tottenham Hotspur of Archibald and Crooks – Chivers and Gilzean, even. Now they had Neil Sullivan, Ben Thatcher, Chris Perry and Oyvind Leonhardsen. As Jimmy Greaves said, Spurs had turned into 'Wimbledon with fans'.

At the end of October came the 3-1 slaughter at White Hart Lane by First Division Birmingham in the League Cup. Hearing the chants of 'Sugar out' reverberating round the stadium, faced with fans calling for his departure at the main gates and commandeering the radio phone-ins to bitterly condemn him for betraying the cherished Tottenham tradition, being rounded on by shareholders and supporters at the club's Annual General Meeting, feeling that what he had done had gone unvalued, Sugar cracked. Just after a 1-1 draw with Arsenal on 18 December 2000, he handed over control of Tottenham Hotspur to ENIC, an investment company.

He felt, he said later, 'an immediate sense of relief'.

In the parallel universe occupied by football fans, few had heard of ENIC. They were just pleased it had entered the fray. Daniel Levy's English National Investment Company (ENIC) secured control of Tottenham Hotpur with a 27 per cent stake, equating to 274 million shares for a premium price of £22 million, in partnership with Joe Lewis, a Bahamas-based billionaire. ENIC had built up a portfolio of European sides. As well as Spurs, they owned substantial interests in Glasgow Rangers, Slavia Prague, AEK Athens, Vicenza and FC Basel. Over time these holdings would be relinquished and ENIC's finance director would become Tottenham Hotspur's finance director as Spurs became ENIC's focus.

But for the fans, what counted was that Levy was a season-ticket holder at White Hart Lane. 'Being a Spurs fan was an advantage when I came in because I understood straight away what the club was all about, what made the fans tick and what the expectations were,' he said later.

As for the man who was now Sir Alan Sugar, four years after the bruising experience at Tottenham, there were still puffs of steam coming out of his ears; in an interview with the *Daily Telegraph* in 2005, he was describing footballers as 'scum, total scum. They're bigger scum than journalists, don't you understand? They don't know what honesty or loyalty is. They're the biggest scum that walk on this planet and, if they weren't football players, most of them would be in prison, it's as simple as that'.

It was not a character sketch recognised by some of his former players. Gary Mabbutt called it 'astonishing' and added, 'Perhaps, when he took over, he didn't realise what he was letting himself in for. I think he found it very difficult to run the club like he did Amstrad and obviously he learned very quickly it was totally different.'

Later, Sugar reflected more temperately on his years at Tottenham, years, he said, that had cost him the light-hearted sense of humour he had as a younger man. 'I wasted 10 years trying to do something great for that football club. Yes, I put Tottenham into a sound financial position, but as far as performance on the pitch was concerned, we did nothing,' he said in his autobiography *What You See Is What You Get*. 'The emphasis changed from me being that horrible man who wouldn't invest any money in the club, to me being the horrible man who'd brought George Graham in and ruined it.'

But although along the way he made some well-intentioned managerial appointments that went badly wrong, it's important to recognise the debt that Tottenham owe Alan Sugar. He snatched the club from the abyss of extinction. And from Robert Maxwell, which would, as events proved later, have probably amounted to the same thing. And that, really, was the achievement that mattered.

The boardroom changed, but at first the mediocrity on the pitch did not. Spurs didn't win away in the Premier League until February, a 1-0 victory at Manchester City. That came after a run of four consecutive 0-0 draws. If Danny Blanchflower's signature quote was 'The game is about glory', George Graham's was 'Move along there, nothing to see'.

'In the cup games, Spurs were always strong,' says Freund, 'but we couldn't play consistently in the Premiership. We had Les Ferdinand up front, Ginola, Sol Campbell, Ian Walker . . . our team was good. We were good against top teams, then we'd lose to low-down sides.

'My feeling about George in the beginning was, yes, I liked him. When he came into the room, he had charisma. He looked strong. His personality was strong. He was good at man-management. If you didn't like him because you were a bit shy, it wasn't George's fault. You could come to him with every problem. I think some of the players didn't realise that.

'Towards the end, I think the turning point was when the new assistant coach, Stewart Houston from Arsenal, came in. He was too close to George. We couldn't have a laugh on the pitch any more. Everything was intense, really hard work. Towards the end of the season we were always a little bit tired, we weren't fresh.'

The new board felt Graham had to go. But in March he was saved – for the time being, that was. The reason for his stay of execution was an FA Cup quarter-final win at West Ham, a fantastic, rampant Spurs victory in which Rebrov came good at last with two goals. It was a match which was almost as exhausting to watch as to play in, and featured backs-to-the-wall defending with even Ferdinand covering in defence at one stage as West Ham whittled down Spurs' lead. West Ham 2 Tottenham Hotspur 3. As the final whistle blew, as Freund climbed into the crowd to join in the celebrations, as Sullivan and Rebrov and Clemence cavorted in joyful delirium, Graham must have privately exulted. He had now taken the club to its second FA Cup semi-final in three years. He was now, surely, unsackable. In the build-up to the semi-final against Arsenal, he complained to the press, laying the blame for his team's poor performance on his transfer budget. He needed, he claimed, £50 million to take Spurs where it was meant to be.

The wrong button had been pushed. Graham had been warned in writing by the board for similar activities before. There were only three weeks left to the meeting with Arsenal, but it was hard to see how he could stay. And he didn't. At the end of a 15-minute meeting on 16th March, Graham was sacked. After two-and-a-half years in charge, the man in the raincoat was gone.

And meanwhile Spurs started the hunt for a new manager. Again.

CHAPTER THIRTY-TWO

WHAT PRICE LOYALTY?

The press talked up Joe Kinnear's chances, they suggested Luca Vialli might be in with a shout, they longingly floated the prospect of a comeback for Terry Venables. But really there was only one possible choice after George Graham. The polar opposite of the last man in the job. The man the fans knew as 'God'.

Glenn Hoddle had 15 months left to run on his contract at Southampton, a club which he'd managed to turn, in 18 months, from annual nominees for relegation into an outfit that stood eighth in the Premier League, in contention for Europe. And they stood five points above Spurs. Southampton, said their aggrieved chairman, Rupert Lowe, upon learning of Tottenham's intentions, had given him the chance to rebuild his career after his job as England manager had derailed so spectacularly in 1999. Now he was being lured away by these 'north London yobbos'.

As far as Hoddle was concerned, though, this was something he couldn't pass up. He was *the* Spurs man, *the* Spurs player, part of the Holy Trinity – Nicholson, Blanchflower, Hoddle. He'd turned down Alan Sugar's offer of the job in 1993. He might never get the chance again. He quit Southampton on 28th March and two days later signed a five-year deal.

The tabloids were well pleased, obviously. They had the chance to reprise the controversies of Hoddle's time as England boss: leaving Paul Gascoigne out of the 1998 World Cup squad, installing a faith healer, Eileen Drewery, as part of his staff. If England had progressed in France instead of going out in the second round to Argentina on penalties, everything probably would have been overlooked. But when, unguardedly, Hoddle aired some off-the-wall theories about reincarnation and disabled people to a journalist from *The Times*, which then drew criticism from Tony Blair, the Prime Minister, that was the end of his England reign.

But nobody around White Hart Lane bothered about that. With John Gorman, his former Spurs team-mate, as assistant, Hoddle arrived to the sound of ringing applause. 'Glenn is an excellent coach, a very forward-thinking coach,' said Ray Clemence. 'Glenn is an idol through and through with the supporters and you only have to look at the job he has done at Southampton to see what a good manager he is,' said Gary Mabbutt. 'He has all the credentials needed to manage Spurs.'

Steve Archibald called it 'an excellent choice for Spurs and Spurs fans.' Graham Roberts described him as 'probably the best player that Spurs have ever had', adding, 'If he wins the FA Cup semi-final, he'll be even more of a hero with fans.' For Alan Mullery, Hoddle was answering the call of destiny. 'I would think,' he said, 'that when Glenn first came out of football as a player, the first thing on his mind would be that one day he would become manager of Spurs.'

Hoddle's first game in formal charge was a tasty one: the FA Cup semi-final at Old Trafford on 8th April. Arsenal v Tottenham Hotspur. In fact, the two had met just eight days before at Highbury, when Spurs had lost 2-0. This, though, was on neutral soil. The press happily pointed out the connections. As a player, Hoddle had left Spurs for Monaco, managed at the time by Arsène Wenger. Now they were meeting for a second time in under two weeks as equals. Or as equal as Hoddle could be with what George Graham had left him, a side that lagged behind all the major teams and that needed both a boost in confidence and a major reconstruction job.

On the plus side, Sol Campbell was back from injury. That had to put Spurs in with a chance. Then, minutes after kick-off, they took the lead through Garry Doherty getting on the end of a Steffen Iversen shot. It was all good.

Too good. Though Neil Sullivan kept Arsenal at bay for most of the first half, Campbell crocked himself again while fouling Ray Parlour. And from the Robert Pires free kick that followed, Patrick Viera headed the equaliser. Late on, Pires tapped home Sylvain Wiltord's cross to make Arsenal 2-1 winners. It wasn't even close. Arsenal had missed a glut of chances. The scoreline flattered Spurs.

Hoddle would have needed no telling about the immensity of the task he had taken on. In the weeks to follow, it became immeasurably harder. His captain, the leader who had kept the club from complete meltdown in a long sequence of barren seasons, the blue-chip talent he could have built a new side around, was about to walk away. The Sol Campbell transfer saga was reaching a conclusion. In doing so it would stir emotions so powerful that they have become an ineradicable part of the Tottenham Hotspur psyche.

Around a year earlier, there had been another north London derby, a 1-1 draw at White Hart Lane that had grabbed everyone's attention because it featured five Spurs players who had come up through the youth ranks: Steve Carr, Sol Campbell, Stephen Clemence, Ledley King and Alton Thelwell.

Thelwell and Clemence went on to be fringe players, and Carr was a modest success. The other two possessed greatness. King was, at 19, already a player of substance with a mature mastery of the art of game-reading to add to simply-executed but effective ball-winning skills. George Graham had been using him in central midfield – in the December just gone, he had scored his first goal for Spurs in a 3-3 draw away to Bradford City. Not only that, but he did it 9.7 seconds after the kick-off, the Premier League's quickest-ever goal. But everyone could see what a defender he would make. Especially in partnership with Campbell.

By the time King had worked his way into first-team contention, Campbell had been there for for eight years. An East End lad who was a schoolboy player with West Ham, he had signed as a trainee in

1992, in the last days of Venables's reign, speedily announcing himself in his debut that December by coming on as a sub for Nick Barmby and scoring. Spurs lost 2-1 that day but Campbell was obviously destined for big things. He had it all: pace, timing, muscle, presence. By the time he settled as a central defender, he was already an England international, winning his first England cap in 1996 and in 1998 becoming, at 23, their second youngest ever captain (Bobby Moore beat him to the record by one year and 27 days). Within a year, though, stories were circulating that Alan Sugar had fended off an approach from Manchester United and it was being speculated that Tottenham might lose him when his contract expired in the summer of 2001.

To avoid him leaving on a Bosman, Spurs offered him a contract which would make him the club's highest-paid player ever. Negotiations went on for months but Campbell never committed himself, in spite of public assurances that he would stay at Spurs. Then, saying he had been advised by the then England manager Sven-Göran Eriksson that it was the right thing to do, he confirmed he wanted to leave so he could play Champions League football.

For the fans, this was depressing but hardly a surprise. There was grudging acceptance of the inevitable, an acknowledgement that he had given Spurs 10 years of distinguished effort unrewarded by major honours. The talk was that he would go to Milan.

For Spurs fans of my generation, one of the unifying moments of experience is the question: 'Where were you when you heard John White had been killed?' I was home for school holidays at the time and can still remember the absolute shock. Similarly, Mat Snow, a generation later, recalls with precision the day he found out Sol Campbell had signed for Arsenal. 'As he walked around the pitch after his last game, I'd thought, "This is it, we're not going to see him again",' says Mat, who had just taken over as editor of *FourFourTwo* magazine. 'At that semi against Arsenal at Old Trafford, when we were outclassed, he did everything he could, he was the *only* good player we had. It would be sickening to see him go to Milan but he thoroughly deserved to. You could easily see how he could prove one of the best centre-backs in Europe, working alongside Maldini, that would really polish him up.

'I was at work when I heard the news. Someone said: "You're not going to believe this but Arsenal are having a press conference and they're going to announce they've signed Sol Campbell." I was speechless. I was very, *very* upset. Anger. And a feeling of betrayal. The last we saw of him he was taking the lap of honour, and everyone was waving – it was a genuine, emotional Spurs fans' farewell. It was your wife moving in with your best friend. He could have gone to any club in the world. But he chose that one.'

'When he left, my quote was on the back of *The Sun*,' says Daniel Wynne. 'The Ultimate Act Of Betrayal.'

They weren't alone in feeling that. All the fans looked on it the same way. Angry with Campbell, angry at Arsenal. Some of us were angry with ourselves, too. We'd believed Campbell when he'd said in an interview with *Spurs Monthly* that one club he'd never play for was Arsenal, when he said his heart and soul was at White Hart Lane. What Campbell had done had not just wounded us, it had made us feel foolishly naive. No wonder so many Spurs fans still find it hard to forgive.

In what was, for a Spurs fan, a gloomy summer, there was one chink of light. On 13th July, 2001, Spurs played a pre-season warm-up against Stevenage Borough. The team, a mix of young hopefuls and veterans, included Steffen Freund.

That day in July, the result was Stevenage 1 Tottenham Hotspur 8. The last of the Spurs goals was very special. After 100 games and three seasons of trying, Freund had scored at last.

Hoddle's rebuilding work that summer featured a battle with his former chairman at Southampton, Rupert Lowe, for the services of the defender Dean Richards, who cost Spurs £8.1 million to release him from his contract. It also included the re-signing of a 35-year-old Teddy Sheringham from Manchester United. The 33-year-old Gus Poyet arrived from Chelsea to link up with him and the 34-year-old Les Ferdinand from midfield. Christian Ziege, almost a boy-child by comparison at 29, came in from Liverpool as left wing-back though he spent most of the season on the treatment table, as did Stephen

Carr. Partly as a consequence of that, the 2001/02 season didn't take off the way Hoddle hoped. Spurs needed to be challenging for the top places, and they weren't.

For the fans, though, three significant games lodged the season in memory just the same. One was the home game against Manchester United at the end of September. It was Dean Richards marking his debut with a goal, it was Les Ferdinand putting Spurs two up after Gustavo Poyet sprung United's offside trap, it was Christian Ziege's free header beating Fabien Barthez a minute before the break. And then it was United coming back from 0-3 down to win 5-3. 'God help the rest of us if they start keeping clean sheets,' said Hoddle afterwards.

Another landmark was the home derby against Arsenal in November, Hoddle's first league derby in charge, Campbell's first in red. A sulphurous, emotionally-charged affair with a late goal by Arsenal was redeemed only by Poyet's last-gasp equaliser. It was a game, says King, that the fans' reaction ensured he'll never forget. 'They gave my name a huge cheer, the loudest ever, because I suppose they wanted to let me know they trusted me and let Sol know they didn't care any more. It was difficult because I admired and liked Sol, but I could see where the fans were coming from.'

The third landmark came with the League Cup semi-final second leg against Chelsea on 23rd January, 2002. The background was this. Chelsea held a 2-1 advantage after the first leg at Stamford Bridge. The fans were pretty much resigned to Chelsea going through on aggregate – Spurs hadn't beaten them in any competition for 12 years. But on a cold, rainy, windy night at White Hart Lane it wasn't just that they beat Chelsea, it was the way they did it, attacking from the start (a goal from Iversen within two minutes) to finish, by which time the tally was Spurs 5, Chelsea 1. Tim Sherwood scored, Sheringham scored, Simon Davies and Rebrov did too, inspiring a chant still sung to this day.

So Spurs, the great under-achievers for so long, had thrashed Chelsea for a place in the final. That, though, was as good as the season got.

At Cardiff's Millennium Stadium in February, wasteful finishing (Les Ferdinand missed a sitter) and chaotic defending handed a 2-1 victory to Blackburn. There was no silverware, and no qualification for Europe via the league.

The lack of success did nothing to diminish Hoddle's standing. Not among the fans, and certainly not in the press, who when the new season got under way made him August Manager of the Month for an unbeaten run which, bolstered by the arrival of Jamie Redknapp on a free transfer from Liverpool, had Spurs briefly topping the league. A month later, Robbie Keane joined from cash-strapped Leeds. Twenty-two years old, already a veteran of a handful of clubs – before Leeds there had been Internazionale, before that Coventry and Wolves – he was a player Hoddle saw as bringing youth and zest to a forward line that by football standards practically had liver spots.

Which he did. Thirteen goals, accompanied by his trademark cart-wheel celebration, made him the club's top scorer in a season that fizzled out with early exits from both the cups and another mid-table finish. In the dressing room, meanwhile, dissatisfaction was growing.

An inventive, forward-thinking coach, perhaps where Hoddle struggled was in the area of man-management. According to the Southampton midfielder Matthew Oakley, 'Glenn was always working with us, but he never got to us on a personal level. He always let John (Gorman) do that. It's not criticism of Glenn. It's just the way he operated. Players are just the people he operates with, a bit like pieces on a big chess-board.'

'When I was at a football training centre in Marbella I met a bloke who used to be his assistant at Swindon,' says *Guardian* journalist David Lacey. 'He told me, "He was all right, Glenn, but when we were watching a match he would never allow anyone to sit next to him. There had to be spaces on either side."'

There were rumours that Hoddle's relationship with director of football, David Pleat, was tetchy at best and tales of strife at the training ground were already surfacing in the press. When Tim Sherwood, one of George Graham's signings, was shunted out in the close season, it was with the words, 'No one would shed a tear if Glenn Hoddle was sacked tomorrow.' Freund went back to Germany and Kaiserslautern.

More money was spent on an overhaul of the forward line for the 2003/04 season – Bobby Zamora from Brighton, Freddie Kanoute from West Ham, and the Porto striker Helder Postiga. Which made it all the more dispiriting when, six games into the season, the new side was resting third from bottom of the league. Managed by one of the greatest attacking players of all time, Spurs had scored six goals and conceded 25. The last three, at White Hart Lane, were scored by Southampton.

Hoddle knew it was curtains. 'I'm out of a job,' he said to Gorman when the third of them went in. Sacked a day later, after two-and-a-half years in the job, he was the first Premier League manager that season to be booted out.

King's summing up of the Hoddle era is typically fair. 'I had always admired him as a player and was keen to work with him. When he trained with us he was still the best player on the pitch by a mile, which was hard to take sometimes. What was great about Glenn Hoddle was he always tried to play good football and his formations were geared towards expressing yourself. I was a young player and it gave me the chance to bring the ball out and have more freedom.

'I never had a problem with him, but I know some of the older players didn't feel the same way. It became a bit awkward because there was some obvious tension between Hoddle and the more experienced players. As a young player you just kept your head down.

'But I honestly don't think we were mentally strong enough under him. We never truly believed we could force our way into the top six. Yes, we thought we could play great football and win games, but too often we would go away from home and do nothing. We were too open and made it too easy for opponents, so you don't need to look for any other reasons for why we didn't do too much.'

'Hoddle didn't like me,' says Freund. 'He didn't believe I could do it. My first game with him as manager, I was the only first-team regular dropped to the reserves. Glenn didn't know how that would push me: "I will show him that I'm good enough to play for Spurs."

'With George, it was, "Don't go forward, because you're not good enough! Stay there to be the balance, in front of the back four." I won the ball and played it to the back four or the goalkeeper. With Glenn, it was, "Steffen, when you receive the ball in midfield, play forward." And the crowd started singing, "Steffen Freund is a football genius", because I played not bad with a ball, because it was allowed now for me. So that was my situation with two completely different coaches.

'But my relationship with Glenn didn't work well. I didn't sign a new contract because we didn't get on. Which was my mistake, because I could have finished my career here. I was too strong, our ways clashed and we couldn't come back together to find a compromise.

'My replacement wasn't good enough. I wasn't so bad that you leave me out completely. We didn't have a holding midfielder. Get rid of me if you want, Glenn, but sign someone! If you replace me, you have to buy someone like me, someone good. Six weeks later, Glenn was sacked!'

Nothing that had happened over those two-and-a-half years could endanger Hoddle's status as one of the greatest players in the history of Tottenham Hotspur. His majestic talent ensured he would always remain a treasured icon in the hearts of fans, but his ability to manage at the club he adorned as a player was summed up by Daniel Levy. 'Following two seasons of disappointing results, there was significant investment in the team during the summer. Unfortunately, the start to the season has been our worst since the Premiership was formed and the current lack of progress and [lack of] any improvement are unacceptable. It is not a decision we have taken lightly. However, we are determined to see this club succeed.'

Restoring Tottenham Hotspur to its rightful place was still a work in progress. And there were a few obstacles to be surmounted yet.

CHAPTER THIRTY-THREE

HELLO GOODBYE

Losing 4-0 away to Newcastle in December. Drawing 4-4 at home to relegation-bound Leicester in February. A 3-1 loss to a struggling Everton at Goodison in April. Spurs in the 2003/04 season were not a rewarding side to support. The new regime's first managerial appointment, the one that had seemed so right, hadn't worked out. Investment in new players hadn't improved the side's performance. They had young Ledley King, they had Jamie Redknapp and Jermain Defoe and Robbie Keane. But the team lacked heart and direction, there were arguments on the pitch and the fans were booing. A nadir was reached with a fourth-round FA Cup replay defeat by a 10-man Manchester City, when Spurs converted a 3-0 half-time lead into a 4-3 defeat. 'Tottenham just lay down and died,' commented Alan Hansen on *Match of the Day* that night. Plus Arsenal finished up champions. Spurs, clearly, still faced a long road back.

Because of the disappointment over Hoddle, the club had stepped away from making a swift replacement and put David Pleat and first-team coach Chris Hughton in interim charge. Over the barren weeks, all kinds of guesses had been hazarded as to the identity of Hoddle's successor. Some of the names in the frame were neon-lit – Giovanni Trappatoni, the manager of Italy, and Fabio Capello of Roma. The press indicated that Spurs were thinking big.

They were. The new set-up turned out to be strikingly unexpected, though. There was going to be a continental system at White Hart

Lane. Jacques Santini, coach of the French national team at the time of the appointment, was going to work in partnership with Frank Arnesen, PSV's Danish talent scout. Arnesen was to be sporting director, with overall control of football matters and transfer strategy. Santini, as head coach, would pick and train the players provided by Arnesen.

With Santini fulfilling his commitment to France in the 2004 Euros, it was Arnesen who arrived in north London first and did all the talking. The last time he had been at White Hart Lane it was 1984 and he was losing to Spurs on penalties, as part of the Anderlecht side who lost the UEFA Cup Final.

'Since that UEFA Cup Final,' wrote Alex Hayes in *The Independent on Sunday*, 'Tottenham have been sliding relentlessly towards mediocrity. Within weeks of guiding the club to European success, the then manager, Keith Burkinshaw, had a disagreement with the board and left the club. That was followed by the rift between Alan Sugar and Terry Venables in the early nineties, and more recently by the awkward times under David Pleat and Glenn Hoddle. Meanwhile, the trophy cabinet has remained bare of the game's biggest prizes. There have been no more European titles, and not a sniff of a chance in the league. Instead, Spurs have relied on domestic cups for silverware, although it has been 13 years since they lifted the one that really counts.'

No pressure then.

The problem was that Tottenham Hotspur in 2004 lacked the status and resources to attract established galaxy-class talent. If they wanted Champions League football, it was going to have to start with the mining and polishing of hidden gems. But it seemed like Arnesen could deal with that. When he retired as a player – having won three Dutch titles in a row with PSV Eindhoven as well as the 1988 European Cup – he became the assistant to their manager, Bobby Robson. During his two years in the job, PSV won the league title and the Dutch Super Cup. But it quickly became obvious that his real skill was working the transfer market. After PSV shifted him into the role of director of football, the club won 12 domestic trophies and qualified for the Champions League every season with sides featuring players unearthed by Arnesen. Among his discoveries were Ruud van Nistelrooy, Jaap Stam, Arjen Robben and Eidur Gudjohnsen. Van Nistelrooy arrived at PSV from Heerenveen for £2.3 million in 1998 and, three years later, it cost Manchester United £19.8 million to take him away. A good proportion of Arnesen's finds brought big money to the club.

That said, the two-man structure was new to English football. Not that there was any reason to doubt it would work. Hoddle had found it difficult to operate alongside Pleat as director of football, but he and Santini, said Arnesen, were two Europeans working in a typical European framework; they were combining their strengths.

And what had to come first were the results. Only then could they think about refinements such as playing The Spurs Way. It was, said Arnesen, about striking a balance. 'When we at Anderlecht lost to Tottenham in 1984, they had very skilful players, but also there was Graham Roberts behind the front players. Attacking players like Jermain Defoe are nice to watch, but behind him you need midfield players with legs who can win the ball.' Arnesen drove his fist into the palm of his other hand. 'Not everyone can play pretty.'

In the hunt for a forceful presence in midfield, Arnesen quickly picked up Michael Carrick from West Ham. Behind him, other players started crowding in, led by the Swedish full-back Erik Edman, the tough veteran Moroccan centre-back Noureddine Naybet and bets on the future like Reto Ziegler. Pedro Mendes arrived from Porto and Helder Postiga went the other way after one disappointing season. The transformation was immediate. True, there had been rumours of strained communications between Arnesen and Santini pre-season but Spurs, once they were out there on the pitch, looked reborn. Over eight games in the opening weeks of the 2004/05 season, tightly-organised, no longer flaky at the back, they only lost once, narrowly, to Manchester United.

But the streak of form was all it was – a streak. Four defeats out of five followed, and behind the scenes there were rumours of more friction as Santini proved less enthusiastic than Arnesen about playing Carrick. In October, Spurs lost at home to Bolton – the day Bill

Nicholson died. Santini refused to speak to the press, opting to watch a video of the match.

The press slaughtered him. Two weeks after that came his resignation, which was accompanied by an abrupt announcement: 'My time at Tottenham has been memorable and it is with deep regret that I take my leave. Private issues in my personal life have arisen which caused my decision.'

There had been no hint given, apparently, no warning. 'It was unbelievable,' Paul Robinson said. 'There was no indication at all.'

There was speculation, mind. When, in his farewell statement, Santini had thanked Arnesen for his understanding, the talk in the press was that he was being massively sarcastic. Santini and Arnesen, it seemed, couldn't work together and Santini had lost the power struggle. Meanwhile, it was left to *The Sun* to sum it all up: 'Santini Jacques It In.'

Twenty-four hours before Santini's walkout, Bill Nicholson's memorial service took place at White Hart Lane. The comparisons were telling. Eight thousand people turned up to show their love and respect for Nicholson: family members, chairman Daniel Levy and the Tottenham Hotspur board of directors, players and ex-players, staff past and present, supporters, even an Arsenal cohort led by David Dein and including Terry Neill. Nicholson's ashes – and later those of his beloved wife of 60 years, Darkie – were buried under the pitch. Even when the pitch was relaid in the summer of 2012, and the ground dug all the way down to the undersoil heating pipes, the ashes were carefully dug around and left undisturbed.

In contrast, Santini came and went so quickly that most Spurs fans barely knew what he looked like. He had been in charge for just 13 matches before he announced he was getting his coat. It was the shortest stint by any Tottenham manager ever. Nicholson had put in 16 years.

By the time he died, aged 85, on 23rd October, 2004, Bill Nicholson had moved out of the end-of-terrace Creighton Road house he had shared with Darkie to sheltered housing in Potter's Bar. But apart from two years there, and a childhood growing up in Scarborough between the wars, Nicholson had spent his whole life in Tottenham. Most of that life – apprentice, player, coach, manager and consultant – was given to Tottenham Hotspur. Of his final role as scout, John Fennelly, head of publications at Tottenham Hotspur, recalled in *61: The Spurs Double*: '[Tony] Galvin was snapped up because Bill braved a wild and snowy night across the Derbyshire hills to watch him play.'

'In the end when he had to drive a long way for these scouting trips, Darkie would come with him,' says Brian Scovell, Nicholson's biographer. 'They'd be driving home from Darlington, three o'clock in the morning, she'd be giving him sandwiches and coffee in a Thermos flask to keep him awake.'

He had retired as scout, finally, at the end of the 1996/97 season. At 78, his mind was as sharp as ever, but the old footballer's legs had begun to betray him. He remained club president, and in 1999 the short approach road from Tottenham High Road to the stadium's main gates was named Bill Nicholson Way as a tribute. In 2001, with the club passing into the more thoughtful hands of Daniel Levy, Nicholson was granted a second testimonial. The man who held Nicholson steady as he raised his arms to acknowledge the standing ovation from a 35,877 crowd was Martin Chivers. The years since the dramas in the dressing room had brought about a rapprochement so total that Nicholson and Darkie had been special guests at Chivers's 50th birthday bash.

In *Big Chiv*, Chivers confesses his regrets about the sourly embattled scenes that had dominated his years as a Spurs player. 'Today, I truly think that it was a real shame we didn't get to know each other better at Spurs. If I am honest, I think the real problem is that we were both stubborn. We never sat down and tried to iron out our differences. I know Bill once said that I never reached my true potential and this was obviously the source of much frustration for him. Who knows what sort of player I would have been if that aggression that Bill yearned for had been part of my make-up?'

It's impossible to imagine the relationship between a modern player and manager enjoying either such longevity or such a touching conclusion.

When it came to being honoured nationally, Nicholson received an OBE, but the knighthood of which he was truly deserving inexplicably failed to come his way the way it had come to Sir Alf Ramsey, Sir Matt Busby, Sir Alex Ferguson and Sir Bobby Robson.

But if any football manager should have been honoured, it was Bill Nicholson. The Double, the trophies, the glory nights, the confident, emphatic assertion that an English club could be the equal of any in Europe – Nicholson's Tottenham Hotspur did it all first. Until its achievements in the early 1960s, it was unheard of for a British club to take on and destroy the elite sides of the continent. In the words of Jimmy Greaves: 'It just didn't happen. It was pioneering sort of stuff, and when you look at it in that light you see it for the great achievement it was.'

What's more, every side Nicholson put together espoused flair, panache and simplicity. It was pass and move, it was a team true to that line of descent that began with John Cameron more than 100 years before and is still recognisable now in a Tottenham Hotspur side of the 21st century. No Bill Nicholson team would drain the life out of a game by playing to win 1-0. Neither would it cheat. Nicholson's sense of fair play was rigorous. Enough of a realist to include soldiers and bruisers such as Dave Mackay and Bobby Smith along with elegant ball-players like John White and Alan Gilzean, Nicholson was even so the archetypal romantic who sent out his teams to play the beautiful, multi-passing game. Football, The Spurs Way.

I started my first job as a football reporter in August 1973, just at the time when Nicholson's time as manager was coming to an end. Though I got to know Danny Blanchflower, his great captain, as a fellow hack – he was writing for the *Sunday Express* – Nicholson, my other childhood god, remained an intimidating, grumpy figure to whom the closest I got was hovering on the edge of the huddled group of sports journalists in the White Hart Lane car park as he barked and grumbled his way through reluctantly given post-match press conferences.

Ten years on from that, freed from the pressure of trying to maintain his scrupulous standards in a changing world, he had lightened up. 'In those days he smiled so much,' wrote John Fennelly, 'and that's how I'll always remember him – with a smile.' The former *Daily Mirror* journalist Ken Jones remembers being at a committee meeting set up to discuss the arrangements for Nicholson's first testimonial, the one that happened in 1983. Things had been dragging on in the way committee meetings tend to and Jones, facing a two-hour drive home, got up to leave.

'No, stop and have another drink,' said Nicholson.

'I can't, Bill, I'm driving.'

'Just one more – that'll be all right, surely?'

Jones was incredulous. 'Bill, why weren't you like this before?'

'Like what?'

'Like this,' repeated Jones. 'All the years I've known you, you were such a miserable bastard!'

'I'm not miserable,' said Nicholson. 'I'm dour. It says so in the papers.'

That same year, I met Nicholson properly at last, at a private pre-release screening of *Those Glory Glory Days*, the semi-autobiographical account of my childhood passion for the Spurs Double-winning side. There were four of us in an otherwise empty cinema – the producer David (now Lord) Puttnam, the director Philip Saville, Bill Nicholson and me.

Nicholson looked exactly as he had ten years back – the same haircut, the same immaculate way of dressing: jacket, shirt and tie with precision-creased trousers, a mac neatly folded over his arm, shoes so well-polished you could use them for mirrors. I was amazed that he'd actually agreed to come – the cinema had never struck me as one of his likely interests. I was nervous, too. I knew he had always believed that women didn't belong in football, and was wondering what he would think of my film.

As the story unfolded of the 12-year-old schoolgirl so desperate to get hold of tickets for the 1961 FA Cup Final she resorted to lies, theft and trespass, Nicholson watched in complete silence, apart from one moment when the heroine repeats his mantra: 'When not in possession, get into position.' 'That's right!' Nicholson's voice boomed out from the seat behind mine. So that was a good sign, but in the light of Nicholson's reputation for telling it like it was, I still couldn't help worrying. What would he say after it was over? I had visions of him ticking us off the way he did the players after they'd beaten Leicester to win the Double, telling us that we were way below par, that this film about Spurs was going to be seen all over the world and that we should have put on more of a show. When the lights came up, I faced him with trepidation.

He looked at me and gave his trademark barking laugh. 'I'd have given you the tickets!' he said.

And I'd have given him that knighthood.

CHAPTER THIRTY-FOUR

THE LASAGNE
WAS INNOCENT

After Santini became the fifth manager in 10 years to get a cardboard box and clear his desk, no one had to use binoculars to spot his successor. He was already at White Hart Lane.

Martin Jol had arrived in the summer, brought in from the Dutch club RKC Waalwijk on Arnesen's recommendation to act as back-up coach to Santini. Now the one-time midfielder with West Bromwich Albion and Coventry was put formally in charge of the first team. He had already won over the fans by showing up at Bill Nicholson's memorial service and, not long after, at the Spurs AGM he told the shareholders how he wanted to emulate Nicholson. 'I want,' he said, 'to be part of the history.'

Unlike Nicholson, though, Jol lacked complete control. Arnesen was at pains to emphasise he was still running things. 'I am responsible for Martin,' he told the media assembled to welcome the newest incumbent of the Spurs hot seat. 'We will talk about things together but I have the last word. If I like a player and the coach does not, I will convince him it is the right man.'

Cards marked, Jol scrapped the defensive approach briefly put in place by Santini and led the team through a season of the usual highs and lows while Arnesen carried on bulking up the squad, making ready-to-play signings like Michael Dawson and longer shots like 18-year-old Tom Huddlestone, while protecting Ledley King from Chelsea's grasp and dispatching Jamie Redknapp to Southampton. Mido, the Egyptian striker, arrived from Roma on a loan deal. 'Mido almost hit me once,' says Paul Coyte, the Spurs match-day announcer. 'I was on the mic and I said he'd been billed in the *Evening Standard* as the Egyptian David Beckham. He came storming up: "How dare you! I am not the Egyptian David Beckham! I am Mido!"' In fact, he turned out to be more the Egyptian Helder Postiga – after scoring twice on his debut against Portsmouth, he only got two more goals the rest of the season. Which Spurs finished in ninth place.

The arrow was pointing upwards, at least. Then came more upheaval. In June 2005, Arnesen left for Chelsea who, rather than have Spurs lodge a complaint with the Premier League, were persuaded to stump up several millions in compensation. Damien Comolli arrived to take over as director of football, in time to witness Jol's most successful spell with the club. It was also one of Spurs' unluckiest.

That season, the midfield included Edgar Davids, on a free from Inter Milan. Here was a player with a proper pedigree – AC Milan, Juventus, Barcelona, 11 years as a Holland international – and attitude. On the pitch he was unmistakeable. He had those swirling, whipping dreadlocks, he wore those tinted goggles. They weren't an affectation, they were there to protect his eyesight as a glaucoma sufferer, but they made him seem even more scary and purposeful. So did his nickname, 'Pitbull'.

'When Edgar Davids came to Spurs, it made me think that we were becoming a really serious club,' says King. 'He gave the whole place a lift. He was a big, big player who helped to bring a winning mentality with him. We all saw his brilliant work ethic and approach to the game. The first question he asked me was, "Can we win anything?"'

The answer looked like being a 'Yes'. With Carrick and Jermaine Jenas alongside Davids, with Dawson alongside King in the centre of defence, and Mido and Keane up front, a solid run in the league had Spurs in fourth place for most of the second half of the season. When they beat Bolton on 30th April, they were seven points ahead of their nearest rivals, Arsenal, in the battle for Champions League qualification. Even though Arsenal won their two games in hand, Spurs had only to match their result in the final game of the season in order to grab fourth place and take themselves into the Champions League for the first time.

Arsenal were playing at home that day. Spurs had to play West Ham at Upton Park. The night before, the team mustered at the Marriott Hotel in east London's West India Quay. 'I wish I'd been at home that night,' says Michael Dawson. 'But we had our routine meal and we went to our rooms. Around one o'clock I woke up, I didn't feel too good and I was sick, so I phoned the doctor. The next morning I went for a walk and I thought, "I can't play this game." Had I been the only one I wouldn't have played, but there were a lot of players feeling that way. To be going into a football match like that and missing out, that was a massive blow.'

The lasagne they had eaten that night has become part of Tottenham folklore, despite it subsequently being proved to be innocent of causing Dawson's bout of sickness and at least half a dozen players in addition vomiting their way through Martin Jol's pre-match talk the next day. The actual culprit, it was concluded after tests, was a bout of gastroenteritis that raced round the team with the efficiency of a gang of pickpockets on the London Underground.

'I was injured, but decided to go to Upton Park to support the lads,' says King. 'I was about to set off when JJ [Jermaine Jenas] phoned to tell me to stick *Sky Sports News* on because they were saying the team had been laid low with food poisoning. When we arrived at the ground, you could tell there was no life in the dressing room, the players were really struggling. This was our biggest game for years, but they were lifeless and some were being physically sick.'

Spurs had tried to get the game postponed, but were ordered to go through with it by the Premier League chairman, Richard Scudamore, who was lending his presence at Highbury that day for Arsenal's last game there. The outcome was predictable. 'I was playing at the back with Michael Dawson, who wasn't feeling great,' said

Anthony Gardner, the central defender, 'and Michael Carrick was struggling too – he had to go off.'

So a drained, weakened Spurs staggered to a 2–1 defeat while across town Arsenal, after trailing 2–1 to Wigan, finished up 4–2 winners to leapfrog into fourth place.

'I will never forget it,' said Jol later. 'Daniel Levy came to the hotel, then the police, which showed it was serious, and we had eight players down. Davids said to me, "It's no problem, but I feel ill as well." We had a meeting, the players wanted to delay kick-off until 5pm, but it wouldn't have made any difference, so they said, "Okay, we'll do it."

'It was my darkest day since I came to Spurs. We couldn't win, we didn't want to play but we had to. I hope in the future the authorities will make an exception. I can't believe it was a virus because it didn't last three days like a virus does. I still can't believe it. Nobody will know what really happened.'

The fans had their suspicions, mind. 'At the time we were thinking that this was the biggest conspiracy since Lee Harvey Oswald,' says Paul Coyte, 'though now I've come to the conclusion that there was no second shooter on the grassy knoll! All you need to do is look back at history and realise that it was just another one of those horrible Spurs twists of fate that could only happen to us. As much as I'd love to think that we were nobbled, I just put it down to that old Spurs luck again.'

Even so, the order to go ahead with the game felt staggeringly unfair to a lot of fans. Many were left asking the inevitable question: would the same thing have happened if the situation had been reversed and the Arsenal players had been the ones who were taken ill? 'Had we been able to field a fully-fit team or postpone the match, we would *probably* have come fourth, and competed in the Champions League the next season,' reasons Ivan Cohen. 'It would have made a world of difference to Martin Jol's standing as a manager. On such relatively small incidents does the history of football often turn.'

That summer, Carrick left for Manchester United but, intent on maintaining the push for the Champions League, Spurs lashed out a club record £16.5 million on Darren Bent, along with Pascal Chimbonda, Younes Kaboul and a gangling teenager called Gareth Bale. Another arrival, for £10.9 million from Bayer Leverkusen, was the Bulgarian striker Dimitar Berbatov, a deceptively languid player who intuitively knew where to be when it mattered.

The bad news, though, was Ledley King's injured knee. His season didn't start until mid-September. Then a broken metatarsal kept him out from Boxing Day until mid-April and, without him, Spurs were distinctly short of clean sheets. Even so, a run of form brought 27 points from their final 12 league games. With only one defeat in those dozen games, they made it into fifth place. Unbelievably, Jol was the first Spurs manager since Keith Burkinshaw to qualify for European football in successive seasons. Meanwhile, Berbatov ended the 2006/07 season with 12 goals in 33 appearances in the league, and was rewarded with the Tottenham Hotspur Player of the Season award, a place in the PFA Premier League Team of the Year, and a great deal of interest from Manchester United.

As the 2007/08 season got under way, there were categorical denials from United that a bid for Berbatov had been made, but the player's discontent was highly evident. So was Jermain Defoe's – Darren Bent's arrival had relegated him to fourth in the striker queue and he was backing away from signing a new deal. Along with the mutterings in the dressing room, Jenas was struggling for form, King was still missing after undergoing surgery in the summer and behind the scenes Jol was clashing with Comolli about some of his signings.

This was the season it had to happen. After two fifth-place finishes, it was Champions League or bust. But in fact, Jol's run at Spurs had stalled. Away to Sunderland, they lost to a goal in time added on. At White Hart Lane, Everton beat them 3-1. They thought they were up and running when they beat Derby 4-0 – the win featured Darren Bent's first goal – but then they lost 1-0 at Old Trafford, threw a 3-1 lead away at Craven Cottage in the last 13 minutes to draw 3-3 with Fulham and got beaten 3-1 at home to an Arsenal side who, with Thierry Henry gone, just had kids in the team.

But Spurs had their own kid. Gareth Bale made his debut at

left-back, scoring three goals in his first four starts. But he was to lose the rest of his season to an ankle injury and Martin Jol's Spurs carried on down the same disastrous path. After turning a 1-0 lead into a draw against struggling Bolton, they were 18th in the league. Unable to defend a free kick, unable to preserve a lead in the final minute of a game, the side was in trouble.

So was Jol. Jose Mourinho was linked with his job after exiting from Chelsea.

'I have to come up with the goods, that is what I have done,' countered Jol. 'No one could've done better, I firmly believe that. Not even Mourinho.' Meanwhile, club officials had been observed talking to the Sevilla coach Juande Ramos. Ramos admitted he had been made 'a dizzying offer'.

In the middle of this rumour–riddled uncertainty, Spurs celebrated their 125th anniversary against Aston Villa at White Hart Lane. 'You couldn't get a fixture more redolent of the Double side and Spurs' history than that,' says Rob White. 'The club gave out silk flags, 36,000 of them, and it was actually stunning to see.

'First off they began with a presentation of legends – Dave Mackay, Cliff Jones and Steve Perryman – and brought the cups out, and there aren't many clubs where that can happen. Then Bill Nicholson's picture appeared on the jumbotron and we all joined in a minute's applause. Thirty-six thousand people, mostly men, expressing their love and gratitude to another male.

'The team wore a commemorative blue-and-white halved strip – the same colours worn in 1884 in honour of Blackburn Rovers. We went 2-1 down, 3-1 down, then 4-1 down, but amazingly I was still thinking, "We can do this," because I know Spurs. Kaboul got the equaliser in time added on, and it was brilliant, euphoric theatre. I came out thinking, "There aren't many clubs when you can see a 4-4 draw full of the good, the bad and the ugly." For pure entertainment over the years, Spurs haven't a rival, and Bill was the cause of that, which is why we put so much store by him. He built this club.'

But for all the buzz left by that 125th anniversary game, the fans had to face the fact that Spurs were still in the bottom three.

At Anfield, an unmarked Fernando Torres scored in time added on to wipe out a 2-1 lead Spurs had never looked like conceding up until then. It left Jol's grip on the window ledge loosening by the day. Then Newcastle kicked away the ladder. Woefully short on confidence, defence and their frailties pitifully exposed, Spurs were beaten 3-1.

Jol's last game was the 2-1 home defeat against Getafe in the UEFA Cup. Or one half of it, anyway. The game went down in the annals as the one where the manager was sacked at half-time. Jol said when he started the job that he wanted to be part of the history. Now he was.

Juande Ramos arrived at Tottenham with a massive reputation. Fifty-three years old, winner of the UEFA Cup with Sevilla in each of the last two seasons, this master tactician had taken them into the Champions League for the first time after they finished a close third behind Real Madrid and Barcelona the previous year. 'A Mourinho-in-waiting' was the opinion of Michael Robinson, the former Liverpool striker now working as a football commentator in Spain.

Or Christian Gross Mark Two. Ramos insisted that his fitness coach at Sevilla, Marcos Alvarez, came along as part of the package. 'Ramos has taken away the philosophy that "fancy" or "precious" players don't work,' asserted Michael Robinson. 'From the first second to the last, every single player gives 110 per cent.'

One of the first things Ramos did was get the tomato sauce bottles removed from the tables at the Spurs Lodge dining room. The message was clear. Not only would this hard taskmaster kick the backside of ketchup-sated slackers, he would also would take Spurs into the Premier League top four, make them Champions League regulars and introduce the winning mentality. Oh, and do something about Spurs' limp-wristed defence.

On Sunday, 28th October, 2007, Ramos watched them lose 2-1 to Blackburn at the Lane. The defeat kept them in the relegation zone, but away draws to Middlesbrough and West Ham, plus a 4-0 win over Wigan at White Hart Lane featuring two goals from Jenas lifted Spurs to a marginally less humiliating 14th in the table. By the end of the year, they were through to the third round of the UEFA Cup, had chalked up their first away win at Portsmouth, lost by a goal at the Emirates, beaten Fulham 5-1 on Boxing Day, and come off the better of a breathtaking 10-goal binge at Reading, who having led 2-1, 3-2 and 4-3 were ultimately battered into submission 6-4 with the help of four goals by Berbatov.

Plus they knocked Manchester City out of the Carling Cup. Which in January meant a semi-final against Arsenal. The first leg, at the Emirates, was just like all those other north London derbies Spurs hadn't won since 1999, a tantalising vision of triumph giving way to crushed hopes. With King back after all his injuries, and a simultaneously languid and thrilling Berbatov emphasising that when he led the attack Spurs were streets ahead, whatever their flaws elsewhere, they outplayed Arsenal and led through Jenas's goal until, getting on towards the end of the first half, the usual misfortune intervened in the shape of Lee Young Pyo forcing the ball off the largely ineffectual Theo Walcott and seeing it fly into the net.

Wenger put out the kids again for the second leg, though on the bench he had all the ones who'd started shaving. They were going to be needed. That night, Arsenal were demolished with a classic demonstration of The Spurs Way, all speed and movement, a 5-1 trouncing that was Spurs' widest margin of victory over their great rivals for 25 years. The game was just three minutes old when Jenas's goal began the rout. Pressured by Dawson, Nicklas Bendtner headed into his own net before half an hour was up. Keane made it 3-0 just after the restart and Lennon added another on 60 minutes, by which time Spurs held the game in such a grip that even a goal from Emmanuel Adebayor left them unfazed. So shredded were Arsenal that towards the end Adebayor and Bendtner were fighting with each other, leaving Steed Malbranque to add Spurs' fifth as a stoppage time afterthought.

Inevitably, Arsenal fans countered that it was only the Carling Cup, that they had higher priorities. No one cared. Ramos had done it, he had turned us into Sevilla, we were on our way to being a great cup side again.

That was the mood, anyway, as Spurs headed for Wembley to take on Chelsea, with a new January arrival in the form of Jonathan Woodgate and with Paul Robinson back in goal after being demoted after carrying Hunt's long kick over the line in the FA Cup game against Reading. Robinson held out until six minutes before half-time, when Didier Zokora stood on Didier Drogba's toe, Drogba dropped as though he'd stepped on an IED, then miraculously recovered to bang in a free kick from 30 yards.

So Chelsea led at half-time and Ramos used his tactical nous to reshuffle the side. Coming up to 61 minutes, Tom Huddlestone came on for Chimbonda, who disappeared down the tunnel in a fit of pique. With 70 minutes gone, Aaron Lennon, who up until then had been having one of those games when all his charges up the right came to nothing, switched to the left. As Jermaine Jenas hustled Michael Essien into losing posession, Lennon crossed deep and Huddlestone harassed Wayne Bridge into a handball. Penalty!

Berbatov pottered up to the penalty spot and made it 1-1.

Younes Kaboul came on to strengthen the defence. This wasn't The Spurs Way; it was park-the-bus, band-of-steel, five-at-the-back defending. And it worked. The game went into extra-time. Four minutes into it, Spurs won a free kick after a foul on Lennon. Jenas took it and Jonathan Woodgate left Drogba behind. The ball seemed to spin off his hair towards Petr Cech, who punched it back against Woodgate's face. And it was in the net. Woodgate had scored with his nose.

So then Spurs had to hang on. Woodgate stuck so close to Drogba they might as well have been having a candlelit dinner. Robinson came up with the sort of save that makes you forgive everything when King headed a ball straight into the path of Joe Cole. Then, after three agonising minutes of time added on, the waiting and tension was over. Spurs had won their first trophy for nine years.

The fans enjoyed two sights in particular. One was that of John Terry leading his beaten team up the 107 steps, shaking his head from side to side. The other was Ledley King hobbling up to lift the cup with Robbie Keane. Chimbonda reappeared, too, brazenly inviting himself to the celebrations.

Before the game at Wembley, Ramos had said: 'To have a trophy now would take a lot of pressure off the team so they can work more calmly with the aim of then fighting to be up there with the best teams to be in the top four, to go for the Champions League, to win more trophies.'

That was the plan. Now they had the trophy to go with it. But after that came a 4-1 defeat in the league by Birmingham City, who were headed for relegation. Then Spurs lost at home to PSV Eindhoven in the UEFA Cup and came off the worst in a penalty shoot-out in the away leg. The rest of the 2007/08 season petered out. Spurs went out of the UEFA Cup; in fact, they only won two out of their next 21 games. In the final game of the season, Liverpool beat them 2-0 at White Hart Lane.

The trouble was that while Jol had come over as warm and genial, Ramos was most visibly not the cuddly type. Even when Spurs were winning, he looked like an undertaker sternly keeping check of his emotions at a particularly harrowing funeral. Then there was his continuing problem with his English. He made Fabio Capello sound like Stephen Fry.

Spurs were 11th in the league in January. They were still in the same position in May. The fact that Arsenal had been humiliated and Chelsea outwitted wasn't enough. The fans didn't need any more transitional seasons. They didn't need a relegation season, either. By the autumn of 2008, that was what it looked like being.

This is what happened. Having signed the Croatian midfielder Luka Modric, slight and whippet-thin like John White, and already recognised in England for the remarkable vision, passing range and creativity he had shown in international performances, Spurs lost Robbie Keane to Liverpool. It wasn't a bombshell. Rumours that Liverpool manager Rafel Benitez had been romancing him behind the scenes were confirmed when he pledged his loyalty to Spurs. He left at the end of July. Then, at the start of September, Dimitar Berbatov left for Manchester United after a long and drawn out transfer saga.

Without their potent, feared strike force, with the squad in mass rebellion, with King now struggling to play two consecutive games because of his knee injury, and with Modric deployed by Ramos out of position deep in midfield where heavier opponents steamrollered him and where his first few weeks passed in a blur of anonymity, Spurs continued their most catastrophic start to the season in 53 years. Players were openly questioning Ramos's methods on the training ground and confiding their misgivings to board members. By the time they lost at Stoke, in a game that featured the sendings off of Bale and Dawson, they had two points from eight games and were five adrift of everyone else. The *Daily Telegraph* was running a 'Spurs Sackwatch Special', and the joke doing the rounds went like this: A man was found dead floating in the Thames, wearing a blond wig, full make-up, bra, knickers, suspenders and a Spurs shirt. Before informing the next of kin, police removed the Spurs shirt to save his family embarrassment. 'It has,' summed up David Bentley, Keane's intended replacement from Blackburn, 'been a bit s***.'

Spilling the beans in *talkSport* magazine, Bentley spoke of a difficult start in which out on the pitch 'we've not been together, we didn't know where people were running, what people were doing'. Ramos's response was to leave him out of the squad to play Udinese in the away leg of the UEFA Cup, a fixture that ended in a 0-2 defeat.

Just when Ramos must have thought it couldn't get any worse, Christian Gross jumped to his defence. From his homeland, where he was now coach of Basel, the Swiss said: 'I can imagine how Ramos is feeling. Living and working in that sort of environment is not easy. I think he must feel very isolated.'

Shortly afterwards, Ramos felt very sacked. Departing with Marcus Alvarez, he released a brief dignified statement: 'The results are what counts in football and we all know how this world works.'

'Although it didn't work out well, at the time Juande filled the bill perfectly,' says Paul Coyte. 'Daniel Levy went out to get the best manager that he possibly could for our club. At the time that man was Juande Ramos. But I think that the lack of spoken English and culture difference worked against him. He had a great start as many new managers do, but after the cracks appeared I think everyone knew that he wasn't the right man for the job.'

For Levy, it followed, the way forward was starkly simple. 'At this stage where Tottenham is,' he said, 'we need a fighter. We need someone who has inspiration.'

They got him. And the first thing he did was put the ketchup bottles back on the tables at Spurs Lodge.

CHAPTER THIRTY-FIVE

TAXI FOR MAICON

Three weeks before the end of the 2009/10 season, eight minutes before the end of the game against Manchester City, it dawned on the fans that Harry Redknapp's Spurs really could do it.

It had come down to one moment, a blur of movement in the goal area after Marton Fulop, on temporary loan from Sunderland, had pushed out a deflected cross from Younes Kaboul. In the minutes leading up to that moment, Spurs had kept on attacking when it would have been easier to have settled for a draw. Settled for having to go to Burnley the week after and hoping there wasn't a cock-up. Settled for taking the chance that they wouldn't be true to their recent history of snatching soul-crushing failure from the jaws of glory, best summed up by the heartbreak of semi-final defeat to Portsmouth in the FA Cup semi-final. The clubs above them in the Premier League had enough in hand to go for that sort of easy option. Spurs didn't. If they chose, even so, to settle for a draw, perhaps they didn't really want the prize badly enough.

Perhaps as they launched themselves into another attack with only a few minutes of the game left on the clock they knew, collectively, that if they didn't take the risk now they would never ever have such a chance of Champions League again. And that feeling was embodied in the half-man, half-Meccano figure of Peter Crouch out-jumping Vincent Kompany.

GOAL!

Manchester City 0 Tottenham Hotspur 1
And the blue-and-white half of north London went bonkers.

When Spurs last made it into the top European competition, it was 1961, and they'd just done the Double. They had never clinched a place in the top four since the inception of the Premier League. On the way to fourth spot they had thumped Wigan 9-1 and beaten Arsenal in the league for the first time in more than a decade.

'I can see the Manchester City game now,' says Michael Dawson. 'It was massive.'

'It was like we'd won the league,' says Gareth Bale.

It was also an incredible turnaround. When Harry Redknapp became manager in October 2008, Spurs had two points from their first eight games of the season and were rooted to the foot of the table. The team was in freefall. From his first game in charge, a 2-0 win over Bolton, Spurs recovered to reach the Carling Cup Final, in which they matched Manchester United before losing the penalty shoot-out, and finished eighth in the table. Now, in 20 months, they had gone from bottom of the heap to Champions League qualifiers. And they had done it not by playing it safe or relying on kick and chase to get out of trouble; they had done it with swagger, imagination and drive. With romantic football. Spurs football.

'I think he changed the mentality of the players,' said Graham Roberts. 'I went to the training ground when Ramos was in charge and saw that it was very difficult for him to get his message across. Harry puts his arms around people and treats players with respect.'

'Some managers are tacticians,' said the journalist David Lacey. 'Harry's a motivator and he knows how to get the best out of players.'

'He builds up players' confidence, telling you every day you can be a world-beater,' agreed Peter Crouch. 'Eventually you start to believe it. Harry is an honest fella. If you're crap, he'll tell you. If you're playing well, he'll tell you. Everything is simple. He resurrects players' careers like that.'

'The good thing about the gaffer,' said Gareth Bale at the time, 'is that if you're good at something he wants you to do it.'

AFC Bournemouth was Redknapp's first proper job in charge (all he'd done before that was give his old West Ham team-mate Bobby Moore a hand during one of Mooro's doomed stabs at management at Oxford City). Under his guidance, the Third Division side produced one of the most celebrated FA Cup shocks when they knocked Manchester United out of the competition in January 1984. Even back then, the man gave a good press conference. *Apres-match* Harry-style, full of one-liners and gusts of laughter, was often better than the game.

In the summer of 1992, he moved on from Bournemouth to Upton Park, the backdrop to his years as a player. At first he was assistant manager to Billy Bonds but, two seasons later, the board moved Bonds aside into an admin job and put Redknapp in charge of the team. It was not a comfortable arrangement for Bonds, who ultimately left the club. But Redknapp's ability to get the best out of strong-willed turbulent personalities was clear in his handling of Paolo di Canio, the hot-headed striker who arrived from Sheffield Wednesday in January 1999 and proved to be a crucial element as, by the summer of 1999, they had achieved their second-best-ever top-flight finish — fifth.

Along the way were learning experiences, too. The first centred around the expensive signing of Marco Boogers from Sparta Rotterdam. Boogers celebrated his second appearance for the club with a red card for a horror tackle on Manchester United's Gary Neville, promptly went AWOL and was tracked down a few weeks later to a hideout in a Dutch caravan park.

Bill Nicholson would never take on a player until he had had him watched at least 13 times. Redknapp had signed Boogers off a video. 'He was a nutter,' commented Redknapp later. 'The video didn't show that.' After that he didn't sign any more players off videos.

The second thing Redknapp learned was never to make unguarded remarks to editors of fanzines. Some he made in the 2000/01 season came to the attention of his chairman and resulted in his leaving Upton Park before the last game of the season had been played.

Redknapp took over at Portsmouth and got them into the Premier

League for the 2003/04 season. But behind the scenes there were clashes with the owner, Milan Mandaric, over Redknapp's assistant Jim Smith, then, more irretrievably, over Mandaric's appointment of a director of football.

Redknapp resigned in 2004. Shortly afterwards, to the chagrin of Portsmouth fans, he became manager of adjacent Southampton. And then ricocheted back again to win the FA Cup with Portsmouth in 2008, the club's first silverware of note for nearly seven decades. Two days before he was due to receive the Freedom of the City award, he left for Tottenham Hotspur.

Returning to a more traditional style of football management – Damien Comolli had left the club along with Ramos – Redknapp got them out of the drop zone with essentially the side he inherited, revitalising the careers of Luka Modric and Gareth Bale on the way. Plus he made a few useful additions. Wilson Palacios came in to add a bit of granite to midfield. Robbie Keane returned after six disappointing months at Liverpool. Jermain Defoe boomeranged back from Portsmouth. But it was another player signed by Redknapp who turned out to be key. A player who, if you're telling the story of Spurs' exploits in the Champions League, is the thread that links the narrative from beginning to end. A 6ft 7in thread called Peter Crouch.

An angular, at times seemingly uncoordinated presence – playing for Liverpool, his nickname had been 'Coathanger' – Crouch was the darting and predatory Defoe's physical opposite. He'd been famous for a goal celebration, the robotic dance first performed after he scored for England against Hungary in May 2006. He trotted it out for a month, then announced he'd only dance it again if he scored in a Champions League Final. Now was his chance.

Compared to the career-long commitment of the likes of Steve Perryman, Gary Mabbutt and Ledley King, that goal against Manchester City in May 2010 meant it took Crouch barely more than a nano-second to achieve status as a Spurs legend. In the qualifying round later that year, his hat-trick against Young Boys of Bern took slightly longer to accomplish. One hundred and sixty-eight minutes, in fact. The first ninety of those minutes were harrowing ones. On an artificial surface that made the ball travel like a pea shooting across a carpet, Spurs were three down before half an hour was up.

Then, after 14 minutes of exquisite torture, Spurs seemed to realise the drawbacks of giving up so feebly and started to haul themselves back. Sebastian Bassong scored with a forceful header. After that, another long wait – until the 83rd minute, when Roman Pavlyuchenko played a one-two with Robbie Keane and banged the ball in at the near post. In the next day's *The Times*, the headline was Young Boys 3 Lucky Boys 2.

'At half-time I felt a sense of humiliation,' says John Crace, one of the fans who travelled to watch all or most of the Champions League games (and wrote about it in *Vertigo*, a fantastic book that sums up with poignant accuracy all the angst of being a lifelong supporter of Tottenham Hotspur). 'I could almost feel the laughter of Arsenal and Chelsea fans at our failing to get past the first hurdle. It was like Everton going out before the competition proper even started. It was far, far worse than being 4-0 down to Inter later, because they were the holders. There was also the feeling that everything we'd worked so hard for last season – that wonderful game at Man City – was going to be tossed away before the end of August and there would be nothing to look forward to.'

'After their third goal went in, it kind of hit us and we woke up,' says Gareth Bale. 'We always believed we'd turn things round at White Hart Lane. The crowd was rocking.'

Bale was right. At the Lane, the real Champions League buzz began. Crouch's three-goal binge, plus a fourth from Defoe, saw Spurs into the group phase on an aggregate 6-3. Crouch was the only scorer wearing a Spurs shirt in the 2-2 draw away to the Bundesliga side Werder Bremen. For the other Spurs goal that night, he merely had to produce an ominous lurk that so frazzled Werder's Petri Pasanen he turned the ball past his own keeper.

There was no goal from Crouch at White Hart Lane later on that September, in Spurs' first home Champions League game and, it followed, a landmark in their history. He did make an essential contribution, though. In a tussle with the FC Twente defender Peter

Wisgerhof he went to ground with sufficiently convincing flair to win Spurs a penalty early on in the second half. Rafa van der Vaart stepped up to take it and saw it turned round the post by Nikolay Mihaylov. After which it was Crouch's knockdown that enabled van der Vaart to atone two minutes later, powering it home with a shot on the turn. Now that Spurs were in the lead, they went on to a relatively easy 4-1 win, with two penalty goals from Roman Pavlyuchenko and one from Bale almost on the final whistle.

Champions League holders Internazionale, their next opponents in Group A, were arguably the toughest. But Inter v Spurs at the San Siro wasn't Crouch's game. The night of 20th October, 2010, was the sole property of another Spurs player entirely. Inter were already one up through Zanetti's second-minute goal when, with 10 minutes gone, goalkeeper Heurelho Gomes saw red for fouling Jonathan Biabiany inside the area. Sacrificing Modric, Redknapp sent on Carlos Cudicini to stay rooted as Samuel Eto'o's penalty put Inter two up. There was barely enough time for Spurs to lift their morale off the floor when three minutes later, Dejan Stankovic added a third. With 35 minutes gone, Eto'o poked in the fourth.

'Every now and again I worry that the fire that burns in my heart for Tottenham Hotspur is beginning to fade,' says Paul Coyte. 'After 35 minutes of that game, I had that feeling again once we'd lost our goalkeeper, were down to ten men and losing 4-0. The rest is history, of course. The second-half comeback was one of the greatest Spurs performances I've ever witnessed.'

Because to anyone who thought, as they had in that first game against Young Boys, that Spurs were on their way out of the Champions League, only two words needed saying: Gareth Bale.

That night he almost produced a miracle – and certainly saved Spurs from total wipeout – with a hat-trick that began seven minutes after the restart with a 50-yard run down the left and an angled shot. And then he repeated the process in the final minute. The second goal was almost the twin of the first. Bale barely stopped for a breather – why put off what had to be done? – to score his third. Bale 52; Bale 90; Bale 90+1. From pain to euphoria. From four goals and a man down after 35 minutes to, well, a defeat still. But as such, it had to be one of the greatest defeats in Spurs' history. One that felt like a victory.

'I think that night made him, worldwide,' says Michael Dawson. 'It put his name on the big stage.'

One of the stand-out things about the first leg against Inter was the number of fans who travelled over for the game. They always have, right from the start of Tottenham Hotspur's adventures in Europe back in the early 1960s, when Aubrey Morris's Riviera Holidays laid on charter flights.

'I think there were about 12,000 fans there,' says John Crace. 'It was a big Spurs day out. When were we next going to see Spurs play Champions League? The San Siro was huge, huge, intimidating concrete. Matthew, my mate, described it as "the Death Star". I think Spurs were intimidated. Then they woke up.'

'I went with my mates Gerry and Daniel and it was fantastic,' says Rob White. 'The stadium wasn't very full because I don't think the Milan fans were very interested in the early stages, but there were so many Spurs fans there that with 10 minutes to go, it was pandemonium, it was fantastic, it makes you realise why you follow Tottenham; you go from the agony to almost winning the thing. Absolutely marvellous – this was what we thought Champions League was going to be.'

Rick Mayston was there too. 'It was the most amazing performance by anyone wearing a Spurs shirt,' he says. 'To see someone with that burst of pace by a player who a year before we were talking about selling [astonishingly, Bale played 25 league games before he experienced a victory in a Spurs shirt]. And to think it was against Maicon, a defender who was the greatest right-back in the world. It was incredibly impressive because it looked like we were dead and buried.'

'We came in at half-time and the talk was, "Just go out there and stop getting embarrassed. Gain some pride,"' says Bale. 'I think we showed in the second half we could battle back. We knew we were capable, and in a way once they had that lead they were switched off.

'From that night, everyone was scared of playing Tottenham Hotspur.

They did not want to come to White Hart Lane. We already had the upper hand psychologically, and in a game that's massive. The performance at White Hart Lane was fantastic.' Most definitely it was. Two weeks on at the Lane, Bale ripped Inter apart again. This time it was not with his goals – he left the scoreboard free to accommodate the names of van der Vaart, Crouch and Pavlyuchenko – but with a performance of devastating athletic power on the left flank that confirmed him as a talent of world class and brought shouts of 'Taxi for Maicon' as he put years on the legs of the celebrated Brazilian right-back. They're still selling the T-shirts outside the ground.

From then on – almost strangely, given Spurs' record of turning things into a rollercoaster ride – it was simple. Towards the end of November, in the home match against Werder Bremen, Spurs ensured their place in the last 16 with goals from Kaboul, Modric and, inevitably, Crouch. Two weeks later, on a freezing night in Holland, Defoe's two goals and a bizarre own goal from the FC Twente keeper brought a 3-3 draw and with it the status of top finishers in Group A. Their attacking football had ignited the habitually pedestrian group stages of the Champions League. Not only had they finished first, they'd done it The Spurs Way.

Back at the San Siro again in the knockout phase for the away leg against Serie A leaders AC Milan on 15th February, 2011, Crouch continued the thread, scoring the only goal of the game after 80 minutes from a storming run and pass by Aaron Lennon. 'I swear if you rewatch that goal he scuffs the ball into the net,' says John Crace. 'But who cares? It went in.'

The pleasure of victory was intensified by a head-to-head after the final whistle between Gennaro Gattuso, the ageing Milan midfielder, and Joe Jordan, Redknapp's assistant manager. Gattuso, who had begun a combative evening by squaring up to Crouch and then grabbed Jordan by the throat on the sidelines in a clash that followed Mathieu Flamini's two-footed tackle on Vedran Corluka, obviously didn't know who he was taking on.

He saw a balding, grey-haired 59-year old in glasses. But in his playing days Jordan had been 'Jaws', the tough and fearsome striker for Leeds and then Manchester United. Famed for its missing front teeth, this was the face that adorned Heineken lager ads on billboards nationwide before the 1978 World Cup, gnashers miraculously restored, under the legend 'Refreshes the parts other beers cannot reach'. No more docile with age, after joining Tottenham in 2008, Jordan enjoyed touchline dust-ups with a range of adversaries that included, mindbogglingly, Roy Hodgson.

So Jordan was ready. Calmly, he took his glasses off and handed them to a member of the Spurs bench. The look of withering disdain with which he met Gattuso's headbutt made you think of another advertising slogan: Priceless. Rio Ferdinand tweeted: 'Joe jordan done well not to retaliate . . . what is gattusso up to trying to head butt big joe jordan . . . know ya players fella!'

'I don't know why it got so silly,' commented Redknapp. 'Gattuso obviously hadn't done his homework. He could've picked a fight with somebody else.'

Three weeks later, in spite of going with a three-man strike force and dominating most of the play, Milan crashed out 0-0 at White Hart Lane. Spurs were in the last eight, back where they had dreamed of being for more than 50 years.

'The absolute highlight was when we beat Inter at White Hart Lane,' says Mat Snow. 'The entire performance – I'm not sure I've seen Spurs play to that standard of performance for years and years. You really felt, "If we can keep this up, it is not too fanciful to think we can get something." We really did deserve to be there. Madly, I even thought we could go to the final and win.'

'I'd allowed myself a delusionary dream,' says John Crace.

We all had. But that was where the fantasy ended, on 5th April, 2011, in the Bernabeu. Crouch, outjumping Vincent Kompany, had provided the first defining moment when he got Spurs into the Champions League. There had been another when his hat-trick against Young Boys took Spurs into the group phase. Now, 15 minutes into the quarter-final against Real Madrid, it's tempting to say he was highly instrumental in getting them out. Already on a booking, with 15 minutes of play gone and with no realistic chance of winning the ball, he hurled himself feet first with clumsy gusto at Marcelo and earned the fastest double yellow in Champions League history. As he trudged away from the pitch, the Bernabeu crowd mocked him with a chant of '*Tonto, tonto, tonto!*' Stupid, stupid, stupid.

Down to 10 men, already one goal adrift after an Emmanuel Adebayor header after four minutes, short of their key front man, with Lennon absent having fallen sick just before kick-off, Spurs' Champions League run more or less ended there. Exposed against one of the best sides in Europe, Spurs had no chance of comeback.

Spurs held out as long as they could. That single goal from Adebayor was the only difference until the 57th minute. Then Adebayor scored with his head again, and two more blows followed – from Di Maria on 72 minutes, and Cristiano Ronaldo on 87. Real would most likely have won even if Crouch hadn't been sent off. But that was hardly going to be much comfort.

'He was too eager,' says Bale. 'He wanted to impress. The whole occasion was kind of overwhelming, I think we all wanted to impress. Too much to be our natural selves.'

'He's the most inoffensive footballer ever, isn't he?' said Redknapp at the time. 'He's certainly not one for getting red cards or making rash challenges. But he's lunged in for the second one and it's cost us dearly. Better teams than us would have struggled. It was an uphill task – an impossible task.'

Over the eight days that intervened between that evening at the Bernabeu and the second leg, the fans tried convincing themselves that it wasn't necessarily over. They thought back to Bale's near-miracle at the San Siro, of his destruction of Maicon in the return game. But really no one sane seriously entertained the possibility of seeing Real's lead overturned. At White Hart Lane, Spurs never stopped battling but the brutal truth was that the game was up after those 90 harrowing minutes in Madrid. There was no sudden, spirits-lifting demonstration of the poacher's art from Defoe to give them early hope. No hat-trick from Bale. No penalty awarded after Alonso's challenge on Modric, and Albiol's on Pavlyuchenko. Just a nightmare moment from Heurelho Gomes, fumbling a routine effort from Cristiano Ronaldo into the net five minutes after the break. Tottenham Hotspur 0 Real Madrid 1. And, of course, no Champions League Final for Crouch to perform his robotic dance.

In a way, though, Crouch added an ironic postscript. Just under a month later, with Spurs positioned to take fourth place and a Champions League spot for the second successive season, he scored an own goal at the Etihad Stadium. With Spurs missing out after dropping points against West Ham, Wolves, Blackpool and West Brom, Manchester City took fourth place ahead of them.

But no one could diminish what Spurs had achieved during their run in the Champions League competition. No one could deny their reputation as a club known the world over for a distinctive brand of football that has remained true to a tradition of more than a century and a quarter. They hadn't gone out on the peak of glory that everyone had fantasised about, but they weren't found wanting. Fifty years after the season Tottenham Hotspur won the Double, that glory night against Inter Milan at White Hart Lane felt like coming home; and in a way it was. Tottenham Hotspur is not just a football club, it is a kind of collective belief in a romantic and beautiful game, rich in fans' memories and imagination, in which the team of 2010/11, the team of Bale and Crouch, Lennon and Modric and van der Vaart and Kaboul earned a share.

CHAPTER THIRTY-SIX

MY ONE AND ONLY CLUB

Midway through July 2012, the announcement no one wanted but everyone was expecting was posted on the Spurs website. The incomparable Ledley King, centre-half, captain and ultimate loyalist, was retiring.

By the time King lifted the Carling Cup in 2008, he already knew his playing days would have to end early. Lasting as long as he did was a miracle of defiance of pain and chronic injury. He had no cartilage remaining in his left knee and was unable to train with his team-mates, yet thanks to his extraordinary ability to read the game he stayed matchlessly unflappable in the hubbub of defence whenever called upon. Which was often, and not solely by his club – even though King wasn't likely to be up to more than a bit-part role, Fabio Capello included him in the squad for the 2010 South Africa World Cup. On the night in 1963 that Spurs played Atletico Madrid to become the first British club to win in Europe, an injured Blanchflower gave Nicholson the choice: 'It's me on one leg or John Smith on two.' Nicholson chose Blanchflower. Fifty years on, King was similarly essential, whatever the state his body was in. Any Ledley King was better than none at all.

His doctor described him as 'superhuman, a player who defied science'. He was more than that. When Sol Campbell defected to

Arsenal in 2001, it was King who stepped up, his calmness and air of authority belying his youth. Three years later, Jacques Santini, who as manager of France had seen what he could do in the 2004 Euros, appointed him as club captain, a role he fulfilled peerlessly for three more managers and eight more seasons. He was, said Thierry Henry, 'the only player who can tackle me and not foul me'.

His last season, 2011/12, was the definitive Spurs rollercoaster. Michael Dawson summed it up this way: 'It was quite unreal, that season we had. It was just bizarre.' At one point Spurs were talked of as potential title winners, and not by the kind of people who think the universe is ruled by giant lizards, either. The usual open manholes and banana skins were lying in wait on the road to the Champions League, but it was Arsenal falling down them and skidding on their backsides. Spurs had all the pace, conviction and passion, while Arsenal were the pretty, ineffectual ones.

Even Harry Redknapp's disappearance for heart surgery in November didn't stop the heady momentum. Nor did losing to Manchester City at the Etihad Stadium towards the end of January. But 24 hours later, Redknapp was standing trial for tax evasion at Southwark Crown Court, from which he walked out an innocent man 13 days later. Within hours of his acquittal, Fabio Capello resigned as England manager and Redknapp was promptly installed as the favourite to take over.

On 11th February, Spurs beat Newcastle 5-0 at White Hart Lane. Here was endeavour, commitment, finesse. It was the most resounding win of the season, an emphatic demonstration of The Spurs Way, underlining Redknapp's shrewdness in the transfer market as new signing Louis Saha scored twice. But even as the Park Lane Lower End chanted: 'We want you to stay, Harry Redknapp, we want you to stay,' Redknapp seemed already to be considering who he'd like in his England team, or at least he was drawn into mentioning names. And Paul Scholes and Steven Gerrard came before Ledley King and Scott Parker.

Even so, Spurs started the week in February third in the Premier League, 10 points clear of Arsenal and seven free of Chelsea, still noisily imploding over at Stamford Bridge. If Manchester United, five points above them, couldn't quite feel Tottenham's hot breath on their sweating neck, they could definitely hear scary, stertorous breathing.

Then everything started to fall apart. As King faltered at last, so did his team. Arsenal v Tottenham Hotspur, 26th February 2012, was always going to be one of those matches I'd have to watch at home, peeping through my fingers. I was cravenly hanging around in the hall when Saha scored four minutes after kick-off, and had already started playing for time by stationing myself in the kitchen when Emmanuel Adebayor's penalty put Spurs two up just after the half-hour. At this point, I thought, 'Am I dreaming?'

Four minutes after that, Bacary Sagna scored. Arsenal 1 Tottenham Hotspur 2. I tried to will the spirit of Blanchflower onto the pitch, heading back towards the centre circle with that odd, crouching run of his, rallying the team like he did in that FA Cup sixth-round game against Sunderland in the Double season: 'Now keep your heads and let's get going after a goal. We don't want that business down in our goalmouth again.' But instead there was plenty more of that business down in the Spurs goalmouth. Four more from Arsenal, dejection and humiliation among the fans.

'In many ways, this was typical Spurs, snatching defeat from the jaws of victory,' says Ivan Cohen. 'Having gloriously gone 2-0 up in the home of our arch enemy, and having dominated with some magnificent football in true Spurs style, we let slip mentally and before we knew it, it was 2-2. By that time the momentum was all in favour of Monsieur Wenger's boys and it was surely only a matter of time before we would be overhauled. It reminded me very much of the notorious home match against Man Utd when we let a 3-0 half-time lead slip, and lost 5-3. However, while losing a 2-0 lead and giving three points to the Gooners was a dispiriting experience, the cold light of objectivity suggests that this is the obvious downside of trying to play the "Blanchflower philosophy" – it's more risky, leading to magnified glories, but also to major dejection when we lose and/or underperform. I think we expect our teams to play in such a way as to achieve glory that we believe in the underlying philosophy in an almost faith-like way, and when it doesn't come off our belief system is challenged but rarely shattered.'

'The critical moment of that season, when we jumped the shark, was when Arsenal got the first goal back at the Emirates,' says Mat Snow. 'Our sense of self-belief is wafer thin. Earlier on in the season, when we beat Arsenal at White Hart Lane, there was never any doubt. But it suddenly evaporated, like those endless games against Manchester United where we're ahead and then we concede a goal and all of a sudden we collapse in our self-belief.'

'It's the Tottenham way,' says Daniel Wynne. 'You've never had it so good, and then something will go wrong. The feeling in Madrid in the Champions League last time. We thought we were up there, and then we weren't. Richard Gough was a quality centre-half. He got it, he really got it. When he was there, we knew we were safe at the back. Then he left. Losing Klinsmann that first year. That hurt.

'Especially in the last two decades, Arsenal have had it over us by some distance. Then in the 2011/12 season everything was going our way, not theirs. Then Harry gets cleared and, a few hours later, the England manager resigns. It would only happen at Tottenham. It reminds me of the Queen song, *Pain Is So Close To Pleasure*. It's the other way round for us. The pleasure is so fleeting.'

Then, in the FA Cup, Stevenage, from League One, held Spurs to a goalless draw at the Lamex Stadium. Spurs won the replay, but only after going a goal down to an early penalty. Plus Michael Dawson horribly injured his knee playing for England and was out for the rest of the season. They lost 2-1 at home to Manchester United, and 1-0 away to Everton, raising speculation that it would be David Moyes to White Hart Lane if Redknapp took the England job.

Staring glazed-eyed at the prize, at the rapidly receding backs of the two Manchesters, Spurs were hanging on, teeth gritted. They reached the FA Cup semi-final at Wembley in mid-April, where they met Chelsea. Now managed by Roberto di Matteo, who seemed to have a spare voice and pair of arms (which turned out to be John Terry, seated behind him), Chelsea complained that the 6pm kick-off was only three days before their Champions League last-four clash versus Barcelona. Spurs lost 5-1. For the fans who had dreamed of Ledley King lifting the FA Cup in his final season, it was a spirit-crushing blow.

But that was nothing – well, almost nothing – compared to what happened after that. Automatic Champions League qualification was no longer a given as Arsenal rallied. On the final day of the season, Spurs were in third place. To keep it, not only did they have to beat Fulham but they had to rely on Arsenal not winning against West Bromwich Albion. The game at The Hawthorns was to be the last for Roy Hodgson, their owlish manager, who had been bestowed with the England job that everyone had assumed was Redknapp's for the taking. Surely Hodgson's side would wish to give him a fitting send-off?

Tottenham Hotspur 2 (Adebayor, Defoe) Fulham 0. For 43 minutes, Spurs were in third position, with a guaranteed Champions League place theirs. Fans with smartphones spread the news from the Midlands that Arsenal had fallen 2–1 behind. When someone shouted that West Brom had scored again, the Lane went bonkers. Only for the subsequent correction. Arsenal had equalised. Then they got another.

So Arsenal had leapfrogged into third place. But Spurs still had the fourth place that would at least get them into the qualifiers. Probably. One obstacle stood between them and their return to the Champions League in 2012/13: the final of the 2011/12 competition between Bayern Munich and Chelsea. If Chelsea won, they would usurp Spurs' place in the competition despite only finishing sixth in the Premier League.

The final went to extra-time and then penalties. Germans always win penalty shoot-outs. Not this time. It was Chelsea, unbelievably, who came away winners, automatically qualifying for next season's tournament at Tottenham's expense.

'Arsenal's form was better than ours,' Dawson commented later. 'No excuses. I do believe you finish where you deserve to. We were at the receiving end of an awful experience, missing out. But if I'd been in Chelsea's shoes, it wouldn't have bothered me. Chelsea wouldn't have worried. That's football.'

'I hadn't really realised that Chelsea would take our place until Messi missed the penalty for Barcelona in the semi-final,' says Rob White. 'From then on, you just thought, "This is ordained." It almost seemed these great footballing gods had it written.'

It wasn't the high note you would have chosen for King, the most graceful and majestic defender who ever trod the grass of White Hart Lane, to end his playing career on. But if you want to link Spurs of modern times with Spurs when they began, then that career is a good place to start. King was Tottenham Hotspur from beginning to end, a one-club man who joined up at 14 and made his first-team debut in 1999. Eighteen years and 323 senior appearances in all. 'This is my club, my one and only club,' he said, and those words will go on resonating as long as there is Tottenham Hotspur.

But where does all this fit in with Spurs of the 1880s? The first captain of Spurs was also a one-club man. Like King, John Jull was a schoolboy when he joined up. A one-time classmate of the original boys from Tottenham Marshes, he doesn't figure in most of the stories about the early months of the club because he was away at boarding school and just turned out for them in the holidays. But he was part of Spurs at the very beginning, when they played on Tottenham Marshes.

His career, obviously, never got to be documented as diligently as King's has been, but his first recorded game for Spurs was the 9-0 defeat of Brownlow Rovers in 1883. Like King, he was a defender, versatile and pacey. King could play at full-back, in central defence or in midfield. Jull's favoured position was right-back, but he could adapt to whatever role was needed, even wearing the centre-forward's jersey in a friendly against Iona in 1889, when he scored four of the goals in Spurs' 10-0 win. Tall, confident and fearless, he was one of the rocks on which the club was built, playing regularly for the 12 years in which Spurs grew from a schoolboy side to be one of London's top clubs. He became captain in the 1884/85 season and, as part of the committee that ran the club in its early years, was a driving force behind the move to the Northumberland Park ground.

By the time Jull stood down in 1896, Tottenham Hotspur was on the brink of far-reaching change. And 116 years later, as Ledley King threw his jersey into the laundry basket for the last time, this modern Spurs, more than a century later, was again on the brink of change. Turbulent change.

CHAPTER THIRTY-SEVEN

MARCHING ON, ON, ON

At the end of a season that played out as if some celestial Chelsea supporter had seized control of the great PlayStation in the sky, Luka Modric came to the end of a long goodbye to Tottenham Hotspur, and Harry Redknapp bid a much more abrupt farewell.

In place of Redknapp came Andre Villas Boas, or AVB, whose cv boasted one year as manager of Porto, during which he led them to a season unmarred by defeat, collared various items of silverware and became the youngest manager ever to win a European title – the Europa League – in the process. True, what followed was nine months at Chelsea that terminated in acrimonious departure, but most of the Spurs faithful were happy to welcome him, and the noise emanating from the fans that had made the early season trip to Old Trafford was deafening as a goal from new signing Jan Vertonghen helped Spurs to a 3-2 victory that seemed to have been aeons in coming. With the arrival of Hugo Lloris, captain of France, to keep goal, it was the injection of optimism that was needed.

'I was disappointed to see Redknapp go,' says John Crace, author of the wonderful *Harry's Games*. 'I rather enjoyed the way we played under him. It had an old-fashioned, quixotic lack of professionalism that played to my inherent Spurs nostalgia. So when AVB came into the frame, I was moderately pleased. I had lived in fear of us getting a Steve Bruce or Sam Allardyce and thought AVB would be a class above them. I was also at Old Trafford when Spurs won for the first time in what seemed like 357 years so was ready to give him the benefit of the doubt.

'His first season was undoubtedly saved by Gareth Bale. He made that season fun. He remains the best all-round player I have ever seen at White Hart Lane – including Greavsie, Hoddle and Gazza. Opposition teams learned to put two defenders on him and they knew exactly what he would do but time and again were still powerless to stop him.'

There was something else that no one could stop Bale doing, however – leaving for Real Madrid at the end of that season, one that brought Spurs a fifth-place finish and another near miss at Champions League qualification. One moment he was scoring from free-kicks, tap-ins, drives from the halfway line; running to the technical area, man-hugging AVB, the coach who had freed him to roam all over the park in such a deadly way, finishing up Spurs' top goalscorer with 21. The next, he was being paraded to the crowd at the Bernabeu, property of Real Madrid. It was like watching your ex turn up at a party with their new squeeze.

'It felt inevitable,' says John Crace. 'I was personally just grateful if Bale stayed on for one more season than he might have done. The brutal truth was that he was just too good for the rest of the team, and no chairman could have turned down £85million-plus for a player who was only ever one bad injury away from being valueless.'

The Bale money, as it was quickly called, triggered the arrival of a stellar line-up of new players. With a squad that boasted Paulinho, Lamela, Eriksen, Chadli, Chiriches, Capoue and Soldado, the media were tipping Spurs as title-winners. When the season opened at Selhurst Park with Soldado's nervelessly executed penalty against newly promoted Crystal Palace, and three points, expectations soared.

Then they fell to earth again. For fans who had loved Spurs for that beautiful, free-flowing, passing game these were dismal weeks. The stifling fare on offer was bad enough. Worse was the defensive flimsiness that brought dispiriting collapses against sides that one season back looked on Tottenham Hotspur as a team to be feared. Soldado struggled to live up to expectations. Adebayor and AVB fell out. Other players found it difficult to adjust to a new league and new teammates, and though several would go on to prove their worth, months of frustration culminated in the departure of AVB and the promotion of Tim Sherwood from the youth side to interim manager. And with that came the resurgence of Adebayor.

'It was the obvious first step to take – get a good player onside who'd been cast aside by the previous regime,' says the *Evening Standard's* Tom Collomosse, 'but he still did it well. With Adebayor, you have to build your team around him, otherwise you probably won't get a great deal out of him. Sherwood looked at what he had, understood that Adebayor could be his main man, and planned accordingly.'

A big and long-lasting part of that plan was the prompt introduction of the youth players to the first team, starting with the French-born Algerian midfielder Nabil Bentaleb. 'It was probably less of a risk than for most new managers,' says Collomosse, 'because Sherwood had worked at the club since 2008 and would have known exactly how strong the players were. It was also a handy way of showing there was talent in the ranks, if only it could be given a chance. Sherwood has been proved right, too; Bentaleb is probably Tottenham's best central midfielder today. But Sherwood was essentially a man keeping a seat warm for someone else. It was always intended to be a short-term appointment, though if he had managed top four or won a trophy he would have been hard to let go. But though a sixth place finish qualified Tottenham for the Europa League again, results against the top teams were disappointing.'

Sherwood, also, was a Marmite character, loved or loathed. The media might have relished his antics in the technical area, his despairing rants when things failed to go to plan, his jousting with the fans; others cringed. 'Sherwood is brash and has a level of self-assurance that borders on arrogance,' comments Tom Collomosse. 'He didn't help himself at times, of course. Yet people forget he was a rookie manager.

Maybe he wasn't ready for such a big job, but you could hardly expect him to turn it down, could you? All things considered, I think he did a solid job at Tottenham.'

And he was the man who gave Harry Kane his chance. 'Sherwood gave him a run of games in the Premier League, which no previous manager had done. Even though he couldn't have forecast how well Kane would do, and without it he might even have spent the 2014/15 season on loan at another club. The legacy of young players is not only about Sherwood, of course. Chris Ramsey did so much for those youngsters, while both Les Ferdinand and John McDermott deserve credit too. But Sherwood had been in charge of that department and it's only fair, therefore, that if Rose, Mason, Bentaleb, Townsend and Kane are now in the first team, much of the credit should go to him.'

It was Sherwood's successor, though, who really flicked the switch. Mauricio Pochettino, who took over from Sherwood in the summer of 2014, brought with him a training regime of such ferocity that some of the older players were left rubber-limbed. But the youngsters thrived on it. Danny Rose fined down and grew up. Ryan Mason emerged from a peripatetic journey on loan, bulked up and developed into a midfielder of attitude and promise. Harry Kane, though, did more than that.

Even those who had been keeping tabs on the progress of the boy from Walthamstow as he moved from loan club to loan club were amazed. Rapturously amazed. Now hyper-fit and joyfully motivated, he was scoring the kind of goals that made the faithful groan with ecstasy. White Hart Lane, 7th February 2015. Tottenham Hotspur 2 Arsenal 1. Or, to put it another way, Harry Kane 2 Arsenal 1. Right then, you sensed it. Here was someone special. Here was Spurs DNA in the glare of the spotlights. He was a symbol of not just the club's future but its roots, his success our success, because Harry, to use the words of the chant, was one of our own.

There was also, that season, another step that Tottenham Hotspur took into the future. In the spring of 2015, all obstacles were finally cleared for the new stadium at Northumberland Park to go up. And so in time, not all that much time, White Hart Lane, where rebuilding nearly brought about the end of the club on the cusp of the 1990s, will go under the bulldozers. Bill Nicholson's ashes, and Darkie's, will be carefully dug up from their secret resting place, and a new hideaway earmarked for them. Then the pitch, over which a teenage Bill Nicholson used to spend summer dragging a roller, under which urban foxes used to bury burgers, and from which pigeons used to be scared off by the groundsman banging together dustbin lids, will turn into earth, stones and dust. No more that lush green expanse onto which the fans used to release cockerels. No one knew what to do with them once they'd strutted their stuff, so one of the staff was appointed cockerel catcher. He kept them in the garden of his terrace house behind the ground, where their regular early morning chorus of cock-a-doodle-doo didn't go down too well with the neighbours.

The East Stand, with the roof where Gazza fell through some rotten floorboards onto the seating below one day in 1989 when he decided to go pigeon-shooting; with the mini-police station complete with a few cells; with the kestrels' nests in the rafters; and the north-east corner that had housed the mortuary for Blitz victims in World War Two, where at night the air still grows cold and makes the hairs stand up at the back of your neck, will be reduced to rubble. So will what is known as The Room Full Of Crap, the former Salvation Army Centre on the corner of Paxton Road, ceiling-high with old turnstiles and dugouts and piles of ancient, unread magazines.

So will the West Stand, with the boardroom where powerful men battled for control, and the tunnel with its inspirational messages: 'The Game Is About Glory'; 'To Dare Is To Do.' The bronze bust of Bill Nicholson will be moved to a new home from its current billet in the Bill Nicholson Suite. Last time it had a shift of position, it took six men to move it and one got a hernia.

It will be the end of the long office occupied by Nicholson, the man who in Perryman's words 'had the shiniest shoes, creases in his trousers that you could cut with, and a hatred of anything red'. The end, too, of the home dressing room where he gave his final instruction before every game: 'Remember, you are going to run out in front of the people who pay your wages. Their expectancy of you is high, their value of you is high and their opinion of you is high. So do not let them down. Entertain them and you can only do that by being honest with yourself, respecting your team-mates and your opponents, and by, as a team, playing as one.'

But the new ground will offer the prospect of creating fresh memories, fresh triumphs and building on our history. The point is not the place itself, it's what we experience there, as the crowd, *with* the players, not just watching them from the outside.

What will never change is Tottenham Hotspur itself, a team that is worth watching, that believes, with Danny Blanchflower, that football is all about glory, it's about doing things with style and flourish. You support them because the way they play is more exhilarating and uplifting – and, yes, sometimes alarming and exasperating – than any other. Because at some moment when you were a kid you saw Martin Chivers accelerate from his marker, hit a defender with a charge from those powerful shoulders and curl a 30-yarder around a keeper's outstretched hands. Or Paul Gascoigne, bursting from midfield like some dishevelled cherub, switching the ball between his feet. Or, if you're not yet an age when a pub landlord can legally pull you a pint, Gareth Bale, one of the most thrillingly gifted footballers alive, careering down the flank against Internazionale. Some of us are even old enough to have seen the awesomely predatory strikes of Greaves and the battered bravery of Mackay as he played out his last days with Spurs.

Fans who only see a club in terms of titles won and trophies lifted are missing out on something important. People support Spurs and not any other club because the football played is a more life-affirming and intoxicating experience. Which is not to say that we've been blind to their flaws. But when things weren't going their way, we loved the good players in the bad teams, and some of the bad players as well, for their idiosyncrasies and laughs they gave us. As Ledley King said, 'I have been here since I was a boy, I have always considered it my club and have always found it hard to imagine wearing the shirt of another team.' We are, and will continue to be, Spurs until we die.

And when that happens, who knows? In that fraction of a moment before the lights go out, maybe we'll see it all again. Maybe we'll be steeling ourselves for one of those long unbearable waits, when Spurs are 3-2 up with four minutes of time added on and it's almost impossible to watch, when in some weird way we can hear the voice of Danny Blanchflower in our heads: 'You've got to believe.'

Or maybe our minds will give the images full play, the whole glorious panorama of Spurs through the decades. Blanchflower to White to Smith. Modric to Lennon to Crouch. Sandro to Dembélé to Defoe. Pass and move, as flowing and exciting as it must have been in the years of Peter McWilliam and Arthur Rowe. Ricky Villa, head down, hair flying, on his way to goal against Manchester City; Glenn Hoddle soaring past the Oxford United defence one long-ago day in April; Jimmy Greaves leaving the Leicester City defenders on their backsides in October 1968; little Terry Dyson beating the giant Peter Swan in the air the night in 1961 the title was decided against Sheffield Wednesday; Alan Gilzean switching direction in the air in wondrous defiance of the limitations of the human body. We'll see Steve Perryman clearing off the line in the 1971 League Cup Final. Alan Mullery, drained with joy, at the end of the 1972 UEFA Cup Final, his last game for Spurs. Tony Parks nearly charging out of the ground with joyful delirium after saving Arnor Gudjohnsen's penalty.

All those marvels of footballing greatness; all those heroes. The wonder of what they did will forever be as vital to the Spurs tradition as the heart is to a human being. Still Tottenham Hotspur, where the game is about glory and the Spurs go marching on.